97
136

BORN OF A VIRGIN

JOHN REDFORD

Born of a Virgin

Proving the Miracle from the Gospels

To Joan
from Fr. John
Welldone on the BA Div.!
God bless.

ST PAULS

The version of the Bible used throughout is *The New Jerusalem Bible*, (hence NJB) except when an author is quoted with a bibical text included, in which case the version used by that author remains in place.

Nihil Obstat:
Rev. John Henry, M.Th., LS.S.
Imprimatur:
The Most Rev. Kevin McDonald,
Archbishop of Southwark, B.A., S.T.L., S.T.D.

The Nihil Obstat and Imprimatur are official declarations that a book or publication is free of doctrinal or moral error. No implication is contained therein that those who have granted the imprimatur agree with the contents, opinions, or statements expressed.

ST PAULS Publishing
187 Battersea Bridge Road, London SW11 3AS, UK

ISBN 978-0-85439-731-0

Set by Tukan DTP, Stubbington, Fareham, UK
Printed in Malta by Progress Press Company Limited

ST PAULS is an activity of the priests and brothers
of the Society of St Paul who proclaim the Gospel
through the media of social communication.

CONTENTS

The Story   13

1. The Christmas Debunk   15

2. "A virgin will conceive and bear a son": genuine prophecy?   23

3. The Manuscripts   44

4. Born of a virgin: the earliest tradition   55

5. The "silence" of the New Testament apart from Matthew and Luke   70

6. The birth narratives: history, *midrash* or myth?   93

7. Assessing the evidence against   134

8 Assessing the evidence for   150

9. The virgin birth: a miracle   177

Bibliography   202

Abbreviations   209

Index of Authors and Subject   211

Scriptural Index   216

ACKNOWLEDGEMENTS

This book uses and develops the principles of Gospel criticism which I have already established in my previous volume published in 2004, *Bad, Mad or God? Proving the Divinity of Christ from St John's Gospel.* I carry those principles of interpretation over into *Born of a Virgin*, providing historical reasons to confirm the theological credibility of the miracle of the virgin birth.

This means in particular that all those I thanked in the Acknowledgements of *Bad, Mad or God?* I also thank here, since this book would not have been published without their help in researching, writing and publishing that first work. But particular mention must be made again of the indefatigable and totally reliable Mary Bull, who proofread the final text and composed the index, also my wonderful secretary Ann Weston, my right hand and my memory.

Also again I would like to thank Cardinal Avery Dulles, for his perceptive reading of the draft manuscript and wise suggestions; and Fr John Henry, the Southwark Diocesan Censor, whose comments went way beyond the duty of a censor to being that of a most helpful critical reader. Finally, once again, I thank my colleague Andrew Beards for his continuous encouragement and most helpful suggestions, and once again Professor Jack Scarisbrick.

I have been particularly grateful for encouraging comments about *Bad, Mad or God?*, from those within philosophical and theological disciplines, as well as from biblical scholarship. I do not believe that historical Jesus research can fruitfully take place without such interface.

Finally, I must thank once again the Maryvale Institute staff and students, especially our Director, Fr Paul Watson, who provide the environment for good biblical and theological reflection; and Fr Andrew Pudussery, the Director of St Pauls Publishing, together with Annabel Robson, Commissioning Editor, and Teresa Rees, our diligent typesetter.

Both *Bad, Mad or God?* and *Born of a Virgin* have subtitles using the word "prove". The 1990 edition of the *Concise Oxford Dictionary* has a variety of meanings for this word. The first meaning given is "to demonstrate the truth by evidence or argument". That is precisely what I am attempting to achieve in both books, the first producing reliable evidence for the divinity of Christ in St John's Gospel, and now in this volume demonstrating the historical authenticity of the accounts of the announcement of the miracle of the virgin birth in the Gospels of Matthew and Luke.

But the dictionary gives a second meaning for "prove" which is also relevant to my agenda. No.3 is "(maths) test the accuracy of (a calculation)", and No.4 is "establish the genuineness and validity of (a will)". In this book, I will be testing out the testimony of Matthew and Luke that Jesus was born of a virgin, putting that testimony through various historical tests. I submit that those accounts will come through those tests with flying colours.

To my Maryvale colleagues
and to our Bridgettine Sisters
Beloved in the Lord

DEMONSTRANDA

1. By "the virginal conception of Jesus in the womb of his mother Mary", we simply mean that Mary did not have intercourse with any male before the birth of Jesus.

2. The conception of Jesus in the womb of the Virgin Mary without male intercourse is credible, but only if the subject of the virgin birth, Jesus of Nazareth, has already been reasonably demonstrated as God become Man for our salvation.

3. Once one has demonstrated that the virginal conception of Jesus is *per se* credible, then the historical evidence for it is more than adequate.

THE STORY

Matthew 1:

NJB 18This is how Jesus Christ came to be born. His mother Mary was betrothed to Joseph; but before they came to live together she was found to be with child through the Holy Spirit.

19Her husband Joseph, being an upright man and wanting to spare her disgrace, decided to divorce her informally.

20He had made up his mind to do this when suddenly the angel of the Lord appeared to him in a dream and said, 'Joseph son of David, do not be afraid to take Mary home as your wife, because she has conceived what is in her by the Holy Spirit.

21She will give birth to a son and you must name him Jesus, because he is the one who is to save his people from their sins.'

22Now all this took place to fulfil what the Lord had spoken through the prophet:

23Look! the virgin is with child and will give birth to a son whom they will call Immanuel, a name which means 'God-is-with-us'.

24When Joseph woke up he did what the angel of the Lord had told him to do: he took his wife to his home;

25he had not had intercourse with her when she gave birth to a son; and he named him Jesus.

Luke 1:

NJB 26In the sixth month the angel Gabriel was sent by God to a town in Galilee called Nazareth,

27to a virgin betrothed to a man named Joseph, of the House of David; and the virgin's name was Mary.

28He went in and said to her, 'Rejoice, you who enjoy God's favour! The Lord is with you.'

29She was deeply disturbed by these words and asked herself what this greeting could mean,

[30]but the angel said to her, 'Mary, do not be afraid; you have won God's favour.

[31]Look! You are to conceive in your womb and bear a son, and you must name him Jesus.

[32]He will be great and will be called Son of the Most High. The Lord God will give him the throne of his ancestor David;

[33]he will rule over the House of Jacob for ever and his reign will have no end.'

[34]Mary said to the angel, 'But how can this come about, since I have no knowledge of man?'

[35]The angel answered, 'The Holy Spirit will come upon you, and the power of the Most High will cover you with its shadow. And so the child will be holy and will be called Son of God.

[36]And I tell you this too: your cousin Elizabeth also, in her old age, has conceived a son, and she whom people called barren is now in her sixth month,

[37]for nothing is impossible to God.'

[38]Mary said, 'You see before you the Lord's servant, let it happen to me as you have said.' And the angel left her.

CHAPTER ONE

THE CHRISTMAS DEBUNK

It goes along with Christmas tinsel, Nativity plays at the local primary school, Christmas stockings, office parties, and Santa Claus. It is the annual media debunking of the Christmas story.

The star of Bethlehem, the three wise men from afar, the shepherds feeding their flocks by night when the angels sang on high, the stable with the ox and ass, the slaughter of the innocent babies in Bethlehem by the wicked King Herod. Come on, you don't believe this, do you? You must realise that it is all myth.

Above all, you don't believe that story of the virgin birth of Jesus, do you? At Christmas 2003, the BBC put out a programme on Mary, in which it was suggested that Jesus was born from sexual union between Joseph and Mary, not from a divine act of the Holy Spirit bringing Jesus to birth in Mary without male intercourse. I was asked to defend the orthodox teaching of the Church at 7 a.m. on the BBC's second channel; while the programme itself was going out on prime time that evening.

The programme attacked in particular what it called the "Blue Mary", that is the Mary of popular devotion. We were given the amazing revelation that the real Mary was not dressed in blue with a crown on her head, but was a simple Palestinian girl of perhaps only fourteen years of age; information I had already been taught at the Catholic seminary, but which the BBC seemed to consider was a serious challenge to my faith.

The next year, Christmas 2004, *Time* magazine, was at it again. David Van Biema investigated *Behind the First Noël*, and introduced us to the maze of opinions about each element of the Nativity narratives in the Gospels of Matthew and Luke. He said, "One might be tempted to abandon the whole Nativity story as 'unhistoric', mere theological backing and filling." He did not seem to give any alternative whereby we might take them seriously as history.

That same year, in England, the London *Daily Telegraph* published an article by Geza Vermes, whom it called "the leading Biblical scholar". He argued that "the traditional Christmas story is based on fable and flawed translation." Vermes argued that the doctrine of the Virgin Birth of Christ was based on a mistaken translation of Isaiah 7:14, where the prophet promises that "a virgin shall conceive...":

> According to the prophet, a child called "Immanuel" would be born of a virgin. The crucial point here is that Matthew is quoting the Greek translation of Isaiah: "Behold a *parthenos* [virgin] shall conceive and bear a son and shall call his name Immanuel." But Isaiah wrote in Hebrew, not in Greek, and in the Hebrew Bible, the mother, of Immanuel is not a virgin – the Hebrew for this would be *betulah* – but a young woman, *'almah,* already pregnant. She is to give birth to a son, Immanu-EL meaning "God is with us".

The newspaper article gives the impression that Vermes' argument is a sudden Christmas revelation disturbing to christians. But the view that the Christian doctrine of the Virgin Birth arises from a mistranslation of Isaiah 7:14 has been around for a long time.

Nearly two thousand years ago, in the early days of Christianity, the apologete Justin Martyr was arguing against his Jewish rival Trypho who was insisting, against the Christian doctrine of the virgin birth of the Messiah, that the Septuagint (LXX) Greek translation of Isaiah 7:14 (the Greek translation of the Old Testament used by the early Christians) was wrong. Trypho insisted that *'almah* should have been translated by the Greek word for "young woman" and not by the Greek word for "virgin". Indeed, the second-century Jewish translations of the Old Testament into Greek by Theodotion, Aquila, and Symmachus actually had the former translation (in Greek *neania*), possibly at least in conscious opposition to the Christian use of the Septuagint at this point.

The newspaper article also gives the impression that

orthodox Christians have yet to answer this objection. But in 1930, J. Gresham Machen in his classic defence of the virgin birth acknowledged the fact that, in his own day, many scholars held that the opponents of Justin Martyr were correct and in the opinion of many modern scholars these versions are right.

Machen argues that the question is by no means so simple. He agrees that *betulah* is the usual word in Hebrew for "virgin". On the other hand, he argues, there is no instance in the Hebrew Bible where *'almah* certainly refers to a woman who is *not* a virgin. Machen argues that the use of *'almah* in Isaiah 7:14 points rather to the prophet's belief that the woman to bear a son was indeed a virgin:

> But on the other hand one may well doubt, in view of the usage, whether it was a natural word to use of anyone who was not in point of fact a virgin. C.F. Burney aptly compares our English use of 'maiden' and 'damsel,' terms which do not in themselves connote virginity, yet would scarcely be used of any but an unmarried woman. If a married woman were referred to in Isaiah 7:14, it does seem as though some other word than *'almah* would naturally be used.[1]

But does the use of *'almah*, albeit if the young woman was still a virgin at the time of the prophecy, necessarily imply that the author of Isaiah 7:14 considered that she was still a virgin in giving birth to the one to be called Immanuel?

The Roman Catholic biblical scholar Daniel J. Harrington certainly thinks not:

> The Septuagint's use of the Greek word *parthenos* ("virgin") for *'almah* ("young woman") indicates that she was perceived to be a virgin at the time of the oracle. But in both texts the assumption is the natural mode of conception, not virginal conception.[2]

Davies/Allison agree: "According to the LXX, 'a virgin will conceive and bear a son'. The LXX probably means only that she who is now a virgin will later conceive and give birth; no miracle is involved."[3]

However, for these modern authors, such an apparent misreading of an Old Testamenttext does not threaten the credibility of the story of the virginal conception in Matthew and Luke. On the contrary, it only confirms it. These scholars would on the contrary see the obscurity of the meaning of Isaiah 7:14 as an argument *for* the early origin of the tradition of the virginal conception of Jesus. As Raymond E. Brown says in *The Birth of the Messiah:*

> It has been suggested that reflection on Isaiah 7:14 and on its prediction that a virgin would give birth gave rise to Christian belief in the virginal conception of Jesus. I am maintaining that there was nothing in the Jewish understanding of Isaiah 7:14 that would give rise to such a belief nor, *a fortiori*, to the idea of a begetting through the creative activity of the Holy Spirit, an idea found explicitly in both Matthew and Luke but not in Isaiah 7:14. At most, reflection on Isaiah 7:14 coloured the expression of an already existing Christian belief in the virginal conception of Jesus.[4]

Davies/Allison also concur that there is "some reason for concluding that reflection on Isaiah's prophecy was not a sufficient cause of belief in the virginal conception of Jesus".[5] So, these modern scholars would argue, Matthew and Luke read into Isaiah 7:14 the idea of a virgin birth because they already believed it. They were reflecting on an already existing Christian tradition.

Thus we have a classic case of "Which came first, the chicken or the egg?" Vermes would say that the early Christians invented the story of the virgin birth because they saw it as a fulfilment of a prophecy of Isaiah; and in fact Isaiah had made no such prophecy. Brown and Davies/Allison would say rather that Matthew and Luke saw in Isaiah 7:14 a prophecy of the virgin birth precisely because they already believed that Mary had conceived Jesus in her womb without intercourse with a man.

So which did come first, the chicken or the egg? Did the prophecy produce the myth of the virgin birth of Christ? Or did the early Christian belief in the virgin birth of Christ create the prophetic interpretation of Isaiah 7:14? Still more, if we adopt the second alternative, was that early Christian belief in the virginal conception, which preceded the writing of the Gospels of Matthew and Luke towards the close of the first century AD., itself based upon fact or the creative imagination of those first Christians? Thus we have outlined the agenda of the present little volume.

"Virgin birth" or "virginal conception"?

One initial point of definition: I will refer indiscriminately to the "virgin birth" of Christ or to his "virginal conception" in the womb of Mary. There was a patristic view that Jesus was not only conceived miraculously, but also born miraculously, viz., that Mary's hymen was not broken when Jesus was born, and that Mary did not therefore suffer birth pangs. This could be a possible meaning of "virgin birth". For this reason, when the question of the historicity of the virginal conception became a controversial issue in Catholic exegesis and theology in the second half of the twentieth century, those discussing the issue referred to "the virginal conception".[6] This was to make sure that it was the miracle of the virginal *conception* being discussed rather than the miracle of the manner of the *virgin birth* of Jesus without the hymen being broken, as some of the Church Fathers had believed.[7]

However, I shall continue to use interchangeably "virgin birth" together with "virginal conception" to refer to the faith of the Church that Mary gave birth to Jesus while she was still a virgin, in the usually accepted sense that she had not had intercourse with any man before Jesus was born. This is the usual meaning of "virgin birth", and I do not see any reason to change this common usage.

Mary's perpetual virginity

Nor do I wish to discuss fully in this book the whole question as to the *perpetual virginity* of Mary. It is Catholic dogma that

Mary did not have intercourse with any man not only *before* the birth of Jesus but *after* it also. This doctrine was defined by the Council of the Lateran 649 with the authority of Pope Martin I.[8] This remains the teaching of the Orthodox Church also, and was the teaching of the early Reformers Luther and Calvin, Protestants accepting the perpetual virginity of Mary until the biblical critical movement post Enlightenment.

From the viewpoint of the strict exegesis of the text of the Gospels, there are three main possibilities, all of which have been contended in the history of the Church:

1. Jesus had "brothers and sisters" in the sense that Mary had more children by Joseph after she gave birth to Jesus. This was a view first proposed by Helvidius in 382.[9] This would deny the Catholic doctrine of the Perpetual Virginity of Mary, but it could leave intact the tradition held by most Christians, and indeed also by Moslems, that Mary had no intercourse with any man before she gave birth to Jesus.

2. The "brothers and sisters" of Jesus were children of a former marriage of Joseph, Mary's husband. This was the view of Epiphanius Bishop of Salamis,[10] and later advocated by the nineteenth-century New Testament scholar Bishop Lightfoot,[11] and it is the explanation accepted by the Orthodox Churches. It has the virtue of saving the doctrine of the Perpetual Virginity of Mary while at the same time making the "brothers and sisters" of Jesus real brothers and sisters of the same father Joseph.

3. The "brothers and sisters" of Jesus were cousins or some less close relationship than children of the same natural father Joseph. This is the viewpoint of the Western Church, proposed first by St Jerome in his vitriolic defence of the Perpetual Virginity of Mary against Helvidius.[12] The Pope John Paul II's *Catechism of the Catholic Church* reaffirms this explanation:

CCC 500 Against this doctrine the objection is sometimes raised that the Bible mentions brothers and sisters of

Jesus.[13] The Church has always understood these passages as not referring to other children of the Virgin Mary. In fact James and Joseph, "brothers of Jesus", are the sons of another Mary, a disciple of Christ, whom St Matthew significantly calls "the other Mary".[14] They are close relations of Jesus, according to an Old Testament expression.[15]

The exegetical debate is endless, and will probably never be resolved. That is why, it seems to me as a Roman Catholic, it is justifiable to cite Church Tradition, and to depend upon that living tradition in settling the matter. The Perpetual Virginity of Mary is not contrary to Scripture, but cannot be demonstrated with certainty from Scripture. As the Second Vatican Council asserts, "Consequently, the Church's certainty about all that is revealed is not drawn from Holy Scripture alone; both Scripture and Tradition are to be accepted and honoured with like devotion and reverence."[16]

If my Protestant fellow Christians cannot accept the Catholic and Orthodox interpretation of Tradition thus expressed in Vatican II, they surely will agree with me that the complex discussion concerning the evidence for the perpetual virginity of Mary in the New Testament at least has indicated for us how difficult it can be to interpret the Scriptures in this modern age. This makes it all the more significant that I am, on the contrary, convinced that it can be demonstrated with certainty from a sound exegesis of the New Testament, using all the tools of modern biblical research, that Mary gave birth to Jesus without prior intercourse with a man.

This then is the single question of this book. Does the New Testament, in particular the Gospels of Matthew and Luke in their account of the annunciation and birth of Jesus, give us *historical evidence* that Mary, in giving birth to Jesus, had not had intercourse with any man, in particular with Joseph her espoused husband? In answering "yes" to this question, this book will confirm a point of unity between all Christians who accept our common creed, that Jesus was "born of the Virgin Mary".[17]

1 Machen, J., 1958, 289.
2 Harrington, 35.
3 ICC, 214.
4 BM 149. So also Harrington, 35: "For early Christians like Matthew, however, the appearance of *parthenos* in Isaiah 7:14 bolstered their already existing faith in the virginal conception of Jesus."
5 ICC, 214.
6 So Raymond E. Brown, BM, 517-518.
7 Bishop A.C. Clarke, 1975, argued that the mode of Jesus' birth as being miraculous was never part of the Church's definition, only that Mary remained a virgin in the sense that she never had intercourse with a man before, during, or after Jesus' birth.
8 Lateran Council of 649 AD (DS 503): "If anyone does not in accord with the Holy Fathers acknowledge the holy and ever virgin and immaculate Mary as really and truly the Mother of God, inasmuch as she, in the fullness of time, and without seed, conceived by the Holy Spirit, God the Word Himself, who before all time was born of God the Father, and without loss of integrity brought Him forth, and after His birth preserved her virginity inviolate, let him be condemned." http://cfpeople.org/Books/Mary/maryp7.htm
9 ODCC, 631. Cf. MJNT, 200-207.
10 ODCC, 464, MJNT, 208-222.
11 Discussed in MJNT, 208 ff. Lightfoot's view is to be found in his commentary on *The Epistle to the Galatians,* 252-91.
12 ODCC, 731. MJNT, 223-233.
13 CCC n.157 refers to Mark 3:31-35; 6:3; 1 Corinthians 9:5; Galatians 1:19.
14 CCC n.158 refers to Matthew 13:55; 28:1; cf. Matthew 27:56.
15 CCC n.159 refers to Genesis 13:8; 14:16; 29:15; etc.
16 DV, Tanner, II, *975. There was a vigorous debate at the Second Vatican Council, as to whether there are some truths not in Scripture but only in Church Tradition. Finally, the compromise formula was adopted, that the Church does not obtain *certainty* about revealed truths only through Scripture, leaving the view open that all doctrine believed should be in some way related to Scripture.
17 The phrase "born of the Virgin Mary" appears in the Apostle's Creed, dating back at least to 150 AD. "The use of the Creed by Tertullian (North Africa) and Irenaeus (Asia Minor and Gaul) pushes the date well back towards the middle of the second century. At that time, therefore, the virgin birth was part of the creed of the Roman Church; belief in it was solemnly confessed by every convert before baptism." Machen, 1958, 3.

CHAPTER TWO

"A VIRGIN WILL CONCEIVE AND BEAR A SON": GENUINE PROPHECY?

In quoting Isaiah 7:14 "A virgin shall conceive and bear a son", Matthew was not referring first and foremost to the historical meaning of the text. Rather, he was looking at Isaiah 7:14 in the light of his already existing belief that Jesus was miraculously virgin-born.

First, we must discuss an obvious change in the way in which contemporary Christian scholars discuss a text of Scripture.

For early Christians such as Justin the Martyr, who, as we have seen above, defended the doctrine of the Virgin Birth of Jesus against those who attacked it, a direct prophecy of the virgin birth in the Old Testament would have been strong proof of the truth of the doctrine. Justin argued against Trypho that Isaiah the prophet foresaw explicitly the virgin birth of the Messiah; thus the pre-Christian Scriptures proved the doctrine.

Second century Jewish scholars would have accepted the same hermeneutical principle that, if Isaiah had prophesied a virgin birth, the Christian doctrine of the Virgin Birth of Jesus would have been at least advanced, if not demonstrated. Thus Jewish apologetes argued that on the contrary Isaiah did not foresee a virgin birth, thus in their view undermining the Christian belief.

But we have seen modern Christian scholars arguing the opposite way round. They argue that the account of the virginal conception of Jesus in Matthew and Luke is more credible historically, at least as an earlier tradition, if Isaiah 7:14 did *not* clearly refer to a virgin birth of a future Messiah. That is because it could be then demonstrated *by historical criticism* that Matthew and Luke referred back to a still earlier tradition in the first century AD that Mary gave birth to Jesus without intercourse with a male.

Indeed, for one who wishes to defend the truth of the virginal conception of Jesus by historical criticism, such an apologete would seem to be in a no-win situation if one claims that this doctrine is a fulfilment of Old Testament prophecy. If one argues that Isaiah 7:14 refers explicitly to a virginal conception, then it would be easy to say that the Gospel writers invented the myth of the virginal conception of Jesus simply to "fulfil the prophecy". On the other hand, if Isaiah 7:14 simply refers to a "woman of marriageable age", then one could argue with Geza Vermes that the early Christians did not know their Hebrew and made a mistake using the Septuagint Greek translation of the Old Testament taking *parthenos* as virgin, and projecting that faith in a mythical story of the virgin birth of Jesus.

But if one could argue that Matthew and Luke read into Isaiah 7:14 a meaning which Jewish exegetes never had in mind, then at least the possibility arises that Matthew and Luke were referring to an earlier tradition.

The use of this argument would not be acceptable to a more conservative Christian. Wayne Jackson is convinced that to accuse Matthew of giving a meaning to the prophet which is not true would be a violation of the true doctrine of biblical inspiration:

> The suggestion made by some, that Matthew took Isaiah's text and gave it an application alien to the original meaning, is unworthy of a correct view of Bible inspiration. Preachers today who take a text, extract it from its context, and make it a mere pretext for points they wish to establish, are strongly chastised and their credibility is compromised. Yet men, under the sway of modernism, do not hesitate to so charge God's inspired apostle in the case of the virgin birth. This is a shameful circumstance.[1]

Jackson therefore insists that, for Matthew's Gospel to be inspired, the author would have to have understood accurately the meaning of Isaiah. Anything less would not be true "prophecy". This is often referred to as "biblical fundamentalism"; although the meaning of this term is often as ill-defined as its opposite, used here by Jackson, "modernism".

We may take "fundamentalism" as that attitude to divine inspiration which identifies the Word of God with literal truth. Thus a "fundamentalist" would wish to say that the world was created literally in six days. Again, when Matthew says:

> Now all this took place to fulfil what the Lord had spoken through the prophet: Look! The virgin is with child and will give birth to a son whom they will call Immanuel, a name which means "God-is-with-us". [Matthew 1:22-23]

This must be also a fully accurate prophecy. For Jackson, Isaiah had actually to mean that the mother would be a virgin when she gave birth to Jesus. "The passage does not speak of a virgin who would marry (thus surrendering her virginity) and then conceive. She conceives *as a virgin*." Furthermore, it can only refer forward to the birth of Jesus himself, not to the birth of any child contemporary with Isaiah himself. "...The virgin's child was to be called 'Immanuel', which signifies 'God is with us'. If this name applied to a child in Isaiah's day, who was this illusive youngster? He seems to have vanished as soon as he was born!"[2]

Jackson's fundamentalist view was almost universal among Christian scholars until the rise of the biblical critical movement in the eighteenth century. No doubt it also is held as the most obvious view by many Christians in the pews. To be fair to Jackson and those who share his theology, it must be said that some who adopt the critical approach to Scripture do deny any doctrine of divine inspiration. His misgivings are by no means without ground. It behoves us therefore to examine briefly how it is possible to believe as a Christian that the Scriptures are the true Word of God in human language while apparently making Matthew an erroneous interpreter of the prophet Isaiah.

The meaning of Isaiah 7:14

The meaning of Isaiah 7:14 is one of the most notoriously difficult texts to unravel in the whole of Scripture. It becomes even more difficult if we view that text in its context.

The historical background of the verse is the fear, in the eighth century BC, of the southern kingdom of Judah at the growing threat of the Mesopotamian superpower Assyria, located in present day Iraq. Expecting the cruel Assyrian hoards soon to invade, the terrified kings of Syria and of the northern kingdom Israel were attempting to force Judah to form an anti-Assyrian alliance. To this end, Razon, King of Syria and Pekah, King of Israel were leading armies to encircle Jerusalem the capital of Judah.

The prophet Isaiah, however, believed that this alliance would be futile. Pekah and Razon, the prophet jibed, were only "smoking firebrands" [Isaiah 7:4], burning firewood smoking before finally going out. The people of Judah instead should trust God to save them.

The prophet Isaiah meets the cowed Ahaz, King of Judah at a pre-arranged place in Jerusalem:

> [10]Again the LORD spoke to Ahaz, [11]"Ask the LORD your God for a sign, whether in the deepest depths or in the highest heights." [12]But Ahaz said, "I will not ask; I will not put the LORD to the test." [13]Then Isaiah said, "Hear now, you house of David! Is it not enough to try the patience of men? Will you try the patience of my God also?
> [14]Therefore the Lord himself will give you a sign: The virgin will be with child and will give birth to a son, and will call him Immanuel. [15]He will eat curds and honey when he knows enough to reject the wrong and choose the right. [16]But before the boy knows enough to reject the wrong and choose the right, the land of the two kings you dread will be laid waste."

The text bristles with disputed questions:

1. **What is the "sign"?** Ahaz is challenged to ask for a "sign" (Hebrew *'oth*). But is that sign miraculous, referring for instance to the prophecy that there will be a virgin birth? This, as we have seen, would be the view of Wayne Jackson, also of E.J. Young, who thinks that "the birth was supernatural."[3] Or was the sign of a non-miraculous

26

nature, such as the prediction of Jeremiah 44:29 ff. that the King of Egypt will fall into the hands of his enemies? In this case, the sign would be the destruction of the kingdoms of Samaria (the northern kingdom of Israel) and Syria in a very short time, thus demonstrating the futility, as the prophet warned, of an alliance with these two "smoking firebrands". This would be the view of such as Gray, who wrote the classical critical commentary on Isaiah 1-27.[4]

2. **What does "The virgin will be with child" mean?** Does the use of the Hebrew *'almah* translated by the LXX (*The Septuagint Greek Version of the Old Testament*) Greek *parthenos* mean that the woman conceiving the child will be a virgin at the time of conception and birth? This is the traditional view of the prediction of a miraculous virgin birth, defended by such as Jackson, as we have already seen. He says, "She conceives *as a virgin.*"[5] Or rather is Brown correct in concluding that "Therefore, all that the LXX translator may have meant by 'the virgin will conceive' is that a woman who is *now* a virgin will (by natural means, once she is united to a husband) conceive the child Immanuel"?[6]

3. **Who is Immanuel, and who is his mother?** Is this child, "God-with-us", truly an exclusive prophecy of the Incarnation, of God becoming a man in Jesus, his mother being Mary? Machen argues that this view is not impossible.[7] Or is Joseph Jenson correct in asserting that "This is best understood as a wife of Ahaz; the child promised will guarantee the dynasty's future…"?[8]

4. **What does "He will eat curds and honey when he knows enough to reject the wrong and choose the right" mean?** If we take "curds and honey" to mean "the only food available in a devastated land" as does Jenson, we will conclude with him that "The discipline of hardship will teach Immanuel 'to reject evil and choose good' and make him the antithesis of Ahaz."[9] On the other hand, Gray thinks the opposite, that curds and honey "are the

27

two things singled out to indicate the abundance of the land of promise".[10] So, Gray would argue, this infant for a short time would eat the luxury food of the northern kingdom, until God's judgment comes with the Assyrian invasion, when he will truly learn to know right and wrong! Gray's view is attractive, since "We may place the interview (of the prophet) with Ahaz early in 734. Damascus was reduced in 732."[11] If the child was born in 734, therefore, he would be changing his luxury infant diet at the age of two, thus fulfilling the prophecy.

Gray wrote in his critical commentary published in 1912, "The ambiguities and awkwardness of the passage are so numerous as to give little hope of reaching an interpretation that will command general assent."[12] We must regretfully say that he would conclude the same were he writing his commentary today, a century later.

Furthermore, as Gray said then, "and under these circumstances even the traditional Christian interpretation will doubtless continue to find defenders..."[13] We cannot demonstrate exegetically with absolute certainty that Isaiah 7:14 refers to a virgin birth. But neither can we demonstrate the contrary position, that the 'almah concerned was a woman of marriageable age who would in the normal natural way give birth to a child with the name Immanuel. Machen's argument, that 'almah never demonstrably refers to a woman who is not a virgin, still has not been overturned. And while we may conclude with Brown and Harrington that the woman could be a *parthenos* before the conception, but lose her virginity in giving birth to Immanuel in a natural way; we could conclude on the contrary with Wayne Jackson that the sentence reads more easily if we conclude that she was a virgin in actually conceiving and bearing a child. And while we cannot demonstrate that the child Immanuel was definitely God Incarnate, Jesus Christ, God-with-us: neither can we identify this child with any child or any mother giving birth to him known to us at the time of the prophet.

The one thing, perhaps the only thing, which is crystal clear to me, is that the prophecy must have some reference to the time of the prophet, even if we grant that it is in some sense or other *also* a prophecy of the birth of Jesus by the Virgin Mary. The prophecy therefore has an immediate and a remote (Christian) meaning. This is also concluded by the evangelical scholar J.B. Taylor:

> The primary meaning of Isaiah's sign to Ahaz is probably that in less than nine months (reading Revised Standard Version margin 'is with child and shall bear') the tide would turn in such a way that a child would be given the name of Immanuel, 'God is with us'. The messianic interpretation is based on the coincidence of the name Immanuel, which expressed so well the early Christians' belief in the deity of the Christ, and the LXX rendering 'the virgin *(hé parthenos)* shall be with child and shall bear a son', which is a legitimate translation of the Hebrew words but which imports into the sign to Ahaz the implication that the mother of Immanuel was a specific woman who was at the time of writing still a virgin *(i.e.* in at least nine months' time a son would be called Immanuel). The door *is* thus left open for Matthew and the early Church to see a remarkable verbal correspondence with what happened at the birth of Jesus Christ.[14]

The deeper meaning

As we have already seen, from Justin in the second century onwards with his dispute with the Jewish apologete Trypho, Christians and Jews have been arguing about the literal meaning of Isaiah 7:14, "a virgin will conceive and bear a son." Christians argued that Isaiah looked prophetically forward to the virginal conception of Jesus in the womb of Mary. Jews insisted rather that Isaiah looked forward only to a woman of marriageable age who would give birth to a son called Immanuel by natural intercourse. Geza Vermes is only the last in the line to continue this dialogue in literal/historical terms.

Two hundred years of critical scholarship working on the text of Isaiah 7:14 has brought us no further towards discovering the meaning of that text in its historical context. But are we limited in our understanding of Isaiah 7:14 to its literal and historical meaning? Clearly, Taylor, whom we have just quoted thinks we are not. He sees a deeper meaning in Isaiah 7:14 which he maintains Matthew and the early Church saw, beyond the meaning known to the prophet Isaiah in the eighth century BC.

What is remarkable is that there is evidence both in Christian and Jewish thinking of the second century AD onwards that both communities saw a deeper meaning in Scripture beyond the literal, which could be discovered by an enquiry where the researcher had the Spirit of God as a guide. It is perhaps surprising that they did not carry this under-standing of the deeper meaning into their discussions of Isaiah 7:14.

In Christian thought, this concept of a deeper meaning developed in Alexandria in Egypt, a city strongly influenced by Greek philosophy. Clement of Alexandria (c.150-215 AD) was a convert to Christianity who retained his love of Greek philosophy "which he also regarded as a Divine gift to mankind. Christ, the Logos, the second Person of the Divine Trinity, was both the source of all human reason and the interpreter of God to mankind."[15] Thus the Logos could help us understand Scripture more deeply:

> The Doctrine of *Logos* gave Clement a tool to unite Christianity with Greek philosophy. Clement believed that the truth in Scripture is often hidden, and could only be found by the use of allegorical interpretation. But this was the deeper meaning (*gnosis*). Clement did not deny the literal, historical meaning of what the authors of Scripture had said. But the emphasis was on allegorical interpretation to find "spiritual" knowledge (*gnosis*).[16]

But it was not only Greek Philosophy which provided the stimulus for the spiritual interpretation of Scripture. This creative use of Scripture interpretation was paralleled in Judaism itself in the development of the Targums, Aramaic translations which also were commentaries on the biblical text. Often we are not sure of the dating of these Targums,[17] but the use of the technique of exegesis which attempted to find the deeper meaning of the biblical text as well as its literal meaning is already evidenced in the Qumran literature, the first century AD Jewish monastic community on the shores of the Dead Sea whose writings were discovered first in 1947. Maier in his study shows the important link between Qumran and Christian exegesis:

> ...in spite of a presupposed and not contested revelatory authority of the prophet in question, it was not the prophetic text itself which constituted the decisive factor and the real basis of the message. It was the pre-conceived message of the *pesher*, the "biblical text" being rather an instrument to arrange and to set forth what the author already had in mind, presupposing that his interpretation is the message of God hidden in the vessel of prophetic speech.[18]

The spiritual sense: justified?

So far, we have uncovered a remarkable consensus. We have demonstrated that, from the second century AD onwards, Jewish and Christian commentators interpreted the Scriptures in a deeper sense than that discovered by literal exegesis. We have also discovered a perhaps surprising agreement between critical scholarship and what is often called "fundamentalist" or "conservative" Christian scholarship, that an Old Testament prophecy can be interpreted beyond its literal meaning.

The "conservative" Evangelical view is all the more interesting because Martin Luther, John Calvin and the early Reformers disliked intensely the spiritual, mystical, or allegorical sense, since it seemed clearly to conflict with the principle of *Sola Scriptura*, that only the Scriptures can be the source of Christian faith. For Luther, the Scriptures have one meaning, the *sensus literalis sive historicus*, to be discovered, as Calvin insisted, by examining the circumstances of time and place in which the author spoke.[19]

But this did not prevent Philip P. Brown, while warning against the dangers of allegorical interpretation, from insisting that:

> At the same time, I believe that God is powerful enough for Scripture to have deeper meanings that we can find of which the authors themselves were not aware. Hosea may not have been specifically thinking about the coming Messiah when he wrote, "Out of Egypt I called my son" (Hosea 11:1). Yet the fact that Israel was called out of Egypt, and yet remained sinful, was something that Hosea clearly understood. The Holy Spirit gave Hosea this truth and he wrote it down with his words. But later Matthew was lead by the Holy Spirit to use these words in a little different way (Matthew 2:14-15). This in no way denies the truth that Hosea understood. We cannot use allegorical interpretation to deny the truth as understood by the authors of Scripture, because the Holy Spirit gave them this understanding.[20]

But how can we justify such an apparently "unscientific" interpretation of Scripture? It is significant that this principle of the deeper interpretation of Scripture was strongly affirmed by *Dei Verbum,* the Constitution on Divine Revelation of the Second Vatican Council, which was promulgated on 18 November 1965; while at the same time this same document completely endorsed the use of the historical/critical method in biblical hermeneutics.

Catholicism and criticism

The Roman Catholic Church came late into full acceptance of the critical method of the study of Scripture. This is despite the fact that modern discussion concerning the origin of the first five books of the Bible, called traditionally "the books of Moses", was initiated by the Oratorian priest Richard Simon in 1678.[21] Simon insisted that Moses could not have written all the books attributed to him.[22] In justification of his critical position, Simon insisted that a Catholic scholar does not depend on Scripture alone, but also on the living tradition of the Church. This had been affirmed by the Council of Trent in 1645. Nevertheless, Simon was expelled from his Order for his indiscretion.[23]

A similar pioneer was another Catholic priest, Johann Isenbiehl, who, in the last quarter of the eighteenth century, was the first to interpret our text, Isaiah 7:14 in its historical context. As his punishment, although a renowned Greek and Hebrew scholar, "he was sent back to the benches of the theological school, and made to take his seat among the ingenuous youth who were conning the rudiments of theology."[24]

The Modernist crisis at the end of the nineteenth century and the beginning of the twentieth century made Pope Pius X nervous at any use of the new biblical criticism. It was not until the encyclical *Divino Afflante Spiritu* ("With the breath of the Holy Spirit") of Pope Pius XII, that Roman Catholic biblical scholars felt liberated from fundamentalism. Two paragraphs are considered by many Roman Catholic biblical scholars the *Magna Carta* of Catholic biblical studies:

> 35. What is the literal sense of a passage is not always as obvious in the speeches and writings of the ancient authors of the East, as it is in the works of our own time. For what they wished to express is not to be determined by the rules of grammar and philology alone, nor solely by the context; the interpreter must, as it were, go back wholly in spirit to those remote centuries of the East and with the aid of history, archaeology, ethnology, and other sciences, accurately determine what modes of writing, so to speak, the authors of that ancient period would be likely to use, and in fact did use.

> 36. For the ancient peoples of the East, in order to express their ideas, did not always employ those forms or kinds of speech which we use today; but rather those used by the men of their time and countries. What those exactly were the commentator cannot determine as it were in advance, but only after a careful examination of the ancient literature of the East...[25]

The Second Vatican Council, in its key document *Dei Verbum on Divine Revelation*, to which we have already referred, promulgated unanimously by the bishops in 1965, not only confirmed the use of the historical/critical method in Catholic biblical scholarship, but added what was perhaps an even more important theological underpinning of that method. The Church had always insisted that the Scriptures of the Old and New Testament were truly the Word of God. This was reaffirmed by *Dei Verbum*. But the traditional interpretation of divine inspiration had often given the impression that the authors were taken over by a kind of ecstasy in order to be the passive vehicle of the Word of God. This might have sometimes been the case, as for example the prophet Ezekiel, when "the hand of the Lord" was upon him [Ezekiel 8:1, 33:22].

But *Dei Verbum* asserted that in addition to being the Word of God, the Scriptures were truly a human word. Paragraph 11 states:

> In composing the sacred books, God chose men and while employed by Him they made use of their powers and abilities, so that with Him acting in them and through them, they, as true authors, consigned to writing everything and only those things which He wanted.

Vatican II therefore teaches a kind of dual authorship of scripture; God and the human author. There is a union of wills between the divine and human author, which means that what the human author intended to say, God intended to say. This makes it all the more important, as *Dei Verbum* says in the same paragraph, "since God speaks in Sacred Scripture through men in human fashion, the interpreter of Sacred Scripture, in order to see clearly what God wanted to communicate to us, should carefully investigate what meaning the sacred writers really intended, and what God wanted to manifest by means of their words."

This gives full theological justification for the kind of research into the historical meaning of Isaiah 7:14 which we have undertaken in this chapter. But then, *Dei Verbum* goes on to insist that the biblical exegete is not limited in his researches to that historical meaning:

> But, since Holy Scripture must be read and interpreted in the sacred spirit in which it was written, no less serious attention must be given to the content and unity of the whole of Scripture if the meaning of the sacred texts is to be correctly worked out. The living tradition of the whole Church must be taken into account along with the harmony which exists between elements of the faith.

Inspiration and revelation

This clearly is a reference to the deeper meaning of Scripture. As with Philip Brown's interpretation, because the Holy Spirit is the author of Scripture, that same Spirit can guide us to a deeper meaning than that which we can uncover from the historical study of the sacred books. This is true not only for ourselves as modern interpreters of Scripture, but even more must it be true of Matthew in writing his Gospel.

But how can this deeper meaning be justified? In his detailed exposition of *Dei Verbum* paragraph 12, Ignace de la Potterie, S.J., insists, with Philip Brown, that this is precisely because Scripture is God's Word and not simply a human word:

> This means that we can now conclude that the causality of the Spirit (first cause) through his action on the sacred writer (secondary cause) is equally exercised on the *actual* text of scripture, which the ancient writer has *written*, and which believers today *read* and *interpret*. This amounts to saying that there is an indwelling of the Spirit in Scripture itself, that the text that has been written is the bearer of the Spirit, and that it must then be read and interpreted in the Spirit.[26]

The words of Scripture can therefore have a meaning beyond the meaning intended by the author because through those Scriptures, we are told of God's divine plan, and the interconnection of salvific events such as the Exodus as compared with the death and Resurrection of Christ. The "living tradition of the Church" enables us to make these connections because of the Church's continuous reflection on Scripture.

Why is this possible and justified? Precisely because, for Catholic theology, the Scriptures *contain* revelation,[27] rather than *are* revelation. In coming to terms with biblical criticism, Catholic scholars developed the idea of the distinction between *inspiration* and *revelation*. The faith of the Church is that the Scriptures are the inspired Word of God. But they are not revelation as such. Rather, they contain revelation. A glass contains a drink, but it is not identifiable with that drink.

For an example, Catholic scholars would point to historical books such as 1 and 2 Kings. Much of these books are histories of kings and battles, presumably obtained, from annals written by court scribes.[28] Reference is continually made in Kings, for instance, to the "book of Annals" either of "Solomon" [1 Kings 11:41], or of "the Kings of Israel" [1 Kings 14:19], or "the Kings of Judah" [1 Kings 15:7], sources no longer extant. This, the theologians insisted, was not "revelation", but human history. But the Holy Spirit wished these recorded and selected Annals to come under the spotlight of the prophetic judgement. Each king was judged – and usually found wanting! – by the criterion as to whether that king helped to preserve the true religion of YHWH, or not, for example King Nadab of Israel, 1 Kings 15:

> [25]Nadab son of Jeroboam became King of Israel in the second year of Asa king of Judah, and he reigned over Israel for two years.[26] He did what is displeasing to Yahweh; he copied his father's example and the sin into which he had led Israel.

This was the revelation, the prophetic judgement of the King's life. The whole text of the book of Kings was inspired, because God's Spirit guided the pen of the writers, even when they were only selecting "secular" history. But they contained revelation, insofar as they were able to interpret that history in terms of the history of salvation.

The Christ event

This distinction between inspiration and revelation is already to be found clearly stated in the thirteenth century, in St Thomas Aquinas' commentary on St John's Gospel. For Thomas, the most important revelatory event is Christ himself. As Nicholas M. Healey says:

> Accordingly, Thomas takes issue with John Chrysostom who, interpreting John 10:1-13, which speaks of the door through which the sheep are to enter, says that it is Scripture which is the door. With Augustine, Thomas insists that it is Christ alone who is the door.[29]

This very much accords with Jesus' own words in John, where he rebukes his hearers with the comment: "You pore over the Scriptures, believing that in them you can find eternal life; it is these Scriptures that testify to me, and yet you refuse to come to me to receive life!" [John 5:39-40].

For Christians, it is the "Christ event" which is the most important principle of the interpretation of Scripture. God's plan from the beginning was "that he would bring everything together under Christ, as head, everything in the heavens and everything on earth" [Ephesians 1:10]. The Scriptures therefore "contain revelation" ultimately because they tell us how this final plan, of "heading up [Greek *anakephalaiósasthai*] everything in Christ" is to be fulfilled. As the *Catechism of the Catholic Church* puts it:

> CCC 129. Christians therefore read the Old Testament in the light of Christ crucified and risen. Such typological reading discloses the inexhaustible content of the Old Testament; but it must not make us forget that the Old Testament retains its own intrinsic value as Revelation reaffirmed by our Lord himself.[30] Besides, the New Testament has to be read in the light of the Old. Early Christian catechesis made constant use of the Old Testament.[31] As an old saying put it, the New Testament lies hidden in the Old and the Old Testament is unveiled in the New.[32]

For this reason, the Church puts the books of Scripture into a hierarchy of importance. Although all the Scriptures are the inspired Word of God, not all are of equal significance in the plan of salvation, in which schema the four Gospels are primary:

> DV 18. It is common knowledge that among all the Scriptures, even those of the New Testament, the Gospels have a special pre-eminence, and rightly so, for they are the principal witness for the life and teaching of the incarnate Word, our saviour.

Rabbinic Judaism has a similar hierarchy of sacred books in which the five books of Moses, the Torah, are primary, the Prophets are second, and the Writings (for example the book of Proverbs) third. Scholars sometimes call this "the Canon within the Canon". All the books of the Bible are sacred and canonical; but within that canon there are some books which have special importance as principles of interpretation of the rest of Scripture. The *Catechism of the Catholic Church* sums up:

> CCC 107-8. The inspired books teach the truth. "Since therefore all that the inspired authors or sacred writers affirm should be regarded as affirmed by the Holy Spirit, we must acknowledge that the books of Scripture firmly, faithfully, and without error teach that truth which God, for the sake of our salvation, wished to see confided to the Sacred Scriptures." [33] Still, the Christian faith is not a "religion of the book". Christianity is the religion of the "Word" of God, a word which is "not a written and mute word, but the Word is incarnate and living".[34] If the Scriptures are not to remain a dead letter, Christ, the eternal Word of the living God, must, through the Holy Spirit, "open [our] minds to understand the Scriptures".[35]

Matthew's understanding

We can easily conclude that uncovering this deeper meaning of Scripture and bringing it alive was part of Matthew's plan in writing his Gospel, critical scholarship dating that work not later than the end of the first century AD,[36] and particularly his account of the birth and infancy of Jesus. There he has five formula citations from the Old Testament,[37] and they do not seem to scholars to have prime reference to the historical context of those prophecies.

For instance, Matthew tells the story of the slaughter of the babies by the wicked King Herod. "Then were fulfilled the words spoken through the prophet Jeremiah: A voice is heard in Ramah, lamenting and weeping bitterly: it is Rachel weeping for her children, refusing to be comforted because they are no more." [2:17-18] But Matthew links this story with a prophecy of Jeremiah where, after the slaughter of the children of Israel, there will be a time of joy, with the return from Exile. Perhaps one could argue that there is a parallel between the promise of redemption after the Exile and the promise of an even greater Redemption with the birth of the Messiah, even if the immediate consequence is the murder of many innocent babies. But surely most would agree that Matthew is adapting an Old Testament prophecy with great latitude.

Raymond E. Brown's comment on these Old Testament citations is most apt:

> For Matthew, these citations did more than highlight incidental agreements between the Old Testament and Jesus. He introduced them because they fit his general theology of the oneness of God's plan (a oneness already implicitly recognised by the appeal to the Old Testament in early Christian preaching) and, especially, because they served some of his own particular theological and pastoral interests in dealing with a mixed Christian community of Jews and Gentiles.[38]

It is in this context, the prediction by the angel of the miraculous birth of Jesus, that the prophetic text Isaiah 7:14 is interpreted by Matthew. I repeat that we have not yet in any way demonstrated the historicity of the virginal conception in our investigation. But we would surely have to say even now that the most natural interpretation of this account by

Matthew is that he is looking at Isaiah 7:14 in the light of his already existing faith that Jesus' birth was miraculous. Indeed, as Davies/Allison insist, "All presumption favours assuming that already in Matthew's time Mary's purported virginal conception by the Holy Spirit had been seized upon by outsiders and turned into calumny."[39] Matthew first therefore counters this by telling of the angel's revelation to the startled Joseph, who had thought before the angelic revelation that indeed Mary was pregnant by another man. Matthew then sees the promise by the angel of the virginal conception of Jesus as a Christ event enabling him to understand the Scriptures of old. We remind ourselves of Matthew's account:

> [22]Now all this took place to fulfil what the Lord had spoken through the prophet:
> [23]Look! The virgin is with child and will give birth to a son whom they will call Immanuel, a name which means 'God-is-with-us'.

He is not first and foremost considering the historical context of the Isaiah prophecy. He is seeing the wonderful story of the virginal conception of Jesus promised by the angel to Joseph as confirmed by looking at the Scriptures inspired by God.

Matthew in his formula quotation fastens on only two aspects of the Isaiah prophecy; the promise that Jesus will be born of a virgin (*parthenos*), and that the name of this child will be Immanuel, God-is-with-us. For Davies/Allison, the first aspect, Jesus born of a virgin, "offers scriptural confirmation for the extraordinary history narrated in 1:18-25. Isaiah's words, which pertain to the house of David and speak of a virgin, are intended to show that Jesus' origin was according to the Scriptures. This is so important because it implicitly identifies and vindicates the Church as the continuation of Israel; for if Jesus, whom the Church confesses, has fulfilled the Scriptures, then Christians must be the true people of God."[40]

The second important aspect of Matthew's understanding of Isaiah 7:14 is "Immanuel, a name which means God-is-with-us". Matthew spells it out for us. Davies/Allison again: "The mention of Emmanuel gives Matthew one more Christological title with which to work. This is consonant with his desire to open his work by telling us *who* Jesus is. It also permits a sort of *inclusion*. For just as 1.23 speaks of Jesus as 'God *with us*, so the Gospel ends with the promise "I am with *you* always…" [28:20].[41]

So what Matthew achieves in this interpretation of Isaiah 7:14 is to understand the virginal conception of Jesus as much more than just a miracle. The Isaiah prophecy enables him to understand the birth of Jesus theologically; as a sign of a new beginning for Israel. Jesus' miraculous birth is a sign that the Christian Church is the renewed people of God, led by Jesus himself as the Son of God, God-with-us.

But how early is Matthew's account? Even more, how do we know that we have the authentic text of Matthew's account of the Annunciation of the virginal conception, or indeed of Luke's? That is the next subject of our investigation.

NOTES – CHAPTER TWO

1   Jackson, W., 2002, p.2
2   *Ibid* p.2.
3   NBD, 557.
4   Gray, *Isaiah 1-39,* 122.
5   Jackson, W., 2002, 2. Above, p.25.
6   BM 149.
7   Machen, 1958, 292.
8   NJBC, **15:19**, 235.
9   *Ibid,* 235.
10 Gray, *Isaiah 1-39,* 128-129.
11 Gray, *Ibid.* 132.
12 Gray, *Ibid.* 123.
13 Gray, *Ibid.* 123.
14 NBD, art. *Virgin,* 1313.
15 ODCC, 303.
16 Brown, P.B., www.newwine.org

17 McNamara, M., 1968, 11.

18 Maier, J., 1996, 127.

19 Kraus, 1969, 10.

20 Brown, P., www.newwine.org

21 Levie, 1961, 27.

22 Kraus, 1969, 66. "Moyse ne peut être l'auteur de tous les livres qui lui son attribués." *Histoire critique du Vieux Testament.*

23 ODCC, 1277.

24 White, A.D. http://abob.libs.uga.edu/bobk/whitet02.html.

25 BI, 332, 752-3.

26 De La Potterie, I, 242.

27 Cf. Tanner, 2, 806, line 32, First Vatican Council *De revelatione:* the Sacred Scriptures *"revelationem sine errore contineant".*

28 Gray, J., I and II Kings, 26.

29 Weinandy *et al*, ed., 2005, 15.

30 The CCC refers to Mark 12:29-31.

31 The CCC refers to 1 Corinthians 5:6-8, 10:1-11.

32 The CCC refers to St Augustine, *Quaest. In Hept.* 2,73: PL 34, 623f; cf. DV 16.

33 DV 11.

34 CCC refers to St Bernard, *S.missus st hom.*4.11: PL 183, 86.

35 CCC refers to Luke 24:45.

36 BMG, 78.

37 Cf. BM, 98. Matthew 1:22-23 citing Isaiah 7:14: Matthew 2:5b-6, citing Micah 5:1 and 2 Samuel 5:2: Matthew 2:15b citing Hosea 11:1. Matthew 2:17-18 citing Jeremiah 31:15. Matthew 2:23b citing perhaps Isaiah 4:3 and Judges 16:1.

38 BM, 104.

39 Davies/Allison, 220. So also R.E. Brown, "What Matthew did (with possible apologetic aim) was to bring into open discussion the problem raised by a pre-Gospel narrative of the annunciation of the Davidic Messiah's birth from a virgin through the creative power of the Holy Spirit". BM, 161. So also Lagrange, 16: *"Quant à la relation de la prophétie a l'évenement, il faut d'abord constater que Mt.tenait la conception surnaturelle comme un fait, et que ce n'est pas la texte d'Isaïe qui lui en a suggéré l'idée."*

40 Davies/Allison, 212-213.

41 The same link between this verse and the end of Matthew's Gospel is made by Harrington, 36. In saying "Immanuel, a name which means God-is-with-us", is Matthew referring to Jesus as God? Irenaeus, Bishop of Lyons, the great second-century theologian, thought so. *Adv.haer.*3.21.4. Cf. Davies/Allison, 217. Davies/Allison, while giving good reasons for this interpretation, in the end prefer to conclude that "While the passage is not Incarnational in its intent in the sense that it posits a pre-existent being, the Son, who took flesh, it does, in a more general sense, indicate that, through the coming of

Jesus Christ God's Spirit became uniquely present among men". This latter position is also taken by Beare, 72: "...in the Matthaean passage, it does not convey the doctrine that Jesus is himself divine, but the conviction of the evangelist that in Jesus, God is again manifesting his presence in Israel by sending a deliverer".

APPENDIX TO CHAPTER TWO:
MATTHEW'S TRANSLATION OF ISAIAH 7:14

Matthew follows almost word for word the Septuagint Greek of Isaiah 7:14: *idou hé parthenos en gastri exei kai texetai huion kai keleseis to onoma autou Emmanuél* ("Behold a virgin shall conceive and bear a son and thou shalt call his name Emmanuel").

But Matthew has one variation, quite significant: he has *kalesousin* ("they will call") in place of the Septuagint *kaleseis* ("thou shalt call"). In the LXX translation, Ahaz is thus told by YHWH to name the child. This is clearly a reference to a past birth in the time of the prophet, with Ahaz the king naming the father, not a reference to a prophecy hundreds of years in advance.

It seems more probable, therefore, if we accept that Matthew is using the LXX that he has changed the verb to the more general "they will call him Emmanuel" in order to make reference to a future virgin birth, the birth of Christ, "they" perhaps even being the many Christians who will call Christ "God-with-us", Matthew "may have preferred a plural because it is not Mary and Joseph but all those saved from their sins (1:21) who will call Jesu 'Emmanuel', the third person plural having for its subject the church (so Frankemolle, pp.16-18)". ICC, 213-4.

Thus again it is by no means obvious that Matthew has read an Old Testament text and created the idea of the virgin birth from reading that text. Matthew seems to have made the Old Testament text prove his point that Jesus was virgin born, rather than creating the idea of the virgin birth from reading the text.

CHAPTER THREE

THE MANUSCRIPTS

> We can be certain that the text of Matthew and Luke we have before us is substantially what was first published, as with the text of the whole of the New Testament.

When, at the end of 2004, I published *Bad, Mad or God? Proving the Divinity of Christ from St. John's Gospel,* I expected, and still expect, many of its arguments to be questioned. After all, I had gone against two hundred years of scepticism concerning the Gospels. I had argued that Jesus was not, as the critical tradition generally asserts, only a Jewish prophet whom the early Christians elevated in their faith to be the Son of God. Rather, as the Fourth Gospel asserts, Jesus himself claimed to be the I AM revealed to Moses on the holy mountain. "Before Abraham was, I AM" [John 8:58]. For this, he was condemned by the Sanhedrin and handed over to Pilate eventually to be crucified. To claim that the historical Jesus understood himself as God goes against the critical establishment's view and one would expect a counter-argument from someone.

What I did not expect was that a book would appear which attempts to undermine the idea that the New Testament manuscripts are reliable. That surprises me, because generally speaking the most sceptical of scholars would not question that they are. But perhaps I should not be surprised. The phenomenal success of Dan Brown's novel *The Da Vinci Code* should surely indicate to us that at this point in time, the most ludicrous interpretations of Christian origins – that Jesus was married to Mary Magdalene, that the divinity of Christ was invented by the Emperor Constantine, that ritual sex took place in the Jewish Temple[1] – are liable to fly off the shelves of the bookshops. People seem to be seduced by any view which deflects from serious consideration that the

Christian faith might be in fact the truth revealed by God for the entire human race.

So perhaps I should not be surprised that *Whose Word Is It? The Story Behind Who Changed the New Testament and Why*, by Bart D. Ehrman[2] has according to its publisher hit the *New York Times* best-seller list. The back cover of the book proclaims to us: "He (Ehrman) makes the provocative case that many of our cherished biblical stories and widely held beliefs concerning the divinity of Jesus, the Trinity and the divine origins of the Bible itself stem from intentional and accidental alterations by scribes – alterations that dramatically affected all subsequent versions of the Bible."

Ehrman is raising a doubt which must present itself to all who approach the Bible, and particularly the Gospels. The first question people ask is, "The Gospels are now nearly two thousand years old. How do we know that we have the original version?" If serious doubts are thrown upon the veracity of the manuscripts themselves, then the enquirer will wonder whether it is worth reading the Gospels at all.

But Ehrman is on his own with these doubts among biblical scholars. However sceptical about the Gospels the scholar might be, he or she accepts that the text itself is basically trustworthy. Why is this so? Why is Ehrman alone in this doubt as to the authenticity of the text of the New Testament? That is because he does not seem to grasp the implications of the research into the text of the New Testament over the past two hundred years.

May I briefly rehearse the argument I outlined in *Bad, Mad or God?*[3] The most important research, into tens of thousands of manuscripts from before the third century AD until the Middle Ages, was performed meticulously by the German Tischendorf, and even more by the English scholars Westcott and Hort in the nineteenth century. Westcott and Hort classified the manuscripts into families, and eliminated those scripts which were clearly dependant on one previously. So they were able to produce families of texts down the line of origin back to fourth and fifth-century manuscripts. Since their time, the discovery of papyrus manuscripts, more or less complete as the case may be, some as early as the second century AD have been used as a further check on these later and more complete parchment manuscripts.

Ehrman recognizes the importance of these researches.[4] But he fails to understand the significance of the conclusions of Westcott and Hort, confirmed by twentieth-century New Testament paleontology. I summarised what Westcott and Hort have demonstrated thus:

> Thus we have an interesting paradox. Because the Christian scribes made mistakes in their transmission of the text (unlike the Jewish Massoretic scribes who were meticulous copyists[5]), and thus produced families of texts based upon common scribal errors or glosses, we cannot go back to a single original later than the beginning of the second century AD *And because the variations between those early manuscripts are generally speaking minute, we can be certain that the unknown original manuscript on which all depended did not differ significantly from the manuscripts we have before us.*[6]

Again, Ehrman admits that, among the thousands and thousands of variations in the thousands and thousands of manuscripts, few are of any theological significance. Then why does he not side with the huge majority of scholars that we can safely depend substantially on the text before us? As we can see now, his real problem is a faulty view of biblical inspiration:

> Most of these differences are completely immaterial and insignificant. A good portion of them simply show us that the scribes in antiquity could spell no better than most people can today (and they didn't even have dictionaries, let alone spell check). Even so, what is one to make of all these differences? If one wants to insist that God inspired the very words of scripture, what would be the point if we don't *have* the very words of scripture? In some places, as we will see, we simply cannot be sure that we have reconstructed the original text accurately. It's a bit hard to know what the words of the Bible mean if we don't even know what the words are![7]

Ehrman's problem, as he says in his first chapter, is that he was first taught in a fundamentalist college, where what is called *verbal inspiration* was taught. He felt that, to keep his traditional faith, he had to know the exact words of Scripture. Manuscript variations were a threat to his faith.

I find it difficult to believe that even his colleagues in his theological college, however fundamentalist he says it was, had as naïve a view of biblical inspiration as he expresses above. All Christians, I am sure, agree that, in giving his final revelation to the human race, in Jesus Christ, God acted in a human way. As Vatican II puts it, "Indeed God's Words, expressed through human language, have taken on the likeness of human speech, just as the Word of the eternal Father, when he assumed the flesh of human weakness, took on the likeness of human beings".[8]

This is the principle of the Incarnation, that God meets us in our own way as human beings. Thus, when God provides us with the Word of God, that Word comes to us in human language, and is transmitted in a human way; in this case, through ancient documents. In spite of the myriad variations, these New Testament documents have been faithfully transmitted to us down the centuries. We can read the Scriptures substantially as they were written. We need no more, in fact we can achieve no more, granted that they are ancient documents, transmitted to us over two thousand years. In this, if you like messy way, God has communicated his Word, his meaning, to us human beings.

The Church has never claimed more than the *substantial reliability* of the Gospel texts. Church authorities have always encouraged scholars to work on the text, to find if possible the nearest to the original; knowing that such a task will always be ongoing, granted the very nature of ancient documents. The first was Jerome (340-420 AD), the patron saint of biblical scholars, who, as Ehrman correctly says,[9] was commissioned by Pope Damasus to produce the official Latin translation of the Greek New Testament, Latin being the common language of the West. In producing this text, Jerome compared the Old Latin texts of the Bible already to hand, with the original Greek.

Jerome's Vulgate ("common") Version became the common Bible of the West for a thousand years. At the time of the Renaissance and the Reformation, a time of great upheaval, the Roman Catholic Church for disciplinary reasons limited scholars to that Vulgate text only, from which other language translations could be made. But the Council of Trent, meeting for its Fourth Session in 1545, was careful to state no more than that the Vulgate was "to be regarded as authentic".[10] This careful wording does not rule out the possibility *in se* that other versions of the Bible might be authentic. But, in a time of theological conflict, the Catholic Church wished to retain control of the text, to make sure that its own people would have to hand a version which it was safe to recommend in terms of doctrine and morality.[11]

This rule of dependence on the Vulgate was relaxed by Pope Pius XII in 1943, in the Encyclical on Scripture studies, we have already mentioned *Divino Afflante Spiritu.* The Pope commended the labours of textual critics (implicitly those such as Westcott and Hort, who incidentally were not Roman Catholics), and encouraged Catholic scholars to join their number in diligent enquiry to discover the original text *as far as possible:*

> For its very purpose is to insure that the sacred text be restored, as perfectly as possible, be purified from the corruptions due to the carelessness of the copyists and be freed, as far as may be done, from glosses and omissions, from the interchange and repetition of words and from all other kinds of mistakes, which are wont to make their way gradually into writings handed down through many centuries.[12]

Pius XII does not share the fears of Ehrman (which I am sure the Pope would have regarded as irrational) that any change to the text as the result of manuscript study could undermine his faith in the Bible as the Word of God. He is sure that the text as it stands as already transmitted is adequate to convey the message of God to the people of God. But, as with every ancient text, there are imperfections which professional research can often (even if not always) correct. This will not undermine the faith of the reader, but will be part of the ongoing process of better understanding revelation, a process which will not end until the end of the world.

It is quite absurd of Ehrman to suggest (or rather to proclaim) that upon this process of textual criticism depends our faith, rather than progress in it. The text as it stands, in whatever version, of whatever age, is quite adequate to convey the true revelation of God in Christ. If the reader wishes confirmation of this, he or she can look on the one hand at the Douay-Rheims[13] version, translated according to the Tridentine rules of the time, from the Latin Vulgate version. Then look at the King James Authorised Version,[14] which was the translation approved in 1611 for use in the Church of England, and was based upon the Greek New Testament *Textus Receptus* (the Received Text). Then finally look at a modern version such as the *New International Version* or the *New Jerusalem Bible*. You will see that, in whatever translation, you are looking at what is substantially the same text, with the same salvific meaning. So will a scholar find, who, using a modern computer bible study programme, will have access to a hundred different translations of the Bible at the click of a mouse.

Mountains out of molehills

Having informed us quite rightly that nearly all the hundreds of thousands of changes in the tens of thousands of manuscripts do not affect the meaning of the text of the New Testament, Ehrman then confuses unnecessarily the reader unacquainted with New Testament textual criticism by making it appear as if some changes would theologically alter our view of Christ and Christian origins. This is misleading.

There are, indeed, three examples of additions to the text which are significant. But these are well known to the scholars, and are more like three pebbles on a large beach, or three molehills in a large field:

1. **The Woman Taken in Adultery** [John 8:1-11]. C.K. Barrett, in his classic critical commentary on John, first published in 1955, says "this narrative is not an original part of the Gospel... It cannot have been included in the Gospel as at first published", because it is lacking in all the early and better manuscripts of St John's Gospel.[15] Barrett is agnostic as to whether this was originally from Jesus, even though he concludes that it was an ancient story about him. But, as Barrett says, "it represents the character and method of Jesus as they are revealed elsewhere".[16] Most of us believe that somehow this story is genuine, even though it is difficult to prove it from textual criticism. It may have been a lost story about Jesus, later to be inserted in the Fourth Gospel. Far from altering our view of Jesus, it only reinforces the emphasis upon the forgiveness of sins which is quite unique to the teaching of Jesus; especially in Luke, for example 7:36-50, 15:7, 15:10, 15:13. For this reason, some scholars think that it originally belonged in Luke.

2. **The Ending of Mark's Gospel** [Mark 16:9-20]. Scholars are all agreed that this was not originally part of St Mark's Gospel. Hort, Swete, and Lagrange, the pioneering Catholic scholar of the late nineteenth and early twentieth century, all judge that the manuscript evidence for it is poor.[17] Was Mark's original ending lost? Or did Mark end originally at 16:8 (without any Resurrection appearances, unlike the other Gospels), and an ending was added later for a smoother finish? With Ehrman and others,[18] I think that, in keeping with Mark's abrupt style, he wanted to end his Gospel with the startling account of the women finding the tomb of Jesus empty: "And the women came out and ran away from the tomb because they were frightened out of their wits; and they said nothing to anyone, for they were afraid" [Mark 16:8]. Mark leaves the account of the appearances of Jesus to the other three evangelists.[19] Mark 16:9-20, in this view, is a very early scribal gloss, to finish Mark's Gospel in a way more in conformity with the other three Gospels.

3. **The Johannine Comma** [1 John 5:7-8]. Ehrman informs us correctly that Erasmus, the sixteeth century Renaissance scholar, began the debate in the West concerning the authenticity of 1 John 5:7-8.[20] The following verses were in the standard edition of the Vulgate, which verses we show here in the Douay-Rheims translation from the Latin:

> And there are Three who give testimony in heaven, the Father, the Word, and the Holy Ghost. And these three are one. And there are three that give testimony on earth: the Spirit and the water and the blood. And these three are one.

Erasmus was, quite correctly suspicious of this text. He suspected that part of 1 John 5:7-8 was a later addition by a pious scribe. What Ehrman does not say is that manuscript research has modified this text in all modern critical editions of the New Testament to its most likely original. *The New Jerusalem Bible*, a translation approved by the Catholic hierarchy, has in its main text of 1 John 5:7-8:

> So there are three witnesses, the Spirit, water and blood; and the three of them coincide.[21]

NJB includes a footnote regarding what scholars call the Johannine Comma, which it places in italics. "Vulg. vv.7-8 read as follows: 'There are three witnesses *in heaven, the Father, the Word and the Spirit, and these three are one; there are three witnesses on earth:* the Spirit, the water and the blood.' The words in italics, (not in any of the early Greek manuscripts, or in any of the early translations, or in the best manuscripts of the Vulgate itself) are probably a gloss that has crept into the text."[22]

Far from being a threat to our faith, therefore, the history of the rejection of the Johannine Comma, and of the ending of Mark, and of the retention of the account of the Woman Taken in Adultery, are all prime examples of the progress made in textual criticism. Strange that Ehrman, in informing his readers who he assumes are not learned in New Testament manuscripts, does not make it sufficiently clear that these three changes are actually incorporated into our modern Bibles.

Ehrman, even to begin to make his case, has to turn these three molehills into mountains. He adds a few more molehills, what he calls "Theologically Motivated Alterations of the Text",[23] and "The Social Worlds of the Text",[24] a discussion about a few texts which he claims have been changed either for theological motives, for example against those who were Adoptionist[25] who thought that Jesus only became Son of God at his baptism; or who had an exclusive view of women.[26] None of these texts, even if we accepted all of Ehrman's speculative modifications, materially alter the meaning of the text of the New Testament, which stands as substantially reliable.

In fact, in his discussion of 1 Corinthians 14:33-36, where Paul decrees that women must keep silence in church, Ehrman confuses the reader further by not distinguishing between *textual criticism* and *literary* or *redaction criticism.* There is no manuscript problem regarding 1 Corinthians 14:33-36. The text stands in all the best manuscripts. Scholars only debate whether it is a later "post-Pauline" interpolation by a "misogynist" Christian.[27] But this redaction, or later addition, would have taken place before 1 Corinthians was published in the form we have it now. That is not a problem for textual, but for redaction criticism. But we are given the impression by Ehrman, in the context of his whole book, that somehow manuscript studies have thrown doubt on this text, which they have not.

In the course of our discussion of this question of the virginal conception, we will encounter some textual problems which have some possible theological implications. But these variations are minute, We have what is substantially the original edition. As we will now see, Matthew and Luke are to be dated not later than the end of the first century, and most probably are to be dated from 70-90 AD.

1   I refute these incredible hypotheses in my pamphlet, *The Truth About Jesus:* Not *the Da Vinci Code.* London, Catholic Truth Society, 2006. Dan Brown has only written a novel; but many take it seriously from the historical viewpoint.

2   London, Continuum, 2006.

3   BMG, pp.75-78.

4   Ehrman, 2006, 124.

5   Kenyon, 1939, 37-8.

6   BMG, 78.

7   Ehrman, 2006, 10-11.

8   DV 13, Tanner, II, *977.

9   Ehrman, 2006, 74-75.

10 *"quaenam pro authentica habenda sit".* Second Decree. Tanner, II, *664.

11 Pius XII interprets this "authenticity" as "juridical" rather than as "critical": "Hence this special authority or as they say, authenticity of the Vulgate was not affirmed by the Council particularly for critical reasons, but rather because of its legitimate use in the churches throughout so many centuries; by which use indeed the same is shown, in the sense in which the Church has understood and understands it, to be free from any error whatsoever in matters of faith and morals; so that, as the Church herself testifies and affirms, it may be quoted safely and without fear of error in disputations, in lectures and in preaching; and so its authenticity is not specified primarily as critical, but rather as juridical." DAS, 21.

12 DAS, 17.

13 http://www.catholicfirst.com/bibledrv.cfm. The New Testament translation was published in 1582, the Old Testament in 1609-10, at the English College, Douay.

14 http://en.wikipedia.org/wiki/King_James_Bible

15 Barrett, *John*, 589.

16 Barrett, *John*, 590.

17 "The passage is omitted by À, B k sy*, and important manuscripts of the Georgian, Armenian, and Aethiopic versions, and Eusebius and Jerome attest that it was wanting in almost all Gk manuscripts known to them". Taylor, *Mark*, 610. "The 'longer ending' of Mark vv 9-20 is included in the canonically accepted body of inspired Scripture, although some important manuscripts (including Vat and Sin) omit it, and it does not seem to be by Mark. It is in a different style and is little more than a summary of the appearances of the risen Christ, with other material, all of which could be derived from various New Testament writings." NJB, 16 c, 1685.

18 Ehrman, 68.

19 Against those who argue that, because Mark is deemed by scholars to be the earliest Gospel, the Resurrection appearances themselves are a later fiction, cf. BMG, 315: "it might well be possible that buried in Matthew and Luke are traditions earlier than those contained in Mark, even if Mark is accepted as the earliest account within the critical orthodoxy". I then go on to demonstrate, with N.T. Wright, 2003, that the Resurrection stories are authentic and historical.

20 Ehrman, 2006, 8.

21 NJB, 2019, 5e. "The three testimonies converge. Blood and water join the Spirit, 2:20k…"

22 NJB 2019, 5d.

23 Ehrman, 2006, Chapter 6, 151-175.

24 *Ibid.,* 2006, Chapter 7, 177-205.

25 *Ibid.,* 2006, 155.

26 *Ibid.,* 2006, 183.

27 As considers Jerome Murphy O'Connor, NJBC, **49:64**, 811. "The injunctions reflect the misogynism of 1 Timothy 2:11-14 and probably stem from the same circle". "Misogynist" is a strange accusation, even granted a post-Paul redactor as the author of 1 Corinthians 14:33-36. All of us know of the Jewish liturgical custom where women sit in galleries, and never lead the synagogue liturgy. No one, to my knowledge, has accused the Jews of "misogynism"! Is Paul here simply following Jewish custom, in which case it could be genuinely Pauline?

CHAPTER FOUR

BORN OF A VIRGIN:
THE EARLIEST TRADITION

> The Gospels of Matthew and Luke were written not later than the end of the first century AD. There is no tradition earlier than Matthew and Luke to contradict their testimony, that Jesus was virginally conceived by Mary.

The date of Matthew's Gospel

As I maintained in *Bad, Mad or God?*,[1] all scholars agree that the Gospels of Matthew and Mark must have been published in their first edition before the close of the first century AD. We have the testimony of Papias, Bishop of Hieropalis, c.60-130, that Matthew wrote the first Gospel, and that Mark was the 'interpreter of Peter the apostle, and the author of Mark's Gospel'. This statement of Papias, quoted in Eusebius' fourth century *Ecclesiastical History*, the authenticity of whose reference to Papias is unquestioned, demonstrates at the very least that Papias knew of the existence of the Gospels of Matthew and Mark prior to 130 AD, and possibly much earlier.[2] We may add also, with Benedict Viviano, that Matthew's Gospel was probably known to Ignatius of Antioch, who was martyred early in the second century.[3]

How much earlier is a matter of ongoing debate among the scholars, a debate which will probably never be resolved. If the author of Matthew is the same individual as Levi, son of Alphaeus, the taxgatherer, who left his accounting table to follow Jesus [Mark 2:14], called Matthew in Matthew 9:9, the traditional author of the first Gospel, then Matthew's Gospel could have been written as early as the middle of the first century, along with the early letters of Paul.

The majority of critical scholars reject the tradition that the Gospel of Matthew was written by an eyewitness of the events recorded. As Viviano says, "But, since the author of the final Greek text seems to have copied with modifications the whole of the Gospel according to Mark, it is now commonly thought that it is improbable that in its present form it is the work of an eye-witness apostle."[4]

I have never found such an argument convincing. In fact, it is a *non sequitur*. Even if Matthew was an eye-witness, could he not have read the Gospel of Mark, and said to himself, "This is a good account of Jesus' life. I will use it in my work"? How many of us have taken someone else's written description of the proceeds of a meeting, to save ourselves the trouble of writing our own account?

The critical view, that Mark's Gospel was first written, and that Matthew used Mark, is itself not without distinguished dissenters. There is a whole minority movement in Synoptic studies, led by W.R. Farmer and Dom Bernard Orchard, to revive the traditional view first stated by the Church Father Papias, and supported by St Augustine that Matthew was first.[5] If so, then an earlier date for Matthew is even more possible.

But even if we accept the critical orthodoxy, that Matthew and Luke used Mark, an early date for the Gospel of Matthew is still arguable. John A. T. Robinson, in his challenging work *Re-Dating the New Testament*,[6] contests the generally held view that Mark's Gospel is to be dated just before the destruction of the Temple in Jerusalem at the end of the Jewish war 66-70.

This view is based upon Mark 13:1-4, where Jesus prophesies the destruction of the Temple. He tells his astonished disciples, "you see all these great buildings? Not one of them will be left upon another; all will be thrown down." The critical view is that this is an example of a prophecy after the event. The early Christians could see the Jewish revolt coming in the mid-sixties. Mark therefore puts into the mouth of Jesus a prophecy of the destruction of Jerusalem and its Temple. But Robinson argues that, on the contrary, Jesus' prophecy is connected rather to an event which had already occurred, "the desecration of the temple-sanctuary by an idolatrous image under Antiochus Epiphanes in 168-7 BC. This was the "abomination of desolation"…[7]

For Robinson, therefore, Jesus is using the language of prophecy in referring to a past event but forecasting a future disaster in the same terms. There is no specific reference therefore to the Fall of Jerusalem, and Mark for Robinson could therefore be dated earlier.

If Mark is to be dated before the usually accepted 64, then for Robinson the same applies to Matthew, if we presume Matthew is dependent on Mark. Matthew, also Luke, tells the story of the wedding feast where many invited guests refuse the gracious invitation to attend [Matthew 22:1-10 = Luke 14:16-24]. Matthew adds "The others seized the servants, attacked them brutally and killed them. The king was furious; he sent troops to kill those murderers and set their town on fire" [Matthew 22:6-8].[8]

Again, Robinson argues that this does not necessarily refer to the Fall of Jerusalem, any more than does Mark. On the contrary, Robinson follows the view of Rengstorf, that "the wording of Matthew 22:7 represents a fixed description of ancient expeditions of punishment and is such an established *topos* of Near Eastern, Old Testament and Rabbinic literature that it is precarious to infer that it must reflect a particular occurrence."[9] Thus, Robinson contends, Matthew also could be earlier than 70 AD, the date of composition most popular among modern scholars.

I personally agree with N.T. Wright,[10] that the historical Jesus actually predicted the Fall of Jerusalem. Prescinding from any supernatural knowledge on Jesus' part, a reasonably astute politician could have predicted the destruction of Jerusalem within a few decades. The situation in Jerusalem was dangerously volatile when Jesus was himself visiting the Holy City, where he was to meet his death by crucifixion some time between 26 and 36 AD.[11]

Robinson demonstrates to us how precarious any arguments are which try to pinpoint still further the date of Matthew after we have established the latest date, the *terminus ante quem* of the end of the first century. It would seem to me not unreasonable, granted that Jesus actually predicted the Fall of Jerusalem, that those who finally edited the Gospel from traditions about Jesus' words and deeds would emphasise those sayings of his which did seem to have relevance to their own historical situation.[12] Thus it seems most reasonable, where the date of Matthew is concerned, to fix the date of composition, as do most scholars, at 70-90 AD.

This was less than a century after the birth of Christ, the more precise date of which we will discuss later. This is well within the time span of an authentic historical tradition. We would not need to argue strenuously for the authorship of Matthew himself of the Gospel which bears his name. The Church teaches the apostolic *origin*, not necessarily the apostolic *authorship* of the Gospels.[13]

As Viviano says, "The apostle Matthew may, however, have been at the start of the gospel tradition if he gathered the sayings of Jesus together in a collection like Q",[14] Q being the name given by scholars to a hypothetical source which contained material common to Matthew and Luke but not in Mark.[15]

For our purposes, this is quite sufficient initially to establish that Matthew's account of the birth of Jesus from the Virgin Mary is at least possibly historically reliable. If, for instance, we could only have demonstrated a date two or three centuries after the events recorded, then we would be justified in thinking that the faith of the early Christians had created a myth. But, fixing a date within three generations at the latest of the event of the virgin birth at least leaves the question open as to that tradition being authentic.

The date of Luke

The vast majority of scholars date Luke's Gospel contemporary with Matthew. On the one hand, there is no clear evidence from Papias, as there was with Matthew, that Luke's Gospel must have been written well before 130 AD. The earliest mention we have of Luke's Gospel is in the Muratorian Canon of accepted biblical books, which is to be dated 180-200 AD.[16] This canonical list mentions "the physician Luke", i.e. the companion of Paul [e.g. Philemon 1:24] as the author of the Third Gospel.[17] Since the date of Luke from external evidence could be pushed back to the latter half of the second century, this has generated a wider range of dating than that proposed by the critical minimum.

Karris, along with many critical scholars, accepts the traditional authorship of Luke: "One should accept the tradition that Luke composed this Gospel, for there seems no reason why anyone in the ancient church would invent this datum and make a relatively obscure figure the author of a Gospel".[18] This would necessitate a date not later than the end of the first century AD. Kümmel is more sceptical, quoting Cadbury's view that "already at the end of the second century it could have been *inferred* that Luke was the author by reasoning from the presupposition that a canonical Gospel must have an apostolic author..."[19]

But this is surely a case of hyper-criticism. Scholars do actually agree that the author of Luke was also the author of Acts, accepting the evidence from the introduction to both books [Luke 1:1-4, cf. Acts 1:1-2, "In my former book, Theophilus..."]. Raymond Brown also agrees that there is no other serious candidate than Luke to be the author of Acts, so also of Luke.[20]

Brown further insists that the objections to Luke's authorship, that a companion of Paul would have known more of Paul's theology,[21] and that there are historical discrepancies between Paul's letters and the account in Acts, are by no means decisive.[22] Why should not Luke's theology be different than Paul's? Luke presumably had a mind of his own! They share the same faith in Christ, so why should they not express that faith differently? As to historical discrepancies between Paul's letters and Acts, is it not impossible that Luke, himself not a witness to events in the pre-Pauline Church, has uncritically accepted historical traditions handed on to him which are difficult to reconcile with information gleaned from Paul's letters. As we shall see later when considering the infancy stories, there is nothing contrary to the theology of divine inspiration with such an idea.

For this reason, it is difficult to see why Brown must restrict himself to the somewhat grudging conclusion that, regarding the authorship of Acts by Luke the companion of

Paul, and so implicitly regarding Luke's Gospel "This proposal for authorship has more to recommend it than other theories, but 'not impossible' is all that should be claimed."[23]

In any other field of the investigation of ancient historical documents, surely, the evidence of the Second Century Muratorian Canon would be accepted that Luke was the author of the Gospel bearing his name, and of the Acts of the Apostles. This external testimony is at the very latest only one hundred years after the composition of the Gospel of Luke. There is no other candidate to contend seriously to be the anonymous author of both Luke and Acts, than Luke mentioned by Paul in his letters [Colossians 4:14, 2 Timothy 4:11, Philemon 1:24]. There are no insurmountable objections to Luke being the author. We may therefore legitimately conclude, with Karris, that Lucan authorship has been demonstrated, thus dating Luke's Gospel at the latest to the end of the first century.

If we therefore take the birth of Christ at some time about 4 BC, just before the death of Herod the Great, (our present calculation of 0 BC/AD was in fact a monk's miscalculation) then we must estimate that we have no more than one hundred years before we have evidence of the tradition, from both Matthew and Luke, that Jesus was born of a virgin. It is an early tradition.

No-one doubts that Matthew teaches the virgin birth in his account. However, there has been some debate whether Luke's Annunciation could be interpreted rather as a promise of a natural birth. As we shall now see, that view cannot be sustained.

Luke: a virgin birth promised?

Luke does not make his account of the Annunciation of the virgin birth of Christ so obviously a fulfilment of Isaiah 7:14 as does Matthew. Davies/Allison think that Luke's account is dependent upon Isaiah's prophecy.[24] But Raymond Brown is not so sure:

And in the angel Gabriel's words to Mary, "Behold you will conceive in your womb and will give birth to a son, and you will call his name Jesus," is the Lucan *syllempsei* [*syllambanein*] *en gastri* an echo of Isaiah's *en gastri le*[*m*]*pesetai* [*lambanein*]? Is Luke's description of Joseph as a man "of the house of David" an echo of the address in Isaiah 7:13 "O house of David"? Scholars have taken a stance on both sides of this question;[25] but the language of birth annunciations, ranging from the accounts in Genesis and Judges through Isaiah to Luke, is so stereotyped that judgements about implicit citations of one passage (Isaiah 7:14) are very precarious.[26]

Nevertheless, Brown is quite convinced that Luke's account of the Annunciation to Mary, equally with Matthew's account, is that the child born in her will be virginally conceived. This Brown demonstrates by comparing Luke's Annunciation to Zechariah concerning the birth of John the Baptist [Luke 1:5-25] with the parallel account of the Annunciation to Mary [Luke 1:26-37].[27]

This parallelism drawn by Brown eventually convinced J.A. Fitzmyer, the distinguished Catholic scholar, that Luke's Annunciation is of a virginal conception. In an article written in 1973, Fitzmyer had originally thrown doubt on whether Luke 1:26-38 need ever be interpreted in that miraculous sense:

> When this account is read in and for itself – without the overtones of the Matthaean Annunciation to Joseph – every detail in it could be understood of a child to be born of Mary in the usual human way, a child endowed with God's special favour, born at the intervention of the Spirit of God, and destined to be acknowledged as the heir to David's throne as God's messiah and Son.[28]

At first sight at least, such a reading of the text might be possible. If we take the word "virgin" (*parthenon*) referring to Mary in 1:27, as we have already seen argued, it need only mean that Mary is a young woman of marriageable age who is just about to marry Joseph: [1:34]. Where Mary says "But how can this come about, since I am a virgin?" could mean no more than that she has "not known man" (i.e. had intercourse with a man) as yet, but perhaps will do so in the future before Jesus is born. Luke 1:35, referring to the overshadowing of the Holy Spirit, might be interpreted as emphasising the divine power in the event of Jesus' birth and its theological significance rather than the mode of conception of Jesus. Finally, when in 1:38, Mary makes her act of faith in the message of the angel, this could mean simply that she believes again that God is going to be present in the birth and in the life of the promised son, but not necessarily that the birth itself is going to be miraculous.

However, Fitzmyer, in his later commentary on Luke's Gospel published in 1981,[29] exercised the scholar's privilege of changing his mind, and now admits that the step-parallelism in the two announcements demands that the miraculous divine intervention, precisely invoking the creative power of the Spirit, has to result in a more extraordinary conception, hence, "virginal". The parallelism between the Annunciation of John the Baptist's birth and that of Jesus indicated by Brown[30] was convincing for Fitzmyer. Elizabeth, announced by an angel as the mother of John the Baptist, is barren, and so miraculously gives birth: so, argues Brown, a greater miracle (hence the virginal conception) heralds the birth of a greater one than John the Baptist, i.e. Jesus the Messiah.

This makes particularly good sense of Luke 1:37, where the angel tells Mary of the corresponding birth to her barren cousin Elizabeth: "for nothing is impossible to God"; God being capable not only of causing barren women to give birth to prophets, but now showing himself capable of causing the birth of the "Son of the most high" [Luke 1:32], with nothing other than the overshadowing of the spirit[31] coupled with the obedient faith of Mary.

It makes even greater sense of Mary's question in 1:34, "How can this come about, because I am a virgin?" seems a most peculiar question if she is just about to marry Joseph, the explanation offered that she did not know the facts of life being more amusing than persuasive![32] Literally, Mary asks, "How can this come about since *I have no knowledge of man*"

(NJB), i.e. "I have never had intercourse with a man." As Raymond Brown says:

> The verb "to know" is a Semitism for sexual relations; see Matthew 1:25: "He did not know her until she brought forth a son." While the tense is present, it describes a state resultant from a past pattern of behaviour, as the Old Latin version recognised using a perfect tense (*novi, cognovi*) – see the series of articles by Queke. The word for "man" is the specific *aner,* "male, husband", not the generic *anthropos.* Here it should be translated "husband" since Luke's intent is wider: Mary has not known *any* man and so is a virgin [1:27].[33]

The meaning of Mary's question is hotly disputed. Some Catholic scholars follow the patristic and mediaeval tradition that Mary took a vow of virginity before she gave birth to Christ.[34] This is not a dogma of faith,[35] but it is a plausible translation of the Greek present tense. In this case, Mary's question is, "How can this be, since I am a committed virgin?"

At the other end of the spectrum, Vermes argues that "How can this come about, because I am a virgin?" should really be understood as "How can this be for I have not yet begun to menstruate?" He points to rabbinic law that a girl who had not yet attained puberty would still be called a "virgin" in respect of menstruation, i.e. at the time of her first ovulation. Vermes argues that this was the case with respect to Mary, who cohabited with Joseph while still a "virgin" in this sense. He maintains, consistent with his theory, that "the situation could then have been misunderstood by the early Church in terms of virginity with respect to sexual intercourse".[36]

I. Howard Marshall rightly dismisses this view, "But this hypothesis gives an impossible meaning to the present verse; it clashes with Matthew 1:25; and it depends on a possible meaning of virgin which would have been unintelligible to Greek readers."[37]

Therefore, even if Vermes' convoluted explanation is correct – and I do not think for a moment that it is – then the

Christian community must have made the mistake of confusing "virgin" (*betulah*) with "a young girl who had not yet menstruated" at a much earlier stage in the history of the tradition of the virginal conception than the writing of Luke's Gospel. As we have the text before us, Luke wishes to tell us that Jesus was born miraculously of a young woman called Mary who had never had intercourse with a man. He wishes to tell us that this makes her son Jesus truly the son not of any man on earth, but the Son of God.

For Raymond Brown, this insight of Luke is an important stage in the development of the first-century Christology.[38] Mary's question "How can this come about, since I am a virgin?" is answered by the angel simply, "Because God's plan is that, without intercourse with any man, you will give birth to the Son of God." Luke wishes to tell us that Jesus is truly the Son of God, precisely because there was no human male agency in his conception; "the Son of the Most High in whom the Davidic royal promise is fulfilled is the child to be called the Son of God, conceived through the Holy Spirit and power. By moving the Christological moment to the conception, Luke tells us that there was never a moment on this earth when Jesus was not the Son of God."[39]

The Earliest Church testimony

Even more, there is no clear contrary tradition that Jesus was born in the natural way, until the close of the *second* century. The Church Father, Irenaeus, writing at the close of the second century, tells us of a Cerinthus who did not accept the divinity of Christ and together with this denied the virgin birth:

> He [Cerinthus, c.170] also said that Jesus was not born of a virgin but was the son of Joseph and Mary, like all the rest of men, only surpassing all others in justice, prudence and wisdom, that after His baptism Christ descended upon Him in the form of a dove... but that in the end Christ withdrew from Jesus, and Jesus suffered

and rose again, while Christ remained impassible since He was by nature spiritual.[40]

Von Campenhausen[41] speculates that there may have been areas of the ancient Church even at the end of the first century which did not accept the virginal conception. He argues from the silence of the Epistle of Barnabas and the Shepherd of Hermas. But this is no more than silence. Von Campenhausen agrees that, as far as hard evidence is concerned, the only tradition we have relayed from 80-120 is that Mary gave birth to Jesus without intercourse with a male.

This testimony to the virgin birth is confirmed by Ignatius of Antioch, who was martyred early in the second century, with the ink hardly dry on the New Testament books. Bishop Ignatius, on his way to martyrdom, was writing encouragement to the Ephesian Christians:

> For our God Jesus the Christ, was conceived by Mary, in God's plan being sprung both from the seed of David and from the Holy Spirit. He was born and baptised that by his Passion he might hallow water. Now Mary's virginity and her giving birth escaped from the prince of this world, as did the Lord's death – those three secrets crying to be told, wrought in God's silence.[42]

This is to be dated from the first decade of the second century. Ignatius' theology is not in any way similar to the way in which the Church's theology developed. It roots the virgin birth not in Christology, but in the theology of the atonement, and indeed in Ignatius' own unique view of it. Only a few years later into that second century, Justin the Martyr (100–160 AD)[43] was already defending the virgin birth, some think not even dependent on the accounts of Matthew and Luke.[44]

The most immediate assumption therefore should be that Cerinthus and those who agreed with him that Jesus was born in the natural way were countering an already existing tradition. They opposed the apostolic version of the birth of Jesus, claiming that he was naturally born. Those heretical

Christian groups, particularly those called "Ebionites",[45] who opposed the divinity of Christ but who named Jesus as Messiah, were opposing the virgin birth of Christ for theological reasons, because of a low Christology.

That is worth saying at this point. We shall see later that it is a common view among some critical scholars that the doctrine of the Virginal Conception was from the beginning theologically motivated. It was an evolution of an idea to promote the divinity of Christ through the myth of the virgin birth. But our preliminary researches lead us to a different first impression. It seems rather that at least it is possible that those who opposed the early doctrine of the Virgin Birth did so not because they had any hard historical evidence that Jesus was in fact naturally born, but rather because they had theological objections to the full divinity of Christ.

But is there any evidence from the New Testament itself that Jesus was born in the natural way? Some scholars think that some texts from the New Testament can be interpreted so.

NOTES – CHAPTER FOUR

1 BMG, 78.
2 Klijn, INT, 218.
3 NJBC, **42:4**, 631.
4 *Ibid.*, **42:2**, 630.
5 Cf. Orchard, Ed., 1978.
6 Robinson, 1976.
7 Robinson, 1976, 17.
8 I have followed Robinson's translation of Matthew in this instance, 19.
9 Robinson, 1976, 20.
10 Wright, 1996, 417. I support this view in BMG, 128, quoting Taylor, *Mark,* 501, who argues that in prophesying the destruction of the Temple Jesus stands in line with Micah 3:12 and Jeremiah 26:6, 18.
11 That was the span of the prefectureship of Pontius Pilate in Jerusalem, who condemned Jesus to death. BMG, 107.
12 This conforms very much to the teaching of the Second Vatican Council, DV19, which speaks of a process of selection, synthesis and explication regarding the composition of the four Gospels. "They (the

Gospel writers) selected some things from the abundant material already handed down, orally or in writing. Other things they synthesised, or explained with a view as to the needs of the churches (*vel statui ecclesiarum attendendo explanantes*)" Tanner, II, 978*.

13 DV 18, Cf. BMG 159 regarding the authorship of St John's Gospel.
14 NJBC, **42:2**, 630.
15 Cf. NJBC, **40:13**, 590.
16 BMG, 79. INT, 218. "a very ancient list of the books of N.T. first pub. in 1740 by Muratori (*Ant. Ital. Med. Aev.* iii. 851) and found in a seventh or eighth-century MS. in the Ambrosian Library at Milan. A reference to the episcopate of Pius at Rome ("nuperrime temporibus nostris") is usually taken to prove that the document cannot be later than *c.* 180, some 20 years after Pius's death (see *infra*)".
http://www.earlychristianwritings.com/info/muratorian-wace.html
17 Klijn, INT, 218.
18 NJBC, **43:2-3**, 675-6.
19 Kümmell, INT, 103. But Kümmell does contest the very late date argued by O'Neill, well into the second century, Kümmel himself opting for 70-90. That is because Kümmel considers that Luke did not know the letters of Paul, which he would have done if the writing of Luke/Acts was well into the second century, by which time Paul's letters were already part of a canonical list. But surely, as Klein contends (Kümmel, INT, 133), Luke could have known of the letters of Paul without wishing to use them as a source? Why is such a view, as Kümmel contends, "arbitrary"? Surely it is a real possibility?
20 Brown, INT, 326.
21 *Ibid.*, 324.
22 *Ibid.*, 326-7. There is a continuing discussion concerning the famous "we" passages. On the missionary journeys of Paul, c.50 AD, Acts on occasions uses "we" in the narrative, as if the author is himself a companion of Paul. "After Paul had seen the vision, we got ready at once to leave for Macedonia..." [Acts 16:10]. Many objections have been raised to this apparent companion of Paul being Luke, cf. Brown, INT, 325. In any case, Richard J. Dillon denies the relevance of the use of the first person plural in the narrative as necessarily implying that the author claims to be an eye-witness. Rather, Dillon thinks, NJBC, **44:3**, 723, it may have been a literary device emphasising the "pedigree of his narrative". Certainly, the use of the "we" in the narrative is contemporary with the period when Luke, if the author, would have been a companion of Paul.
23 Brown, INT, 326-7.
24 "The Old Testament verse seems to have influenced Luke 1:26-33; for even if Luke 1.31 has parallels outside of Isaiah 7:14 (e.g. Genesis 16.11, Judges 13:3), the description of Mary as a 'virgin', of Joseph as belonging to the 'house of David' (cf. Isaiah 7.17) make dependence upon Isaiah's prophecy plain enough." ICC, 212.

25 BM, 153, n.63: "Neirynck, *Noël*, 30, contends that there is no real evidence that Luke's scene reflects Isaiah 7:14, while Schürmann, *Lukasevangelium*, I, 58ff., is insistent on the influence of the Isaian passage. Vögtle, "Offene", 46, comments on how difficult it is to decide". Also BM, 300: "And so I would agree with Fitzmyer that there is no way of knowing that Luke was drawing upon Isaiah 7:14."

26 *Ibid.*, 153.

27 *Ibid.*, 297. So also Marshall: "The forms of the narratives are so similar that it cannot be doubted that they have been consciously arranged to bring out the parallelism between them.... ", *Luke*, 62.

28 "The Virginal Conception of Jesus in the New Testament." *Journal of Theological Studies*, 34 (1973), p.63.

29 *Luke*, 338.

30 BM, 301-303.

31 Luke 1:35 makes great sense if we see it as the creative power of God present in the virginal conception of Jesus; even if we do not go so far as the intriguing interpretation of John McHugh in identifying the imagery of the Ark of the Covenant in this text (MJNT, 56-63) and particularly in the concept of overshadowing [cf. Exodus 40:34-5, I Kings 8:10-11]; or even more as far as Miguens (Miguens, 1975, 75) in seeing daring parallels even with sexual love in Ruth 2:12, where Ruth asks her husband-to-be Boaz to "spread therefore your wing over your handmaid...", the imagery here in Miguens' view suggesting an analogical marriage between Mary and the Holy Spirit; although, of course, Miguens would be far from any suggestion of sexual contact with the divine, rather the concept of mystical non-sexual union which is strong in both Jewish and Christian tradition. (Cf, e.g. Hosea 2:21: "I shall betroth you to myself for ever, I shall betroth you in uprightness and justice, and faithful love and tenderness." Ephesians 5:31-32, where Paul compares the union between Christ and his Church with marriage.)

32 cf. BM, 303-309.

33 BM, 289.

34 MJNT, 176: "Indeed, among Roman Catholics this interpretation went virtually unchallenged until the beginning of the twentieth century".

35 MJNT, 446-447.

36 Marshall, *Luke*, 69-70.

37 *Ibid.*, 69-70.

38 i.e. "the doctrine of Christ", or "the study of Christ".

39 BM, 315-6.

40 Irenaeus, *Against Heresies*, 1,26, 1 (Harvey, 1, 211-12; PG, 7, 686). Palmer, P. *Mary in the Documents of the Church*. London, Burns, Oates, 1953, p.6.

41 Von Campenhausen, 1964, 19.

42 From Ephesians xviii.2 ff. Boslooper, 1962, 28.

43 ODCC, 770. http://www.newadvent.org/cathen/08580c.htm
44 Boslooper, 1962, 31, quotes Bruno Bauer when he said that Justin did not know Matthew and Luke. Bauer "was probably right". But Bauer accepted an impossibly late date for Matthew, well into the second century. Surely, Justin would have known the Canon of the four Gospels, including Matthew and Luke. But Justin's acceptance of the virgin birth is in any case significant, whether or not he knew Matthew and Luke.
45 ODCC, 438.

CHAPTER FIVE

THE "SILENCE" OF THE NEW TESTAMENT APART FROM MATTHEW AND LUKE

> • There are some texts in the Gospels which speak of Jesus as the "son of Joseph". But "son of Joseph" in the Gospels is always on the lips of Jesus' disciples or his adversaries. The evidence is best explained by the fact that, in the days of Jesus' public ministry, it was generally assumed that he was the natural son of Joseph. This was to prevent ridicule and scandal. He was in any case Joseph's adopted son, which in Jewish Law made him eligible for the inheritance of his father. Both Luke and Matthew claim that Jesus was in the line of David the Messiah [Matthew 1:1, Luke 1:27].
>
> • Only in one text, Matthew 1:16, does an evangelist apparently refer to Joseph as the apparently natural father of Jesus. But this is only in a variant manuscript reading with poor manuscript support.
>
> • As for St Paul, it cannot be demonstrated from his writings either that he believed the virginal conception, or that he did not.
>
> • Even though it cannot be with certainty demonstrated that Mark and John's Gospel give evidence of belief in a virginal conception, their high Christology, together with some hints that they possibly did not believe that Jesus had a human father, makes the existence of their faith in the virginal conception at least a possibility.

Some scholars are of the opinion that, because the remainder of the New Testament apart from Matthew and Luke has no explicit reference to the virgin birth, this demonstrates that there were other traditions within earliest Christianity which did not know of, or did not accept, the tradition of the virginal conception.

To press home this argument, some New Testament texts have been interpreted as at least suggesting that Jesus had been born in the normal way through intercourse between Mary and Joseph.

The line of David and the fatherhood of Joseph

Von Campenhausen claims that the "Lucan and the Matthean genealogical trees [Matthew 1:1-17, Luke 3:23-38] show that they originated in communities that as yet knew nothing of a virgin birth and regarded Jesus as Joseph's child, for, although they differ from each other, they both relate only to Joseph. Only in the last link in the chain have the evangelists attempted an artificial twist by way of correction, so as to accommodate it to the virgin birth." [1]

But it cannot be concluded that, because the genealogies trace the line through David's house, the compiler of the genealogy did not accept the virgin birth. On the contrary, as Beare argues, "The doctrine of the virgin birth, therefore, actually required that the place of Jesus in the Davidic succession should be secured through adoption or acknowledgement by one who was himself a 'son of David'. The genealogy and the story of the miraculous conception, accordingly, are not incompatible with one another, but complementary." [2]

Joseph needed to be descended from David, and he also needed to be the father of Jesus, for Jesus to be the Davidic Messiah. As Davies/Allison rightly say:

> It may surprise that the genealogy is followed by a story which denies Joseph's participation in fathering Jesus. But Matthew has in mind legal, not necessarily physical, descent, that is, the transmission of legal heirship; and the idea of paternity on two levels - divine and human, with position in society being determined by the mother's husband – was familiar in the ancient near east. In addition, the Mishnah relates, "If a man said, 'This is my son', he may be believed (*m.Bat.*8.6; cf. Isaiah 43:1, 'I have called you by name, you are mine'); and according to Matthew (and presumably his tradition) Joseph gave Jesus his name and thereby accepted the role of father. [3]

It is at this point that we come up against a considerable problem with tracing the historical tradition of the virginal conception. If Joseph can be legitimately called the "father" of Jesus, because Jesus is his adopted son, even if not his natural son, then we are led immediately to ask whether there are other instances in the New Testament where Jesus could be called "son of Joseph" and the virgin birth is not thereby denied by the use of that phrase. The mere calling of Jesus "son of Joseph" might not be any kind of threat to the historicity of the tradition of the virgin birth.

Thus, in the story in Luke of the finding of the Child Jesus in the Temple, Jesus' distraught mother Mary, on finding her son, who had been lost for three days, says to him "My child, why have you done this to us? See how worried your father and I have been, looking for you." [Luke 2:48]. Speaking to Jesus, she calls Joseph his "father". Howard Marshall makes the obvious comment, "The reference to 'your father' is also perfectly in keeping (how else would she have referred to Joseph?)."[4]

Thus Mary's use of "your father" to Jesus with reference to Joseph in no way prejudices Luke's account of her own Annunciation where she is promised a Messiah without male intercourse. Joseph is the adoptive father of Jesus.

On the other hand, there is a further complication. Granted hypothetically for the moment that we have proved our case and that the virginal conception actually happened, it is hardly likely that the knowledge of that miraculous event would have been paraded for the whole of Nazareth to hear, at least during Jesus' childhood. It would have caused general derision, and the name of Joseph would have been blackened as a cuckolded husband. The miracle of the virgin birth would surely have needed to have been kept quiet until after the Resurrection at least. Then, and only then, would the virgin birth be credible, and a further revelation of the nature of Jesus as Son of God and as Redeemer.

Thus, in the days during Jesus' life on earth, it would not only have been the case that calling Joseph Jesus' father was not wrong, since he was his adoptive father. It would also have been true that those who knew of the secret of the virgin birth would in no way have wished to discourage the idea, in public at least, that Joseph was the natural father of Jesus. I would suggest that this is not only possible conjecture. If Jesus was truly virgin born, then this would have been the only sensible procedure, to allow the general impression to continue that Joseph was the natural father.

To me, this explains, as we shall see, a great deal of the evidence which is adduced from the New Testament that Joseph was the father of Jesus. There is, however, one text which goes even further than saying that Joseph was the father of Jesus, or that Jesus was Joseph's son. It is a variant reading of Matthew 1:16.

Matthew 1:16

At the end of his genealogy, Matthew, having gone down his genealogical tree by referring always to "Abraham the father of Isaac", etc., ends up by saying:

> And Jacob fathered (Gk *eggenésan*) *Joseph* the husband of Mary: of her was born (Gk *eggenéthé*) Jesus who is called Christ. [Matthew 1:16]

In this text, Matthew is carefully avoiding saying that Joseph was the father of Jesus, in order to prelude the account of the Annunciation of the virgin birth of Jesus to Joseph. The passive tense "was born" is used of Mary regarding the birth of Jesus, to ensure consistency with the virgin birth of Jesus.

But there is a variant manuscript reading for Matthew 1:16, which was interpreted, when the manuscript was first discovered in 1894, as being evidence for another tradition to the effect that Joseph was the natural father of Jesus.[5] This variant reading appears for certain only in one version of the manuscripts, in the Old Syriac (Sinaiticus) version, dated the fourth or fifth century, and may be translated as:

> Jacob fathered Joseph; and Joseph, to whom the virgin Mary was betrothed, fathered Jesus, called the Christ.

A full discussion of this variant reading of Matthew 1:16 is in Davis/Allison,[6] and in the *Birth of the Messiah*.[7] Other minor variants are also considered there, including a manuscript of a fifth century debate between a Christian and a Jew.[8] However, the reader will find in neither commentary any certain conclusion to the debate. It is one of those textual-critical discussions to which we referred earlier when considering New Testament manuscripts in general, to the effect that there is a continual process of refinement of the text, while asserting that we do have the substantially reliable text in our Bibles.

The first clear certainty is that the manuscript evidence favours the usual reading. All the Greek manuscripts, which are generally the most reliable, apart from two inferior groups of manuscripts which have the variant,[9] have "And Jacob fathered (Gk *eggenésan*) Joseph the husband of Mary: of her was born (Gk *eggenéthé*) Jesus who is called Christ" [Matthew 1:16]. Thus the reader of the Bible is not deceived when he or she will read that text in nearly every version of the New Testament today.

However, it cannot be said that the status of the variant reading is of no consequence. A Syriac manuscript of the fourth and fifth century, thus written in the oldest Christian Semitic language, stemming from the Aramaic which Jesus himself spoke, geographically on the Syrian and Galilean border, is not to be ignored.

My own view is that Raymond Brown has the best of the solutions which I have read. He says:

> The Sinaitic Syriac translator was a free spirit who did not hesitate to make major "improvements" in the textual tradition that came to him. A Semitic, he could have understood "Joseph was the father of Jesus" not in a biological way that would contradict Matthew's emphasis in 1:18-25 but in terms of legal paternity (i.e. the view that a man's acceptance of a child as his son is what makes him a father...).[10]

The original Syriac would be much closer to the Hebrew, as a North Semitic dialect. The verb for "begat" or "fathered"

(Hebrew *yôléd*) does not necessarily mean that the father has a biological relationship with the son. It usually does, because the father is usually the natural father of the son, as 1 Chronicles 1:34, "And Abraham begat (conceived) Isaac". But the same verb is used in Psalm 2:7 "I will proclaim the decree of Yahweh: He said to me, "You are my son, today have I fathered you." In this case, where God is concerned, to "father" means formally installing a "king into theocratic rights."[11] This meaning carries over into the Greek translation of the Psalm, referring to Christ in Acts 13:33, and Hebrews 1:5, 5:5, using exactly the same verb *yennaó* as in Matthew. The Old Syriac version of Matthew 1:16 therefore would see Joseph as the father of Jesus in the same sense, that he constituted Jesus in the Messianic line.

There is still a niggling feeling at the back of one's mind, nevertheless. Is this variant Syriac text a fragment, an ancient indication that there was a tradition in Jesus' own area of Galilee/Syria that he was simply seen as the "son of Joseph", first because he assumed all the rights of the son of Joseph, and also because in the early days of Jesus' life and ministry it could not be revealed that he was born of a virgin? As Brown points out, the variant text as it stands is not easy to make self-consistent.[12] That is why critics of the virgin-birth tradition do not use it any more as ammunition against that tradition. While saying that apparently Joseph was the natural father of Jesus, our scribe calls Mary "the virgin Mary". Is he influenced in fact by two apparently conflicting traditions: his old Semitic tradition, the view of the Galileans during Jesus' childhood, that he was the natural son of Joseph; and the apostolic tradition, which he accepted, that in reality Jesus was virgin born?

St Paul

In 1943 Douglas Edwards argued that, because the virgin birth is not mentioned in the New Testament apart from the infancy narratives of Matthew and Luke, it must be doubted whether the apostles all knew of it.[13]

As we have already discussed, it would have been perfectly understandable if the doctrine of the virgin birth was kept secret before the death and resurrection of Jesus, to avoid ridicule and scandal. But after the resurrection, with the growth of the church, how long would it have been before the doctrine of the virgin birth was known among the apostles? And, if they had known it and believed it, how long before they would have used it in their teaching?

St Paul could be a most important witness in this regard. The earliest Christian documents we have to hand are his letters to the incipient Christian communities under his direction. He tells us in his letter to the Galatians, written about 54 AD,[14] that he went up to Jerusalem to meet the other apostles. He tells us that he made two visits, the first visit meeting only Peter and James [Galatians 1:18], and then the second [Galatians 2:1], "after fourteen years" (c.36 AD)[15] when he met privately "with those of repute",[16] i.e. with those who were apostles before him. If the doctrine of the virgin birth was already being taught then, it is difficult to believe that it was not told to Paul, as part of the Jesus-tradition. If so, then Paul would have known of this doctrine from his missionary journeys onwards, i.e. from 45 AD.

Is there evidence, for or against, that Paul believed this doctrine? In my opinion, there is nothing either for or against. Reflecting on Paul's letters, it is difficult to think of a situation where he would have needed to emphasise the doctrine. (How often has the reader heard a sermon in church on the virgin birth?) Again, as we shall see with McHugh, Paul does not present to us a systematic creed. For instance, Paul would not have wished to use the doctrine of the virgin birth as a motivation for celibacy, which he treats of with the Corinthian Christians in 1 Corinthians 6. His recommendation of celibacy for Christians is what we would call "low key". He wishes people to marry rather than give in to temptation, and not to abstain from sex during marriage except only temporarily [1 Corinthians 1:5]. Only if it is their gift are they to follow his example, to be celibate. It is hardly a situation where he needs to quote the virgin birth as a motivation for celibacy.

A better situation would have been in his writing on

Christ as the Second Adam, in Romans 5. Irenaeus of Lyons developed the doctrine of Mary as the Second Eve; but this is indeed a development from St Paul. We would simply have to say that such a development was not yet in Paul's thinking, whether or not he knew of the doctrine of the virginal conception.

Arguments from silence are notoriously flimsy, from the very nature of the New Testament documents, as McHugh indicates:

> It cannot be stressed too often that the New Testament is not an orderly compendium of Christian doctrine, setting out in magisterial form a comprehensive synthesis of all items like the *Summae* of the mediaeval schoolmen; and indeed it is *a priori* possible that an item of historical fact – even an important item, which was widely known in the early church – could have failed to find a place or mention in the apostolic writings by pure accident. Such a total silence (e.g. on the martyrdom of James, the bishop of Jerusalem) is no proof that it never happened.[17]

On the other hand, there is no certain text in Paul which indicates clearly that he believed that Jesus was born out of natural intercourse. Romans 1:3 has been cited as a text which affirms that Jesus had a human father, saying that Jesus "was (born) of the seed of David (*ek spermatos Daueid*) according to the flesh". But John McHugh correctly notes the absence of Paul's usual word for "born" (*gennétheis*) which would give "*begotten* of the seed of David according to the flesh", and which would be evidence that Paul believed that Jesus had a human father. As it stands, where Paul says that Jesus "came to be (*genomenou*)" this could simply be a reference to the fact that Jesus stood in the line of David, where inheritance was concerned.[18]

McHugh notes two other texts in Paul's writings where he claims Paul similarly uses *yinomai*, "become", rather than the expected *yennaomai,* "to be born". In Galatians 4:4, we read that God sent his Son, "coming to be from a woman" (*genomenon ek yunaikos*) instead of "coming to birth from a woman". The phrase "born of a woman", is in Job 14:1,

15:14, 25:4.[19] All these texts in the Septuagint Greek have *yennétos yunaikos*, "*born* of woman". Thus, Paul's use of *yinomai*, "become" may be of significance; except that *yennétos yunaikos*, born of a woman, using the Job formula, might have been an even stronger affirmation of the virginal conception, and indeed was used as such in Christian history![20] The other text is Philippians 2:7, where Paul tells us that Jesus being in the form of God "came in the likeness of men" (*en homoiómati anthrópón genomenos*), rather than, again, "being born in the likeness of men". McHugh argues that one cannot exclude altogether the possibility that Paul wrote *genomenos* because he believed that Jesus' new birth according to the flesh "took place without the intervention of a human father".[21]

We cannot exclude the possibility that, in using in these three texts *ginomai*, "come to be", rather than *gennaomai*, "be born", in contexts where *gennaomai* might have been expected, Paul is referring implicitly to the birth of Jesus without male intervention. But we cannot know this for certain. It may be that Paul's use of *ginomai* in these contexts is rather part of his theology of the incarnation, Christ coming to be in our flesh, rather than any emphasis on the miraculous mode of his birth.[22] Regarding Paul and the virgin birth, it seems to me, the game reaches stalemate. We cannot prove that Paul believed the doctrine, nor can we prove that he did not. But was the fact that he does not with certainty even implicitly mention it mean that he did not believe it? Certainly not, it seems to me. It simply did not form part of his theological thinking. He would not be alone in this among Christian thinkers.

St John

There are two texts in St John's Gospel where the evangelist puts on the lips of various people that Jesus was the son of Joseph:

- Philip found Nathaniel and said to him, 'We have found him of whom Moses in the Law and the prophets wrote, Jesus son of Joseph, from Nazareth.' [1.45]

- (The Jews) were saying, 'Surely this is Jesus son of Joseph, whose father and mother we know. How can he now say, "I have come down from heaven?" [6:42]

Von Campenhausen [23] thinks that, although these are not statements made by the evangelist, but are put by him on others' lips, they do represent his mind "for in continuing his presentation he comes back to them and never disavows them".

Von Campenhausen thinks that, furthermore, this represents the mind of the evangelist in writing the Gospel, since, for him the true decision of faith must come from meeting Jesus and his testimony, "in view of the ineffaceable double significance of his earthly person, without the help of miraculous signs". However, if the author thinks miraculous signs are so unimportant in his Gospel, one must wonder why he includes seven of the most remarkable of them. [24]

Both Jesus' disciples-to-be and the hostile crowd are only expressing what the common opinion of Jesus was in his own region of Nazareth and Galilee, that he was the natural son of Joseph and Mary, or perhaps even the adopted son. Surely, the simplest explanation is that John is simply telling it as it was. In historical fact, people thought Jesus was the son of Joseph. As C.K. Barrett says, commenting on John's use of "Son of Joseph":

> It is in accord with his ironical use of traditional material that he should allow Jesus to be ignorantly described as 'son of Joseph' while himself believing that Jesus had no human father. [25]

Barrett nails his colours to the mast in giving it as his opinion that the author of the Fourth Gospel believed in the virgin birth. Not all exegetes agree, viz., Raymond Brown and Fitzmyer. Miguens quotes their opinion:

> Concerning the fourth Gospel, Brown's view is that "Overall, the scales tip in favour of Johannine ignorance of the virginal conception; and that means the ignorance of it in a late-first-century Christian community that had access to an early tradition about Jesus." Fitzmyer agrees:

"The Johannine Gospel obviously does not deny the virginal conception of Jesus, but does not affirm it either...the Johannine Gospel can still refer to Him (Christ) as the 'son of Joseph' and can remain silent about His virginal conception."[26]

All agree first that there is no *explicit and unequivocal* reference to the virgin birth in either the Fourth Gospel or the Johannine epistles. The verse from the Prologue of John's Gospel which is sometimes quoted in defence of the virgin birth, 1:13, has poor manuscript support.

The usual and best supported reading of John 1:12-13 is in the NJB, as follows:

> But to those who did accept him (the Word) he gave power to become children of God, to those who believed in his name **those who were born** (Gk. *hoi ... egennéthésan*) not from human stock or human desire or human will but from God himself.

The plural form is the best attested, which carries the meaning that all Christians are spiritually born again [John 3:16]. But there is some attestation of the other reading in the singular, read in the Western text, **he who was born** (Latin, *qui...natus est*). Barrett opts for the usual, plural, reading,[27] and claims that the latter singular reading is to be explained as an alteration because of the need seen by the scribe to affirm the virgin birth, which John does not do elsewhere. But Barrett still maintains that the author of the Fourth Gospel did believe in the virgin birth:

> The reading which refers explicitly to the birth of Jesus is to be rejected; but it remains probable that John was alluding to Jesus' birth, and declaring that the birth of Christians, being bloodless and rooted in God's will alone, followed the pattern of the birth of Christ himself.[28]

Barrett here notes the Fourth Evangelist's use of contrasts, such as light and darkness. So Jesus is the "light of the world" [John 8:12], but Judas went out "and it was night" [John 13:30]. Barrett then notes the ironic contrast throughout John's Gospel between the origin of Jesus seen by those who do not understand, and his real divine origin as from the Father. Thus the origin of Jesus really is from God. He is not the son of Joseph; he is the Son of God.

This contrast is reflected in the stressed conversation which Jesus had with his sceptical audience in the Temple [John 8:38-41]:

> [38]What I speak of is what I have seen at my Father's side, and you too put into action the lessons you have learnt from your father.[39] They repeated, 'Our father is Abraham.' Jesus said to them: 'If you are Abraham's children, do as Abraham did.
> [40]As it is, you want to kill me, a man who has told you the truth as I have learnt it from God; that is not what Abraham did.[41] You are doing your father's work.' They replied, 'We were not born illegitimate, the only father we have is God.

Jesus accuses his fellow Jews in the Temple courtyard that their father is not Abraham, as they claim, but the devil, because they do not believe in him.[29] Are Jesus' opponents simply answering his charge against them? Or is there something more sinister behind their affirmation that *they* were not born illegitimate? Brown explains:

> *We were not born illegitimate.* Literally "of fornication". The usual interpretation is that "the Jews" see in the hint that the devil is their father a charge that Abraham is not their father and that they are illegitimate. In this interpretation, their "we" is simply an answer to the "you "[plural]" in Jesus' last statement. But there is another possibility: the Jews may be turning to an *ad hominem* argument against Jesus. He has been talking about his heavenly Father and about their father, but were there not rumors about his own birth? Was there not some question of whether he was really the son of Joseph? ...The Jews may be saying, "*We* were not born illegitimate (but you were). There is an early witness to Jewish attacks on the legitimacy of Jesus' birth in Origen *Against Celsus* I 28 (GCS 2:79); and the *Acts of Pilate* II 3, has the Jews charging Jesus: "You were born of fornication".[30]

If this interpretation is correct, then we have already to revise any notion that Jesus was most likely born of a natural union between Joseph and Mary. Were there already rumours that Joseph was not the natural father of Jesus, and that Jesus was born in some kind of miraculous way? If so, then this may be evidence that the accusation of illegitimacy was not post-apostolic, but in the earliest sources of the Christian faith. Conversely, therefore, this could itself be historical evidence for the virgin birth, which itself gave occasion for such rumours. In this case, implicitly also, therefore, Barrett is correct. The Fourth Evangelist believes in the virgin birth.[31]

Miguens in particular draws this conclusion, developing the contrast in John which we have already seen utilised by Barrett between Jesus' true heavenly origin as seen by the evangelist, and the erroneous judgements about Jesus made by his opponents, even sometimes by his disciples. Miguens notes how often Jesus calls God his own Father, much more than in any other Gospel:

> The Johannine theology certainly understands that there is an element in the "incarnate" Logos dwelling among us that cannot derive from any human father... This is the reason suggested by Tertullian, *Adv.Marc.* 4,10, why a virginal conception was needed in the case of Jesus, Son of God. If this theology is mentioned here, it is to bring into strong relief a definite purpose of the fourth evangelist: he knows and stresses that Jesus has a mother who is a woman, and a father who is not a man but God – Joseph is not mentioned in this fatherly role by the evangelist himself. This is all the more striking that most of the time it is Jesus Himself who calls God His Father, in the strong sense we have seen.[32]

Miguens of course stresses that it is not the evangelist himself who calls Jesus "son of Joseph", but it is either his new disciples [1.45] or indeed his adversaries [6:42]. For the Evangelist, argues Miguens, only God is his Father and Mary his mother.[33] I find this a very persuasive argument, even if we cannot say that John without doubt in his Gospel affirms the virgin birth. It would make the greatest Johannine sense if he did.

Mark

Manuel Miguens[34] argues that it is significant that in Mark's Gospel, Jesus is called "son of Mary" rather than "son of Joseph". Miguens explains this by inferring that Mark has deliberately altered the traditional appellation of Jesus as "son of Joseph", which earlier appellation is preserved by the parallel narratives in Matthew 13:55 and Luke 4:22, which call Jesus "son of Joseph".

Miguens, along with the majority of critical scholars today, accepts that Mark's Gospel was first, and that Matthew and Luke depended on Mark's account. It is therefore even more significant that, according to Miguens, Luke's account, 4:22, calling Jesus "son of Joseph" is earlier in the Gospel tradition than Mark, and is according to Miguens "a more acceptable text from a historical viewpoint"[35] than Mark's text which has "son of Mary". It is more likely that, in Jesus' own time, Jesus was called "son of Joseph". Mark must have changed a traditional Gospel source, perhaps Q.

Obviously, these small redactional changes do not alter substantially the historical character of the Gospels. As the Second Vatican Council says in DV19:

> ...inspired writers composed the four gospels, by various processes. They selected some things from the abundant material already handed down, orally or in writing. Other things they synthesised, or explained with a view to the needs of the churches.[36]

Mark's alteration for Miguens had an important theological reason. Miguens thinks that Mark wishes to emphasise that Jesus is "son of God" exclusively, and so deliberately avoids using the term that Jesus is "son of Joseph".[37]

> The only reason one can think of why Mark departed from the older and otherwise uniform phrasing of the tradition, and why he makes a deliberate effort to eliminate any mention of Joseph at this point, is the same reason which impelled him not to mention Joseph in his entire Gospel, to exclude any human paternity of Jesus, to omit

that Mary had any husband – and to insist on the fact that Jesus is "Son of God." In other words, the reason of his change is his conviction that Jesus is "son of Mary" and "Son of God" exclusively.[38]

This silence of Mark, therefore, while not necessarily implying that he believed that Jesus was born of a virgin, for Miguens certainly speaks for it rather than against it.

These arguments in no way convince Raymond Brown.[39] Brown launches a typically thorough investigation into the meaning of *The Appellation "Son of Mary" in Mark 6:3.*[40] He first admits that the major manuscripts all have "son of Mary" in that text. I follow his translation:

> Mark 6:3 (major codices) "Is not this *the carpenter, the son of Mary,* and the brother of James, Joses, Judas, and Simon? Are not his sisters here among us?"

Brown then throws a textual spanner in the works. He quotes P[45], which is not as in Britain the number of a dreaded dismissal note for an employee, but is the number of an old papyrus manuscript, because of its age, important, and which has a significant variant to the usual text. Brown then compares the other accounts, not only in the parallel Synoptics, but also in John:

- Mark 6:3 (P[45], family 13, OL, Bohairic, Armenian): "Is not this *the son of the carpenter and of Mary,* etc.?"

- Matthew 13:55: "Is not this *the son of the carpenter?* Is not *his mother called Mary,* and are not his brothers James and Joseph, Simon and Judas? Are not all his sisters here among us?"

- Luke 4:22: "Is not this *the son of Joseph?*"

- John 6:42: "Is not this Jesus, *the son of Joseph?* Do we not know *his father and mother?*"

Brown then enters into a complex discussion, to which the reader is referred, as to which was the original reading of Mark 6:3, granted the manuscript variation between the major codices and P[45]. If the reader thinks, with Ehrman, that the Church is nervous of these manuscript variants, and tries to cover them up, then let them see the discussion in the relevant pages of the *Birth of the Messiah*.[41]

Brown concludes in agreement with Miguens, that the original form of Mark 6:3 was the majority manuscript text "son of Mary". But Brown does not conclude at all from this that Mark is arguing to the virgin birth, that Jesus had a divine Father and a human mother only. Miguens entertains the possibility, on the contrary, that calling Jesus "son of Mary" is an implicit illegitimacy charge, since Jesus has no legitimate human father. But Brown rejects this view on the grounds of there being no evidence for such a meaning of the term in Jesus' own time.[42] Brown[43] explains Mark's refusal to call Jesus "son of Joseph" on the more mundane grounds that "Joseph was dead and Mary, the one living parent, was well known to all the villagers."[44] Brown further explains "A good parallel is offered by Luke 7:12 where, in the context, it is perfectly understandable that the deceased is identified as 'the only son of his mother who was a widow'."[45]

We may or may not be satisfied with Brown's explanation of Mark's phrase "son of Mary", but we would also have to agree with Brown that Miguens is arguing a very elusive case. In fairness, Miguens does deal with other texts in Mark where he argues one would have expected more mention of Jesus' human father.[46] In my opinion the most we can conclude here is that it is at least possible that Mark believed in the virginal conception of Jesus, and that there is no evidence whatsoever that he did not. Even this modest conclusion is by no means irrelevant to our case.

Mark and John: high Christology

Mark's emphasis on Jesus as Son of God is not first and foremost a statement about Jesus' birth, but about his divine status. Miguens, therefore, it seems to me, is on much firmer ground when he develops the theme in Mark of his silence about any human father of Jesus, even if we admit the one variant of Mark 6:3 where he refers to *"the son of the carpenter and of Mary…*", in any case on the lips of the crowd, not of the evangelist himself.

Put positively, Jesus in Mark is the Son of God. His only true Father is God. Furthermore and quite correctly, Miguens sees this as much more than a Messianic title, but, in the whole perspective of Mark's Gospel, as "evidence of a deep Christological insight concerning the very person of Christ".[47] Miguens is here referring to the absolute use of "the Son", in Mark 13:32, but this high Christology pervades the whole of Mark's Gospel. We have developed the same theme in *Bad, Mad or God?*[48] Mark is just as important to my case, that the historical Jesus was aware of himself as God become man, as is John's Christology.

In the history of Gospel criticism, Holtzmann used the growing scholarly conviction that Mark's Gospel was the first of the four written as the basis of a new Liberal Protestant Christianity.[49] Mark has no account of the virgin birth, or of the Resurrection appearances of Jesus, apart from the added ending Mark 16:9-20, which we have earlier judged in this book, together with the general critical consensus, to be a later manuscript addition, not part of Mark's original Gospel.

Thus Holtzmann used Mark as the basis of a liberal life of Jesus, to save German Christianity from the ravages of David Friedrich Strauss, who published the first edition of his *Das Leben Jesu Kritisch Bearbeitet,* ("The Life of Jesus Critically Examined") in 1835,[50] translated into English by none other than the novelist George Eliot[51]. Strauss had claimed that the four Gospels were mostly myth, not even, as the rationalists had argued, authentically historical stories with a natural explanation for the miraculous dimension (e.g. that there was truly a feeding of the five thousand, but they brought along their sandwiches). This led some even to doubt the existence of the historical Jesus.[52]

At least, argued Holtzmann, for the new Christian who cannot accept miracles and the incarnation, Mark gives us an acceptable life of Jesus, of a prophet who came to bring in a new social order which he called the "kingdom of God".

We recount in BMG how this compromise image of the historical Jesus was shattered by William Wrede's *Messianic*

Secret.[53] Mark throughout, argued Wrede, was shot through with the faith of the primitive Church, which has to be disentangled before any rational life of Jesus can be constructed.

Wrede, we submitted, was quite right in this: that Mark's Jesus is no Liberal Protestant or Liberal Catholic for that matter. But Wrede was wrong in that he shared the post-Enlightenment prejudice against miracles. God, for all the new "critical" thinkers, could only work through secondary causes. Thus the miracles, and also the concept of God assuming a human nature as taught in orthodox Christianity, was simply impossible.

Thus both Holtzmann and Wrede were closed to the real message of Mark. From the beginning, Jesus for Mark is a supernatural being who,[54] after being baptised Son of God, is accused of blasphemy for curing the man let down through the roof and saying that his sins were forgiven. After performing many miracles and being recognised as Son of God by the devils in those he exorcised, Jesus is revealed as Son of God at his Transfiguration, and plans for his arrest are made after he identifies himself as the Son in the parable he tells of the wicked husbandmen. Finally, at his arrest, Jesus reveals himself as the divine Son of Man:

> The high priest tore his robes and said, 'What need of witnesses have we now? You heard the blasphemy. What is your finding?' Their verdict was unanimous: he deserved to die. [Mark 14:63-64]

But what, as I argue, if Mark is actually recounting historical fact?[55] What if Jesus actually came with those blasphemous claims, and performed miracles to authenticate them? Mark's is the first Gospel written, in critical judgement. In that case, therefore, the earliest Gospel we have is of such a divine-human being, the transcendent Son of God.

I argue the same case regarding the Fourth Gospel. For Strauss, in his *Leben Jesu,* it was the *intention* of the writer of the Fourth Gospel which made his work the most mythical of all four Gospels. John is clearest of all about the divinity of Christ, the constant theme of the whole Gospel narrative. The smaller number of miracles in John for Strauss means nothing. In the evangelist's intention, these miracles are given a much more loaded meaning than in the Synoptics. From the very first miracle at Cana of Galilee, the turning of water into wine, where according to John, Jesus "manifested his glory; and his disciples believed in him" [John 2:11], "it is entirely in the spirit of the fourth gospel, to place in relief the exaltation of Jesus as the divine logos".[56]

This meant that the Fourth Gospel had essentially to be myth. For Strauss, the fundamental myth was the Incarnation itself. As a radical Hegelian, he could not accept that a human individual could be the divine Son of God and remain so for all eternity. This is consistent with the Hegelian view that only the Absolute Idea survives the historical process of thesis, antithesis, and synthesis. Strauss demythologises the Incarnation by turning the God-man into the ideal of humanity.[57]

As I argue in *Bad Mad or God?*, the problem with Strauss, Hotzmann, and Wrede, indeed with the whole of nineteenth-century radical German historical Jesus research, is the prejudice against miracles and against the Incarnation. Once that prejudice is removed, it becomes at least possible to demonstrate that the historical Jesus had a divine self-consciousness,[58] as the Fourth Gospel states unequivocally in John 8:58, "Before Abraham was, I Am", after which his opponents wish to stone him for blasphemy.

Of course, not every miracle, not every incarnation, is thereby validated. That is why, in *Bad Mad or God?*, I go through a process whereby the substantial historicity of Mark and John is authenticated. Taking away post-Enlightenment prejudice, critical criteria[59] can be adduced which confirm that the historical Jesus had a divine self-consciousness as asserted by Mark, and even more clearly by John. I must refer the reader to that book to examine those authenticating criteria.

If Mark and John, therefore, have such a high Christology, which was clearly expressed in their Gospels – Mark dated at 64, John at not later than 110 – then we have an interesting situation. Both those Gospels know of no human father for Jesus, but know only a divine father, God. Only on the lips of those who talk about Jesus is he referred to as "son of Joseph".

Thus we have arrived at an intriguing midpoint in our investigation. On the one hand, knowing in particular the high Christology of Mark and John, together with hints in those Gospels which might imply a belief in the virginal conception of Jesus, it certainly would not be surprising to learn that both those evangelists believed in the Virgin Birth by the time they wrote their Gospels. On the other hand, what was the origin of their belief? Did their belief demand an evolution into the doctrine of the Virgin Birth without any historical justification for it?

We are back to our original question as to the origin of the belief in the virginal conception. Did the belief generate the myth, or was there a miracle which occurred factually of the virginal conception which was the real cause of Christian belief that Jesus was born of the Virgin Mary? We have not answered that question, but we are some way forward. We know now that, central to the Christian message by the end of the first century, that is, by the end of the era of the apostles, Christians believed that Jesus was entirely unique, as the divine Son of God. Thus an entirely unique kind of birth would not be entirely incongruous, nor would also his having no human father but a human mother.

We have also established that there is no tradition within the New Testament, once again the earliest literary testimony of the incipient Christian faith, that Jesus was the natural son of Joseph or of any other man. There is nothing which with any certainty contradicts the testimony of Matthew and Luke that Jesus was born of a virgin named Mary who had not had intercourse with a man.

Our next task is to examine the infancy narratives of Matthew and Luke, to see if, in the accounts of the Annunciation and Birth of Jesus in those Gospels, we can ascertain whether they are writing history or myth.

1 Von Campenhausen, 1964, 11-12.

2 Beare, *Matthew*, 67.

3 Davies/Allison, *Matthew* I, 185.

4 Howard Marshall, *Luke*, 128.

5 BM, 61-64.

6 ICC, 183, n.71.

7 BM, 62-64.

8 i.e. 'The Dialogue of Timothy and Aquila', ICC, 183, n.71.

9 "With the exception of ὁ and the Ferrar miniscules (f 13) all Greek witnesses read what we have printed". i.e. the first text. *Ibid.*

10 BM, 64.

11 BDB, 408.

12 Cf. BM, 63. "If the variant reading meant to make Joseph the biological father of Jesus, why did it not simply say: 'Joseph was the father of Jesus by Mary', the formula employed in the genealogy when women are mentioned?"

13 D. Edwards, 1943, 48.

14 NJBC, **47:6**, 781. Fitzmyer, "A not unlikely date is *ca.* AD 54, not long after Paul's arrival in Ephesus at the beginning of Mission III... An earlier date is often given for Galatians by proponents of the South Galatian theory (see Bruce, *Galatians* 43-56) but it is difficult to reconcile that with all the data... "

15 A very difficult date to determine. Cf. NJBC, **47:17**, 783. Possibly 36 (the probable date of Paul's conversion) plus 14. Fitzmyer, "Yet many problems remain…"

16 NJBC, **47:17**, 784, Fitzmyer, "*privately to those of repute.*" His argument slightly disparages the Jerusalem "pillars", who were apostles before him (1.16)".

17 MJNT, 270.

18 MJNT, 275-276.

19 As Fitzmyer points out, NJBC, **47:26**,787.

20 "Instead of *genomenon*, "some patristic writers read *gennomenon*, and understood this participle as referring to Mary's virginal conception; but this is anachronistic interpretation…." NJBC, **47:26**, 787.

21 MJNT, 276.

22 This is the view of R. Barry Matlock, who takes David Wenham, *Paul, Follower of Jesus or Founder of Christianity?* Grand Rapids, Eerdmans, 1995, 341-3 to task for coming to the same conclusion as McHugh. Matlock concludes that "Paul's usage in these texts, instead of suggesting any principled reflection on the peculiar circumstances of Jesus' birth, is such as rather to diminish any particular focus on the *birth* of Jesus as distinct from his 'coming to be' in the form and function in which he appeared": George J. Brooke, Ed., 2000, 51.

23 Von Campenhausen, 1964,14.

24 (The turning of the water into wine 2:1-11, The cure of the nobleman's child, 4:46-54, The cure of the man at the pool of Bethesda, 5:1-15, The multiplication of the loaves 6:1-15, The walking on the water, 6:16-21, The cure of the man born blind, 9:1-7, The raising of Lazarus, 11:41-44.)

25 Barrett, *John*, 184.

26 Miguens, 1975, 28. Miguens refers to Brown, *The Virginal Conception*, 59, Fitzmyer, *The Virginal Conception*, 560.

27 Brown, *John I*, 12, lists "Boismard, Blass, Braun, Burney, Dupont, Mollet (SB), Zahn and others" as opting for the singular reading, while "J. Schmid… Barrett, Bultmann, Lightfoot, Wikenhauser and others" opt for the plural.

28 Barrett, *John*, 164.

29 I strenuously deny that John's Gospel is being anti-Semitic here. Cf. BMG, 267-295, Chapter 15. I claim that "the Jews" referred to so frequently in the Fourth Gospel are in fact native dwellers in Jerusalem and in Judea. Jesus addresses them as God's specially chosen people, and challenges them to follow him as sent from the Father as the Light of the World. Of course, they reject him, but the Fourth Gospel presents hope for his people. "When you have lifted up the Son of Man", says Jesus, "you will realise that I Am He…" [John 8:28].

30 Brown, *John I*, 357.

31 In Appendix V of BM, 541-2, Brown discusses the illegitimacy charge related to John 8:41. He concludes that such a charge is "plausible", more so than Mark 6:3, "Yet the charge is far from certain".

32 Miguens, 37, 1975.

33 Although curiously, Mary is not named in the Gospel, she is called "the mother of Jesus", Miguens, 1975, 35.

34 Miguens, 1975. 6-27.

35 Miguens, 1975, 17.

36 Tanner, II, *978.

37 For Mark's use of the term "son of God" for Jesus, cf. Mark 1:1, 12:36ff., 13:22, 14:36, Miguens, 1975, 9-14.

38 Miguens, 1975, 21.

39 BM, 519, 537-541.

40 *Ibid.*, 537-541.

41 *Ibid*, 538-9.

42 *Ibid.*, 540.

43 *Ibid.*, 537.

44 *Ibid.*, 540.

45 *Ibid.*, 541.

46 E.g. Mark 10:29, where Miguens argues that one would have expected 'my father' also in the sentence "this is my brother and sister and mother", Mark 3:35, Miguens, 1975, 25.

47 Miguens, 1975, 13.

48 BMG, Chapter 8, *You Have Heard the Blasphemy*, 134-150.

49 *Ibid.,* 47. Cf. NTHIP, 151-2.
50 Hodgson, Ed., xxiv.
51 Cf. BMG, 47.
52 We demonstrate the existence of the historical Jesus in BMG, Chapter 5, pp.103-112.
53 BMG, 49-51. Cf. Trocmé, *Mark,* 123-4.
54 *Ibid.,* 139-141.
55 On the historicity of Jesus' self-consciousness in Mark, cf. BMG, 141-149.
56 Hodgson, Ed., 526.
57 *Ibid.,* 780. "Humanity is the union of two natures - God become man, the infinite manifesting itself in the finite, and the finite spirit remembering its finitude; it is the child of the visible Mother and the invisible Father, Nature and Spirit... It is Humanity that dies, rises, and ascends to heaven, for from the negation of its phenomenal life there ever proceeds a higher spiritual life; from the suppression of its mortality as a personal, rational and terrestrial spirit, arises its union with the infinite spirit of the heavens. By faith in this Christ, especially in his death and resurrection, man is justified before God; that is, by the kindling within him of the idea of Humanity, the individual man participates in the divinely human life of the species."
58 BMG, Chapter 14, *The historical Jesus really said "I am",* 253-266.
59 Cf. especially BMG, Chapters 6-7, *The Critical Minimum,* and *Building up a Profile the Wright Way,* 113-133.

CHAPTER SIX:

THE BIRTH NARRATIVES:
HISTORY, *MIDRASH* OR MYTH?

- **The Infancy Narratives in Matthew and Luke considered generally are not demonstrably fiction.**
- **Historical criticism would admit that at least there is some reliable history in them.**
- **The statement of intent of Luke's Gospel, and the Church's tradition, expressed in *Dei Verbum*, would encourage us to take the accounts seriously from the historical viewpoint.**

How can we know whether or not the Infancy Narratives of Matthew and Luke, which are the only explicit source for the doctrine of the Virgin Birth in the New Testament, are "historical"? In literary terms, are they fact or fiction?

The first important issue which we encounter when we try to discover whether or not the tradition of the Virgin Birth of Christ is historical or not is the whole question of the Infancy narratives of Matthew and Luke, considered as a whole, i.e. Matthew 1-2 and Luke 1-3. If we could ascertain that, in general, the Infancy narratives are reliable historically, then that would incline us towards accepting the historicity of the accounts of the Annunciation of the virgin birth in Matthew and Luke.

There are questions about the Infancy narratives which give rise to doubts about the validity of depending on these accounts as reliable historically:

(a) The Date of Matthew and Luke

If we adopt the Holtzmann, or "two-source" theory, and accept that Matthew and Luke are thereby post-Mark (c.80–100), we must consider the fact that, given a date of 4 BC for the birth of Jesus, there would have been the best part of a century between the event of Jesus' birth, and the writing of the Infancy narratives. Time, many scholars would say, for birth legends to have been created, without basis in the early life of the historical Jesus.

(b) Apparent Inconsistencies in the Infancy Narratives

For Matthew, the announcement of Jesus' birth is to Joseph [Matthew 1:18], his account then continuing with the Visit of the Magi [2:1-12] and the Flight into Egypt [2:13-15], followed by the Massacre of the Innocents [2:16, 18], and the Journey back from Egypt to Nazareth [2:19-21].

For Luke, on the other hand, after the foretelling of the Birth of John the Baptist [1:5-25], the Annunciation is rather to Mary [1:26-38], and is followed by a completely different set of narratives, i.e. the Visit of the Shepherds [2:1-20], the Presentation of Jesus in the Temple [2:22-28], and the boyhood Visitation of Jesus to Jerusalem and his discussions with the doctors of the Law [2:41-50].

This diversity of account is all the more remarkable because, in the remainder of the Gospels of Matthew and Luke, dealing with the public ministry of Jesus, the Gospels are strikingly similar, often identical in wording, for example the account of the Miraculous Feeding of the Multitude, cf. Matthew 14:13-21, Mark 6:32-44, Luke 9:10b-17. That is why the first three Gospels are called the "Synoptic Gospels", precisely because "looked at together" (*syn-opsis*) they look so alike; but not so the Infancy narratives of Matthew and Luke. "Looked at together", they look entirely different from each other.

Moreover, according to Brown, not only are the stories different, but they are difficult to reconcile historically with each other. Brown concludes that "the two narratives are not only different – they are contrary to each other in a number of details."

According to Luke 1:26 and 2:39 Mary lives in Nazareth, and so the census of Augustus is invoked to explain how the child was born in Bethlehem, away from home. In Matthew there is no hint of a *coming* to Bethlehem, for

Joseph and Mary are in a house at Bethlehem where seemingly Jesus was born (2:11). The only journey that Matthew has to explain is why the family went to Nazareth when they came from Egypt instead of returning to their native Bethlehem (2:22-23).

A second difficulty is that Luke tells us that the family returned peaceably to Nazareth after the birth at Bethlehem (2:22,39); this is irreconcilable with Matthew's implication (2:16) that the child was almost two years old when the family came back from Egypt and moved to Nazareth. Of the options mentioned before we made the detailed comparison of the two narratives, one must be ruled out, i.e., that both accounts are completely historical.[1]

(d) The Literary Form of the Infancy Narratives: Midrash?

These difficulties, i.e. the lateness of the accounts in Matthew and Luke, the differences between them, and the difficulties in reconciling historically those differences, lead some scholars to propose that the literary form of the Infancy narratives is not historical, but fictional. In this, for these scholars, is intended no derogation of the worth of the Infancy narratives, but rather indicates the theological intention of the evangelists to understand the mystery of Jesus in terms of stories about his birth.

Those who propose that the Infancy narratives of Matthew and Luke are in general fiction, or *theologoumena*, i.e. fictional stories with a theological meaning, summon the Hebrew concept of *midrash* to their aid, from the Hebrew word *darash* or "investigate". The *midrash* was a form of rabbinic exegesis which explained a passage of the Scriptures imaginatively. As Addison Wright's says, "A *midrash* is a work that attempts to make a text of Scripture understandable, useful, and relevant for a later generation."[2]

For instance, Matthew's story of the magi who saw the star of the Davidic Messiah at its rising is an echo of the Old Testament story of Balaam, a type of magus from the East, who saw the star rise out of Jacob. The story of Herod seeking the life of the infant Jesus and massacring the male children at Bethlehem is a reapplication of the Old Testament story of the wicked Pharoah who sought the life of the infant Moses and slaughtered the male children of the Israelites, even as the story of Joseph, the father of Jesus, who dreams dreams and goes to Egypt is a reapplication of the story of the patriarch Joseph who does the same thing. Luke's description of Zechariah and Elizabeth, the parents of John the Baptist, is taken, at times almost verbatim, from the Old Testament description of Abraham and Sarah.[3]

Nevertheless, Brown concludes that the Infancy narratives cannot be described as *midrashim* in the strict sense of the term. "The birth stories were composed, not to make the Old Testament Scriptures more intelligible, but to make Jesus more intelligible. Part of his intelligibility is that he stands in continuity with and in fulfilment of the Old Testament Scriptures."[4] Brown is therefore prepared to allow only that the Infancy narratives of Matthew and Luke are *midrashim*, not in the strict sense of the term, but in that "The same kind of mind that would compose a *midrash* in order to make Scripture understandable composed birth stories to make that christological insight understandable."[5]

We must question Brown more closely here. He admits that the evangelists have an entirely different theological agenda in their use of Jewish principles of biblical interpretation, i.e. "to make Jesus more intelligible". But would their desire to make Jesus more intelligible lead them to compose *fictional* stories in the midrashic mode? This is the view of Davis/ Allison. They contend that "the haggadic legends surrounding the birth and early life of Moses have determined the content of Matthew's source".[6] Or, on the contrary, would their belief in Jesus make them more concerned to ensure that any traditions handed on about him were *historically authentic*? In this case, they would have composed stories about Jesus using rabbinic principles of exegesis, but were diligent to ensure that these stories were based upon historical fact.

We have already seen that at least there is the real possibility that Matthew's interpretation of Isaiah 7:14 was based upon his prior knowledge of the tradition that Mary gave birth to

Jesus without the agency of a man. Some scholars see other narratives in the Infancy stories historically based. Duncan M. Derrett, for instance[7] sees some historical memory, however vague and inaccurate, behind the stories of the Magi and of the shepherds: and, even more strenuously, Richard T. France argues that the story in Matthew 2:16-18 of the slaughter by King Herod of the innocent children is totally credible:

> The historical evidence, therefore, such as it is, suggests that the incident is not in itself improbable, but very much in keeping with what we know of the last years of Herod's reign. Among the more striking atrocities of that period it was a relatively minor incident, which has understandably not left any clearly independent mark in the very selective records of Herod's reign. It was only its association with the birth of Jesus, and the christological implications which were seen in it, which led to the recording of the incident in Christian circles; otherwise it would have been forgotten.[8]

This means that we cannot flash the term *midrash* in order to settle the question as to whether the Infancy narratives are historical or not. The birth narratives of Matthew and Luke have parallels with Jewish contemporary exegesis, but not so as to settle the question of their historicity.

Brown concludes that the Infancy narratives cannot be described as "factual history" while at the same time he does not fail to recognise "the probable presence of items of historical value".[9] We shall see later that Brown suggests that there is a possibility that the origin of the early Christian belief in the Virgin Birth was a theological reflection on Jesus as Son of God from the first moment of his conception. We shall see that his opinion is that, while he accepts the Virgin Birth as a dogma of faith, we cannot prove beyond doubt that this dogma of faith was based upon an authentic historical tradition. The narratives of the virgin birth in Matthew and Luke, in his opinion, could have been written as fictional *theologoumena* based upon Christological insight rather than factual testimony. We must be clear from the outset that such a view cannot be based upon a straightforward consideration that these narratives were in the literary form of *midrashim.* That literary form could be used in the context of a factually based story as well as of a fictional tale.

Fact or *theologoumena?* The options

With this in mind, therefore, we could come to four possible conclusions regarding the historicity of the Infancy narratives in general:

1. Absolute historicity, namely that every detail in them is verifiable historically.

2. Substantial historicity, namely that the stories of the infancy are historically based (for example that there were "historical Magi" who sought to find a King, that Jesus was actually born in Bethlehem) but that traditions of Jesus' infancy have been handed on in a popular way, with historical details often blurred.

3. Fictionality, namely that the infancy stories are a "myth" with a theological meaning, often called *theologoumena* by the scholars. Some historical data may be discovered in those stories, but their genre is not that of fact, but of fiction.

4. We do not have enough historical evidence one way or the other to make any judgement concerning the historicity or fictionality of the Infancy narratives of Matthew and Luke.

Of course, the option is not a straight choice overall between absolute historicity and total fictionality. There are almost an infinite number of variants of the above positions. One could hold, for instance, that the story of the shepherds with their vision of the angels is demonstrably fictional, while the Flight into Egypt really happened. Particularly regarding the narratives of the virgin birth in Matthew and Luke, one could hold that Matthew's was a *theologoumenon*, while Luke's was ultimately based upon Mary's own testimony that she had not had intercourse with Joseph or with any other man before she gave birth to Jesus.

Clearly, there is insufficient time in this investigation to make any detailed examination of the Infancy narratives in Matthew and Luke in general, nor would that be appropriate. In this chapter, we can only suggest indicators which might lead us to hope to find reliable history in the infancy accounts, which in turn will lead us to take seriously the possibility of the historicity of the accounts of the Annunciation of the virgin birth in Matthew and Luke.

Option one: "Absolute historicity"

In this view, every detail in the Gospel accounts of the infancy is historical, not fictional. It is difficult to define precisely what "absolute historicity" might mean. No account of any factual event could be totally complete. It would be humanly impossible to describe every minute detail of what happened, even of a walk in the park. If an account is not totally complete, then it is necessarily incomplete, and apparent differences might emerge to be explained in any write-up of the event being described.

Let us take, for instance, Brown's difficulty quoted earlier that "in Matthew there is no hint of a *coming* to Bethlehem, for Joseph and Mary are in a house at Bethlehem where seemingly Jesus was born (2:11)." This seems to contradict Luke's account, where Mary "wrapped him (Jesus) in swaddling clothes and laid him in a manger because there was no room for them in the inn" [Luke 2:7]. Davies/Allison agree with Brown, commenting on Matthew 2:11. "If the 'house' is the house of Jesus and his parents in Bethlehem, this would obviously not harmonise with Luke's account, which explains that Jesus was laid in a feeding trough, 'because there was no room for them in the inn' (2:7)."[10]

But Brown and Davis/Allison might be accused here of being too demanding of strict specificity in what is after all a popular account. As Howard Marshall points out, a second century tradition locates the place of Jesus' birth as a cave, upon which the Emperor Constantine built a basilica, the site of the present Church of the Nativity.[11] "But caves were sometimes used to provide accommodation for animals, and houses were built near them, so that they might be used for this purpose".[12] Howard Marshall is cautiously favourable towards the historicity of the tradition of Jesus being born in a cave. Thus one could harmonise the accounts in Matthew and Luke. Matthew calling the place where the Magi found Jesus an *oikos* is simply a vague term[13] for the "house" in Bethlehem close to which the cave where Jesus was born was situated. That is even ignoring the possibility that by the time the Magi came to visit Bethlehem, Mary had moved to a more appropriate "house" away from the lowly birth place where Jesus had been born.[14] Brown says concerning *oikos* in Matthew 2:11, "There have been attempts, often quite forced, to harmonise the information."[15] But Brown admits implicitly that all attempts are not necessarily forced; and one must ask, is attempted harmonisation of two admittedly incomplete popular accounts an illegitimate exercise? Surely not, unless one is pre-disposed from the outset to argue their fictionality.

Likewise regarding Brown's second difficulty, that Luke tells us that the family returned peaceably to Nazareth after the birth at Bethlehem [2:22, 39], which Brown claims is irreconcilable with Matthew's implication [2:16] that the child was almost two years old when the family came back from Egypt and moved to Nazareth, one must ask whether again attempted harmonisation must be deemed forced. Matthew simply tells us, "Herod was furious on realising that he had been fooled by the wise men, and in Bethlehem and its surrounding district he had all the male children killed who were two years old or less, reckoning by the date he had been careful to ask the wise men" [Matthew 2:16].

Luke agrees with Matthew that Jesus was born in Bethlehem. He then tells us that Jesus was taken up to the Jerusalem Temple (walking distance from Bethlehem) when he was eight days old. Matthew does not give us the date when Jesus was taken down to Egypt by Joseph and Mary to avoid Herod's evil intentions to kill one whom he feared might be a rival to his throne. We are not told either how long Jesus, Mary, and Joseph, stayed in Egypt before returning ("peaceably") to Nazareth their home. Thus Jesus could have stayed in Bethlehem for most of the two years, perhaps Joseph finding work there, before fleeing to Egypt. This was by no means impossible. Joseph could then have returned to Nazareth after another year or two, after Herod's death.

This is all guesswork. But can we say that a narrative is incredible, or irreconcilable with another narrative, when so little information is given, and harmonisation is possible if only of necessity speculative? All agree that the Gospels as a whole were not written to satisfy specialist historians; but that does not mean necessarily that they wrote fiction. On the contrary, as we shall see, the tradition of the Church insists that the Gospels are historical documents.

Problems concerning chronology are not confined in the Gospels to the Infancy narratives. In the accounts of the public ministry of Jesus in the four Gospels, there are problems of chronology. For instance, in the Synoptic Gospels, Matthew, Mark, and Luke, Jesus goes up to Jerusalem only once, and is arrested and crucified after that one visit [cf. Matthew 21:1\\]; whereas in John's Gospel, Jesus goes up three times to Jerusalem. [John 2:23, 5:1, 7:1]. And when did Jesus cleanse the Jerusalem temple? It is at least likely that Jesus did so early in his public ministry as John states [John 2:13-22], rather than later, as stated in the Synoptics [Matthew 21:12-13\\].

And it is at least as possible that John [John 19:31] has the date of the Last Supper as right as the Synoptics, who make the celebration of the Last Supper a Passover meal [Matthew 26:18\\]. Brown thinks that this is indeed the case:

> We suggest then that, for unknown reasons, on Thursday evening, the 14th of Nissan by the official calendar, the day before Passover, Jesus ate with his disciples a meal which had Passover characteristics. The Synoptists or their tradition, influenced by these Passover characteristics, too quickly made the assumption that the day was actually Passover; John, on the other hand, preserved the correct chronological information.[16]

This introduces us to the second possibility regarding the Infancy narratives, that they are factual, not "absolutely", but "substantially".

Option two: "Substantial" historicity

The second possibility is what we might call the position of "substantial historicity", namely, that the stories of the infancy are historically based (for example that there were "historical Magi" who sought to find a King, that Jesus was actually born in Bethlehem, in a manger) but that traditions of Jesus' infancy have been handed on in a popular way, with historical details often blurred. Thus, in this view, we must be prepared for the possibility that there are, strictly speaking, factual errors in the transmission of the narratives; but that these minor errors do not detract from the substantial historicity of the story handed on.

Brown's view of the date of the Last Supper, quoted above, is clearly an example of such substantial historicity. According to Brown, the Synoptists made a factual error in saying that the Last Supper was celebrated on the Passover, since in fact the Last Supper was celebrated by Jesus with his disciples on the day before Passover. But this does not undermine the fact that the Last Supper actually took place, but that in the transmission of the narrative, this minor error was made.

If we assume the "substantial" and not the "absolute" historicity of the Infancy Narratives, then the problem outlined above, that Matthew calls the place where the infant Jesus was found an *oikos*, "house", whereas Luke tells us that Jesus was laid in a "feeding trough" (*phatnê*), is easily solved. If we assume that Luke's account is closer to fact, then Matthew calling the place where Jesus was born an *oikos* is simply a minor factual error, Matthew's tradition not even being aware of the fact that Jesus was born in a lowly place not worthy of the name of *oikos*.

Similarly, we could solve the problem of what Howard Marshall calls the "long and inconclusive debate"[17] concerning

Luke's account of the census which demanded that Joseph and Mary travelled to Bethlehem, during which visit Christ was born:

> Now it happened that at this time Caesar Augustus issued a decree that a census should be made of the whole inhabited world.[2] This census – the first – took place while Quirinius was governor of Syria,[3] and everyone went to be registered, each to his own town.
> [Luke 2:1-3]

The historical difficulties regarding such a Roman census at the end of Herod the Great's reign requiring Mary and Joseph to travel from Nazareth to Bethlehem are numerous and well documented.[18] But Howard Marshall nevertheless concludes that "the character of the census described by Luke is far from impossible, and hence many recent writers are prepared to admit that Luke's description of a census reflects historical reality."[19]

Many proposed solutions are dependent on Luke having made some minor historical errors in handing on what many consider to be a substantially historical narrative. One theory is that Luke confused a census which actually took place under Quirinius in AD 6-9 with the birth of Jesus which took place before the death of Herod in 4 BC.[20] Howard Marshall himself speculates that "It is not impossible that this enrolment (of Joseph and Mary) was carried out by Quirinius acting in a special capacity before the death of Herod…"[21] Assuming this latter resolution of the difficulty, Luke was right in stating that Quirinius was overseeing the census in 4 BC, but factually inaccurate in affirming that Quirinius was governor of Syria at the time.

It seems to me most reasonable to argue for the substantial historicity of the infancy narratives in general. If we grant the received critical dating of Matthew and Luke, composed towards the close of the first Christian century, then one would expect that in the hundred years after the birth of Christ around 4 BC, memories would become blurred as to detail (for example what precise census it was which brought the Holy Family to Bethlehem). At the same time, authentic historical memories might feasibly remain as to the substance of what actually occurred (that the Holy Family did go to Bethlehem because of a census). Such, surely, is the very nature of human memory.

We have already quoted the Second Vatican Council's *Dei Verbum* which asserted that, while the Holy Spirit was the author of Scripture, "in composing the sacred books, God chose men and while employed by Him they made use of their powers and abilities..."[22] As truly human authors, Matthew and Luke would have composed their birth narratives from sources handed on to them, without necessarily being able to check every historical detail.

This seems to me commonsense. However, in Catholic theology, and also within conservative evangelical Christianity, the view that the Infancy narratives at least possibly contains minor historical errors, comes up against the theological question of the inerrancy of Scripture.

Inspiration and inerrancy

The first draft of the *Dogmatic Constitution on Divine Revelation*, in 1961, at the beginning of the Second Vatican Council's deliberations, was an affirmation of absolute inerrancy. Any error, even of a minor nature, was excluded necessarily from the Word of God written. This view followed the strictures of the papal encyclical on biblical studies *Providentissimus Deus* ("The Most Provident God") issued by Pope Leo XIII in 1893, which condemned those scholars who limited biblical inspiration to matters of faith and morals:

> For all the books which the Church receives as sacred and canonical, are written wholly and entirely, with all their parts, at the dictation of the Holy Ghost; and so far is it from being possible that any error can co-exist with inspiration, that inspiration not only is essentially incompatible with error, but excludes and rejects it as absolutely and necessarily as it is impossible that God

Himself, the supreme Truth, can utter that which is not true.[23]

The first draft of *Dei Verbum* in 1961 followed the teaching of *Providentissimus Deus* without moderation. But the final draft of *Dei Verbum,* promulgated towards the end of the Second Vatican Council in 1965, is a much more nuanced statement than that of Pope Leo XIII:

> Therefore, since everything asserted by the inspired authors or sacred writers must be held to be asserted by the Holy Spirit, it follows that the books of Scripture must be acknowledged as teaching solidly, faithfully and without error that truth which God wanted put into sacred writings[24] for the sake of our salvation.[25]

This more moderate statement of inerrancy followed debates among Catholic theologians since 1893. While accepting Pope Leo's insistence on the total inerrancy of Scripture, theologians had defined more closely what constitutes an "error". As we have seen earlier, since Pope Pius XII's epoch-making encyclical *Divino Afflante Spiritu,* Catholic exegetes now worked on the principle that not every book of Scripture is necessarily historical. The Bible is not a book but rather a library of books of different types, a coat of many colours. It may, as with the book of Job, be written in the literary *genre* of an epic poem. God can write poetry as well as history. Even if Job had not even existed, if the intention of the author was to tell a fictional parable in poetic form, that author could not be accused of error, any more than the Gospel writers could be accused of error if the inn mentioned in the parable of the Good Samaritan only existed in Jesus' story-telling imagination.

Catholic theologians post-*Divino Afflante Spiritu* made a useful distinction between "material" and "formal" error. The question was; what did the human author of Scripture wish to affirm? Because that was what God wanted to affirm, granted the divine inspiration of Scripture. In telling us that five thousand people were fed with five loaves and two fishes, did the evangelists wish to assert the numerically precise number of people miraculously fed? Or did they only wish to assert an approximate figure, such as saying that "sixty thousand people went to the football match"? In such a case, if there were actually only 4,900 people fed, the evangelists were not stating a "formal" but only a "material" error; just as it would not be an error if in fact 60,521 were actually present at the Premier League match. The crucial question is the *intention* of the biblical writer. Did he intend to assert a precise number, or only an approximate number? He could not be accused of error in the sense condemned by Leo XIII, since the approximate figure was what God's Holy Spirit was actually asserting through him.

On the same principle, therefore, an author of a biblical book could conceivably put into literary form narratives handed on to him which were substantially historical, but which contained minor factual errors. That author would not necessarily check sources, but uncritically accept them. He would accept them without intending to affirm their historical accuracy. Thus the biblical writer could not be accused of error, because he did not intend to commit himself to the factual accuracy of minor details in the account. Here also was a case of "material" and not "formal error".

The Council Fathers affirm equally strongly with Pope Leo XIII the doctrine of "total inspiration", that all the Scriptures with all their parts were written with their authors inspired by the Holy Spirit. No doubt also with *Providentissimus Deus* in mind, they are not saying that the truths of Scripture are limited to matters of faith and morals. A superficial reading of the above text of *Dei Verbum* might lead a careless reader to such a false conclusion. But *Dei Verbum* 11 is careful not to say that the Scriptures only teach "saving truth". That would have implied the limitation of the Scriptures to truths of faith and morals.[26] Rather, it is whatever the sacred writers *assert* that God wishes to assert without error for our salvation.

It is that conformity between the divine will and the will of the human author which is the key therefore to the meaning of the doctrine of inerrancy as developed by Vatican II. That total conformity is what makes the Scriptures entirely unique in the history of human literature. Of no other book can it be said with certainty that every word written is what God actually wanted to say.

If God wished the human author to write a fictional and poetic account, then that is what was written. The truth about the book of Job which the human author, and therefore God, wishes to assert is the truth of God revealing the mystery of himself in the suffering of a just man, if you like, Everyman. But an historical truth may also be affirmed. The truth about Christ's birth is, we will argue, that he was born miraculously of a virgin in Bethlehem.

Similarly, if God wished to allow the human author to include narratives which were substantially historical, but which contained minor factual errors, then that is in conformity with the genuinely human authorship of Scripture. Humans do customarily hand on substantially accurate stories of what actually happened, but with minor historical flaws. These minor factual errors are, in the scholastic terminology "material" errors only, not "formal" errors, because the formality of the author's commitment to the historical fact in question was not present. In terms of *Dei Verbum*, the human author does not "assert" their truth, thus neither does the Holy Spirit in inspiring the human author.

We have already admitted that a literary *genre* of fiction is not excluded within the scope of divine inspiration. Now, is it possible that the Infancy narratives, therefore, are *theologoumena*, fictional stories about Jesus' birth with a theological meaning?

Option three: Complete fictionality, *theologoumena*

This view is that of complete fictionality, in which cases the stories are a "myth" with a theological meaning, often called *theologoumena* by the scholars, with no verifiable historical value. In this view, the Infancy narratives would be classified as legend along with stories of the saints such as George slaying the dragon. There may be some historical fact to be uncovered, such as the fact at least that there was a Christian martyr called George, to whom the legend of slaying the dragon became attached. But the genre of the story must be described as myth or legend.

David Friedrich Strauss excluded dogmatically any possibility of the miraculous. "…the absolute cause never disturbs the chain of secondary causes by single arbitrary acts of interposition."[27] Thus, for Strauss, the virgin birth, as well as the miracles performed by the adult Jesus were rejected as to their authenticity *a priori*, before any exegetical investigation.

Strauss went even further than Reimarus and the rationalists before him,[28] who had argued for some natural explanation for the miraculous events described in the Gospels. Strauss pours scorn on the explanation by the prince of rationalists, Heinrich Eberhard Gottlob Paulus,[29] to the effect that the angelic visitor announcing to Mary that she was to give birth to a son was in fact an all too human male who "passed himself off for the angel Gabriel",[30] and thus became the natural father of Jesus. Strauss quotes with approval Gabler's critique of Paulus' naturalistic explanation: "What! Asks Gabler, is Mary, at the very time she is betrothed, to become pregnant by another, and is this to be called an innocent holy action, pleasing to God and irreproachable?"[31]

Strauss rejected the historicity, not only of the account of the virginal conception in Matthew and Luke, but the entire corpus of the Infancy stories in the Gospels. Strauss allowed some history in the Gospels when drained of their miraculous content, in that the adult historical Jesus believed that "he would visibly make his second advent in the clouds of heaven as the messianic Son of Man and terminate the existing dispensation".[32] But the Infancy narratives for Strauss are pure myth, without any historical value. Regarding the Visitation of Mary to Elizabeth [Luke 1:39-56] he writes "Since then we find all the principal incidents of this visit inconceivable according to the supernatural interpretation; also that they will not bear a natural explanation; we are led to seek a mythical exposition of this as the preceding portions of the gospel history."[33]

It appears at first sight that we do not lack scholars today who seem to come to a similar conclusion. Raymond E. Brown, a Catholic scholar, does not deny in any way as did

Strauss the possibility of a miracle as "an extraordinary action of God's creative power".[34] But, although expressing his conclusions more gently, he seems to agree substantially with Strauss in that, in general, "one may not classify the Infancy narratives as belonging to the literary genre of factual history".[35]

Brown insists that there are facts embedded in the Infancy narratives. For example, he accepts that Jesus was a descendant of King David, in spite of the fact that Brown cannot be certain of the historical value of the genealogies of Matthew and Luke which affirm Jesus' Davidic descent.[36] But he concludes in Appendix III that "The evidence, then, for birth at Bethlehem is much weaker than the evidence for Davidic descent or even (see Appendix IV) for the virginal conception".[37] This is despite the fact that both Matthew and Luke tell us, it seems independently, that Jesus was born in Bethlehem [Matthew 2:1-16, Luke 2:4-15]. The birth at Bethlehem seems to be a major part of the story. To reject the historicity of the birth at Bethlehem must be a reduction of a major part of the Infancy narratives as myth, or, if one would prefer, *theologoumena.*

At first sight, therefore, Brown would seemingly conclude that the Infancy narratives are substantially *theologoumena* rather than substantially history as a literary *genre.* However, as we shall now see, if we examine his views more closely, Brown's position, together with that of a constituency of critical scholars, is much more nuanced than Strauss' dogmatic rejection of any possibility that the infancy narratives might even contain a shred of genuine historical fact.

Option four: We do not have enough historical evidence one way or the other to make any judgement concerning the historicity or fictionality of the Infancy narratives of Matthew and Luke

Brown's own more complicated position becomes much clearer when we take a specific, and it seems to me a crucial, example of his judgement as to the *genre* of the Infancy narratives. The place where Jesus was born would seem to be an important aspect of the narrative. In *The Birth of the Messiah*, R. E.Brown concludes particularly negatively regarding the tradition of Jesus' birth at Bethlehem.[38] In fact, he claims not without reason that this is the common opinion among modern New Testament scholars.[39] But, as we shall now see, Brown in no way rejects the historicity of the birth at Bethlehem as dogmatically as did David Friedrich Strauss.

The case of those who conclude that the birth at Bethlehem is itself a *theologoumenon* would be that Christian tradition had taken an Old Testament prophecy, and made it the basis of the fictional Infancy stories that Jesus was born in the city where the great King David was born:

> But you (Bethlehem) Ephrathah, the least of the clans of Judah, from you will come for me a future ruler of Israel whose origins go back to the distant past, to the days of old. [Micah 5:1]

The Micah text does not necessarily imply that such a future ruler would actually be born in Bethlehem, rather that he would be born in the line of David who was born in Bethlehem. Indeed, there is no first century AD evidence that Jews believed that the Messiah would be born in Bethlehem apart from the New Testament itself. But it would hardly be surprising if, from a reading of such a prophecy within the Jewish community of the time, there was an opinion that the Messiah would be born in "the city of David".[40] Certainly that is implied in John 7:42, during a discussion as to whether Jesus was the Messiah:

> Some of the crowd who had been listening [to Jesus] said, 'He is indeed the prophet,' and some said, 'He is the Christ,' but others said, 'Would the Christ come from Galilee? Does not scripture say that the Christ must be descended from David and come from Bethlehem, the village where David was?' [John 7:40-42]

Brown argues first that we must be cautious before assuming that the story of the birth at Bethlehem was a fiction. He argues that Christians did not need to believe that Jesus was born at Bethlehem in order for him to be the Messiah. He quotes the common belief among the Jews that the Messiah would be hidden, and "would appear suddenly without people knowing where he came from".[41] For the credibility of Jesus as Messiah, therefore, Christians could have easily left the place of Jesus' origin unknown. To invent a story about Jesus being born at Bethlehem would seem to be a particularly gratuitous piece of fiction only two or three generations after the event of Jesus' birth itself.

I would add to Brown's argument a consideration of Luke's account of the birth at Bethlehem. If Luke was inventing the story of Jesus' place of birth, the geography of the narrative appears to be particularly incongruous. The Annunciation of Jesus' birth to Mary takes place at Nazareth [1:26-38]. Why could the narrator, putatively unconcerned with historical fact, not keep her at Nazareth for the birth of Jesus? That would surely better fulfil Luke's message that Jesus was poor and lowly in birth, since, as Nathaniel says in John 1:45, surely reflecting a contemporary Jewish opinion, "Can anything good come out of Nazareth?"

Instead, Luke has to get the Holy Family down to Bethlehem, apparently inventing the story of a census [Luke 2:1-8], which census has no point in the story except to get them down there. How much easier it would have been for Luke to have Jesus born in Nazareth, Jesus' home town, and for the angels to appear not to shepherds in the rough grassland around Bethlehem, but to those labouring in the rich agricultural fields of Galilee, or even to fishermen on the Sea of Galilee.[42]

As Brown concludes with his summary of evidence in favour of the historicity of the birth of Jesus at Bethlehem, "Birth at Bethlehem could never be more than a very secondary motif in the royalty of him who died as "Jesus *the Nazorean,* King of the Jews."[43]

Nevertheless, Brown, after a considerable discussion where he advocates extreme caution before accepting the Bethlehem birth as a pure *theologoumena,* then introduces what seems at first sight to be a more serious objection to its historical credibility. In the rest of the New Testament, there is silence

111

about the birth of Jesus at Bethlehem, just as there is silence regarding the virginal conception, as we discussed in a previous chapter. Brown brings to a climax his discussion of the historicity of the birth at Bethlehem as follows:

> Even if we leave aside the implausible publicity that Mathew 2:3-5 attaches to Jesus' birth at Bethlehem, how can there have been such a general ignorance of Jesus' birthplace in Bethlehem when the parents would have had to come from there as strangers with their child to a small village in Galilee (Matthew's scenario) or to come back to the village with a child born to them during a short journey to Bethlehem (Luke's scenario)?[44]

These objections have some weight. But are they decisive against the Bethlehem tradition, as Brown concludes? In my opinion, certainly not. As Brown freely admits, "the tradition of birth at Bethlehem is considerably more ancient than its present context in the Gospels."[45] And no other birthplace is even hinted at in the rest of the New Testament. Nazareth was his hometown, his *patria*,[46] of course. But, *pace* Brown, this in no way implies necessarily that he was born there.

Is it clear from the New Testament that the citizens of Nazareth *were* ignorant of Jesus' birth at Bethlehem? Perhaps they were well aware of it, but drew no conclusions from that birth as to Jesus' messianic status. Even if all believed that the Messiah would be born in Bethlehem (which is by no means certain, as we have already seen) that did not mean that everyone born in Bethlehem was the Messiah.

It could have been popular knowledge that Mary and Joseph went to Bethlehem because they were "of the house and lineage of David" [Luke 2:4]. But this would not mean, again, that Jesus was claimed to be the Messiah, only that he was in the messianic line, with many other babies of the time. If we assume the historicity of the Massacre of the Innocents, and of the flight of the Holy Family into Egypt, then all that the Nazareth citizens might have known was that the infant Jesus avoided that massacre by the escape into Egypt. After all, those infants slaughtered were not messiahs, only feared to be such by Herod.

It is surely reading too much into the Gospel account to assume with Brown that Luke means to inform us that the Holy Family's visit to Bethlehem was "short". We read that, after "When they had done everything the Law of the Lord required, they went back to Galilee, to their own town of Nazareth" [Luke 2:39]. One might assume from this, as does Brown, that Luke is telling us that Jesus, Mary, and Joseph returned to Nazareth immediately after the visit to Jerusalem when Jesus was eight days old. [Luke 2:22]. But this assumption is by no means necessary. Howard Marshall says simply, concerning Luke 2:39, "Luke says nothing about the visit to Egypt, which according to Matthew 2:13ff. preceded the settlement in Nazareth (Lagrange, 91f.).[47]

It is commonplace knowledge among all scholars of the Synoptic Gospels, that Matthew, Mark and Luke consist mostly of individual short accounts of words and deeds of Jesus (called *pericopes*) which are put together by the final editor of those Gospels into a continuous narrative. Luke 2:39 is an interconnecting verse between two such short pieces,[48] the story of the infant Jesus being presented in the Temple [Luke 2:22-38], and the following narrative about the finding of the child Jesus in the Temple [Luke 2:40-52]. Thus nothing prevents a long period of time having intervened between vv. 38 and 40.

We suggest the following reconstructed sequence of events relating to the history of the birth and early life of Jesus according to Matthew and Luke, assuming their substantial historicity:

1. The Annunciation to Mary in Nazareth according to Luke 1:26-38 and to Joseph in Matthew 1:18-23, also presumably in Nazareth, although Nazareth is not named in Matthew's account until after the return of the Holy Family from the flight into Egypt [Matthew 2:23].[49]

2. The birth in Bethlehem "during the reign of King Herod" [Matthew 2:1, Luke 2:1] in the inn [Luke 2:2-7].

3. The visit of the shepherds [Luke 2:8-20] to Jesus' place of lowly birth in Bethlehem.

4. The circumcision of Jesus [Luke 2:21-38] in Jerusalem, only walking distance from Bethlehem, eight days after his birth, and the Visitation to the Temple according to the Law forty days after his circumcision [Leviticus 12:1-8], in the Temple, where Anna the prophetess and Simeon proclaim Jesus as the one for whom Israel is hoping.

5. The visit of the Magi to Bethlehem, and the flight into Egypt [Matthew 2:1-18], anything up to two years from Jesus' birth.

6. The return to Nazareth [Matthew 2:19-23, Luke 2:39-40], according to Matthew after Herod's death, 4 BC.

7. The visit to Jerusalem of the Holy Family when Jesus was twelve years old [Luke 2:41-50].

8. The return to Nazareth, where Jesus lived until his adulthood [Matthew 2:23, Luke 2:51-52].

The above reconstructed history can only be an artificial harmonisation of two separate accounts of Jesus' birth and childhood which are both only short and popular narratives. That reconstruction leaves open many unanswered questions, and alternative suggestions. For instance, instead of a long period of time in Bethlehem after the birth of Jesus, did the Holy Family rather flee to Egypt from Nazareth after returning to their home town following only a short visit to Bethlehem for the census, where Jesus was born? Were they frightened that the massacre of babies would follow them to Nazareth?

Any reconstruction of the events could only be an hypothesis. But this does not mean that the accounts are necessarily fictional *theologoumena*. The accounts are difficult, but not impossible, to reconcile. For this reason, scholars, even if they eventually decide that the accounts are fiction, honestly admit the tentative nature of their conclusions.

Thus Daniel Harrington says, "the historicity of these episodes remains an open question that probably can never be definitively decided."[50] And again, John P. Meier concludes:

The somewhat contorted or suspect ways in which Matthew and Luke reconcile the dominant Nazareth tradition with the special Bethlehem tradition of their infancy may indicate that Jesus' birth at Bethlehem is to be taken not as a historical fact but as a *theologoumenon,* i.e., as a theological affirmation (e.g. Jesus is the true Son of David, the prophesised royal Messiah) put into the form of an apparently historical narrative. One must admit, though, that on this point certitude is not to be had.[51]

From the strict viewpoint of historical investigation, it may be not. And yet we must ask, have scholars paid sufficient attention to the remarkable historical agreements as between the two evangelical accounts of the infancy?

Positive indications of possible historical content in the infancy narratives

Raymond Brown summarises the agreements between Matthew's and Luke's account as to the following:[52]

(a) The parents to be are Mary and Joseph who are legally engaged or married, but have not yet come to live together or have sexual relations [Matthew 1:18; Luke 1:27,34].

(b) Joseph is of Davidic descent [Matthew 1:16,20; Luke 1:27,32; 2:4].

(c) There is an angelic announcement of the forthcoming birth of the child [Matthew 1:20-23; Luke 1:30-35].

(d) The conception of the child by Mary is not through intercourse with her husband [Matthew 1:20,23,25; Luke 1:34].

(e) The conception is through the Holy Spirit [Matthew 1:18,20; Luke 1:35].

(f) There is a directive from the angel that the child is to be named Jesus [Matthew 1:21, Luke 1:31].

(g) An angel states that Jesus is to be Saviour [Matthew 1:21; Luke 2:11].

(h) The birth of the child takes place after the parents have come to live together [Matthew 1:24-25; Luke 2:5-6].

(i) The birth takes place at Bethlehem [Matthew 2:1; Luke 2:4-6].

(j) The birth is chronologically related to the reign (days) of Herod the Great [Matthew 2:1, Luke1:5].

(k) The child is reared at Nazareth [Matthew 2:23; Luke 2:39].

These common elements are significant, particularly in the light of the fact that all scholars agree that the accounts of the infancy in Matthew and Luke do not depend on each other from a literary viewpoint. For evidence of such literary dependence, we have to wait until the beginning of the public ministry of Jesus, with the mission of John the Baptist and the baptism of Jesus by John (see table opposite).

I have indicated the close verbal agreements between each of the four Gospels in their respective accounts of the beginning of the preaching of John the Baptist by using normal type, italic type, bolded normal and bolded italic type:

1. Where there is no verbal agreement, I have used normal type, e.g. (Matthew 3:1, Mark 1:1, Luke 3:1, John 1:19) The evangelists are individual and unique in introducing the mission of John the Baptist in their own way.

2. Where there is agreement between all four Gospels, I have used *normal italic* [Matthew 3:3, Mark 1:3, Luke 3:4, John 1:23]. Each of the four evangelists quotes the same "proof-text" from Isaiah 40:3-5. Thus, it is obvious to conclude, the entire Christian community by the end of the first century was using this text from Isaiah, no

Matthew 3:1-6	Mark 1:1-5	Luke 3:1-4	John 1:19-23
In due course John the Baptist appeared; he proclaimed this message in the desert of Judaea, ² 'Repent, for the kingdom of Heaven is close at hand.' ³ *This was the man spoken of by the prophet Isaiah when he said: A voice of one that cries in the desert, 'Prepare a way for the Lord, make his paths straight.'* ⁴ This man John wore a garment made of camel-hair with a leather loin-cloth round his waist, and his food was locusts and wild honey. ⁵ **Then Jerusalem and all Judaea and the whole Jordan district made their way to him,** ⁶ **and as they were baptised by him in the river Jordan they confessed their sins.**	The beginning of the Gospel about Jesus Christ, the Son of God. ² *It is written in the prophet Isaiah: Look, I am going to send my messenger in front of you to prepare your way before you.* ³ *A voice of one that cries in the desert: Prepare a way for the Lord, make his paths straight.* ⁴ **John the Baptist was in the desert, proclaiming a baptism of repentance for the forgiveness of sins.** ⁵ *All Judaea and all the people of Jerusalem made their way to him, and as they were baptised by him in the river Jordan they confessed their sins.*	In the fifteenth year of Tiberius Caesar's reign, when Pontius Pilate was governor of Judaea, Herod tetrarch of Galilee, his brother Philip tetrarch of the territories of Ituraea and Trachonitis, Lysanias tetrarch of Abilene, ² and while the high-priesthood was held by Annas and Caiaphas, the word of God came to John the son of Zechariah, in the desert. ³ **He went through the whole Jordan area proclaiming a baptism of repentance for the forgiveness of sins,** ⁴ *as it is written in the book of the sayings of Isaiah the prophet: A voice of one that cries in the desert: Prepare a way for the Lord, make his paths straight!*	¹⁹ This was the witness of John, when the Jews sent to him priests and Levites from Jerusalem to ask him, 'Who are you?' ²⁰ He declared, he did not deny but declared, 'I am not the Christ.' ²¹ So they asked, 'Then are you Elijah?' He replied, 'I am not.' 'Are you the Prophet?' He answered, 'No.' ²² So they said to him, 'Who are you? We must take back an answer to those who sent us. What have you to say about yourself?' ²³ *So he said, 'I am, as Isaiah prophesied: A voice of one that cries in the desert: Prepare a way for the Lord. Make his paths straight!'*

doubt in its catechesis, as a prophetic justification for the ministry of John the Baptist.

3. Where there is very close verbal agreement between Matthew and Mark, I have used ***bolded italic*** [Matthew 3:5-6, Mark 1:5], i.e. the reference to people from Judea and trans-Jordan coming to be baptised by John, and confessing their sins. There are throughout the Gospels of Matthew and Mark a huge number of texts in verbal agreement, or closely approximate verbal agreement. Most of the Gospel of Mark has verbal parallels with Matthew. The majority of scholars conclude that Mark was the first written Gospel, and that Matthew used Mark to write his Gospel.[53]

4. Where there is close verbal agreement between Mark and Luke, I have used **normal bolded type** [Mark 1:4, Luke 3:3], i.e. that John preached a baptism of repentance for the forgiveness of sins. The majority of scholars also conclude that Luke as with Matthew was dependent for a large portion of his Gospel upon Mark. In this case, Luke was dependent upon Mark as one of his "ministers of the word".

As we see from the above, Mark and John have no account of the infancy, but begin with in Mark's case a brief [1:1[54]] and in John's case a substantial [1:1-18[55]] introduction. Their account begins actively with the ministry of John the Baptist and the baptism of the adult Jesus by John. Only Matthew and Luke recount the birth and infancy of Jesus.

So it is remarkable, granted their close verbal agreements from the ministry of John the Baptist onwards,[56] that Matthew and Luke do not agree verbally at all in the first two chapters where they recount the infancy. In terms of our classification above, we would have to produce a two-column table with Matthew 1:1 to 2:23 (48 verses) and Luke 1:1 to 2:52 (132 verses) all in normal type.

What are we to conclude from this established fact that Matthew is not dependent from a literary point of view upon Luke, and Luke is not dependent upon Matthew? As we argued regarding the virginal conception itself, so we could argue that these eleven data arise from a tradition handed on to Matthew and Luke independently, prior to the composition of their Gospels.

It is what C.H. Dodd in relation to St John's Gospel called an "independent historical tradition".[57] He argued from the miracles for example, [cf. John 5:1-14, John 6:1-13], that John did not depend upon the Synoptic Gospels in these accounts but had his own tradition. Dodd hastened to add that he had not thereby demonstrated necessarily the *historicity* of the narratives in question:

> For unquestionably the tradition, in all its forms, *intends* to refer to an historical episode, closely dated *sub Pontio Pilato*, apart from which (this is the uniform application) there would have been no church to shape or hand down such a tradition. It is in this sense an historical tradition, whatever degree of absolute historical or factual value may attach to various parts of it".[58]

Nevertheless, if we agree with Dodd that in any given case a Gospel looks back in dependence not to another Gospel, but to its own source, it becomes a real possibility that it *is* an historically authentic account. Regarding John's "independent historical tradition", if the story in question was legendary, it would have had to have been invented some time between 30 AD, and the date of the composition of the Fourth Gospel, at the latest the first decade of the second century, some seventy years. It is not a long time for such a legend to be created, particularly if eye-witnesses could still have been alive then to verify or even falsify the veracity of such an account.

Regarding the Infancy narratives, granted the fact that Matthew and Luke are earlier than John, most scholars opting for about 70-80 AD, again we only have a time-span of seventy years. Less than seventy years, indeed, for we have to allow time for the "legend" to have become part of the Christian community's life. Matthew and Luke write their Infancy narratives as if all these eleven apparent facts are totally accepted without question.

As Meier correctly concludes:

> In view of all that we have seen, do the Infancy Narratives have anything to contribute to our knowledge of the historical Jesus? Some exegetes would answer: practically nothing. However, a totally negative judgement may be too sweeping. According to the two-source theory, Matthew and Luke did not know each other's Gospels. Moreover, as we have just seen, Matthew and Luke's Infancy Narratives become historically significant, insofar as the criterion of multiple attestation comes into play. Such agreements would, at the very least, go back to earlier tradition and not be the creation of the evangelist.[59]

Meier depends upon criteria generally accepted by scholars post the 1960s New Quest of the Historical Jesus to authenticate sayings of Jesus, one of which is The Criterion of Multiple Attestation. "A saying of Jesus in the Gospels is likely to be historically authentic if it is attested in more than one independent literary source (e.g. Mark, Q, Paul, John), and/or in more than one literary form or genre".[60]

On the one hand, we may argue with Meier that the Infancy narratives are often difficult to reconcile historically. On the other hand, as we see above, they manifest significant historical agreements which do not depend upon one Gospel using another. So how are we to decide for or against their historical reliability?

Who has to prove what?

In a court of law, an accused prisoner is innocent until proven guilty. Who has the burden of proof (the *onus probandi*) regarding the Gospels as to their authenticity? Has a sceptic to prove them false? Or has the believer in the authenticity of the Gospels to prove them true?

This introduces us to the Criterion of Historical Presumption. "This Criterion states that a saying of Jesus in the Gospel is presumed to be from the historical Jesus unless proved otherwise."[61] But Meier comments that in an historical investigation into the life of Jesus, this presumption cannot be employed. Rather, Meier claims, "In the convoluted case of the Gospels, such a criterion simply does not exist."[62] For him, the *onus probandi* rests on one who attempts to prove the Gospels authentic; and, in a case where such cannot be proved, "In effect, this means that critics must allow a galling but realistic third column for a vote of 'not clear' (*non liquet*)."[63]

Of course, we may decide to accept or not to accept the historicity of a given account, without being able to prove that account historically. We must agree with Meier that it is possible to accept X as fact without being able to prove X is fact.

But in *Bad, Mad or God?*, I questioned whether Meier was correct in dogmatically insisting that historical presumption can never be used in historical investigation into the life of Jesus. I argue that historical presumption could validly be used in the cumulative build-up of a case, as does N.T. Wright in his excellent work *Jesus and the Victory of God.* "What is more, this argument advances across the swamp of historical scepticism not by means of the tightrope of isolated sayings, but on the broad and well-built causeway formed out of praxis, stories and sayings taken together as a whole."[64]

As so often, I find Wright's way right.[65] In considering the Infancy narratives, I suggest also that we can use historical presumption from "a broad and well-built causeway" rather than necessarily conclude "not clear" (*non liquet*).

Our study of literary criticism has not settled the case as to whether the Infancy narratives are substantially historical fact or *theologoumena,* substantially fiction. Even if we grant the literary form of *midrash* as characteristic of the *genre* particularly of Matthew's account, that does not settle the question of historicity, as we have seen. Matthew's peculiar, even forced, quasi-rabbinic use of Old Testament proof texts ("a voice was heard in Ramah weeping", and so on) suggests that Matthew is reflecting on events, such as the Slaughter of the Innocents, which have actually occurred, or at least have been reported to him, rather than that he is making up stories from the proof text.

Our studies have also cautioned us against concluding too quickly that the apparent inconsistencies in various accounts of the infancy of Jesus in Matthew and Luke make it impossible or even unlikely that the narratives are factual at least substantially. The historical points common to Matthew and Luke, as we have seen, are all the more striking because there is no literary dependence of one evangelist's account upon the other. Harmonisation is possible, as many "conservative" scholars have proved,[66] particularly if, as we have seen, we admit the possibility that Matthew and Luke have handed on traditions which are substantially factual while containing minor errors of fact, as, for instance, regarding the census. That, to me, makes the accounts more rather than less credible, as, for example, it does regarding the accounts of the Resurrection of Jesus[67] as testified in the four evangelists.

The date of Matthew and Luke is agreed by the scholars as not later than towards the end of the first century AD. This means that there is only one hundred years from the final edition of those Gospels back to a possible eye-witness account of those events in the time of Herod the Great, 4 BC. Admittedly, the events of the life of the adult Jesus, being witnessed publicly, are easier to authenticate, not only because they go back only to about 30 AD, but also because there were many witnesses of those events. But nothing prevents there being witnesses to the events of Jesus' infancy either first or at least second hand. We will discuss the "family tradition" later, and find it a fruitful source of investigation.

In assessing ancient documents, we are often dependent upon straws of evidence which might seem at first insignificant. Even if those straws cannot lead us to certain verifiable historical conclusions in themselves, I submit that they might tip the scales in terms of historical presumption. They may lead us legitimately to presume that the accounts in question are historical, failing stronger contrary arguments.

The historicity of the Gospels

The Second Vatican Council's Dogmatic Constitution on Divine Revelation, *Dei Verbum* appears to declare without question the genre of the Gospels as history, not myth:

> 19. Holy Mother Church has firmly and with absolute constancy held, and continues to hold, that the four Gospels just named, whose historical character the Church unhesitatingly asserts, faithfully hand on what Jesus Christ, while living among men, really did and taught for their eternal salvation until the day He was taken up into heaven (see Acts 1:1). Indeed, after the Ascension of the Lord the Apostles handed on to their hearers what He had said and done. This they did with that clearer understanding which they enjoyed (3) after they had been instructed by the glorious events of Christ's life and taught by the light of the Spirit of truth. (2) The sacred authors wrote the four Gospels, selecting some things from the many which had been handed on by word of mouth or in writing, reducing some of them to a synthesis, explaining some things in view of the situation of their churches and preserving the form of proclamation but always in such fashion that they told us the honest truth about Jesus. (4) For their intention in writing was that either from their own memory and recollections, or from the witness of those who "themselves from the beginning were eyewitnesses and ministers of the Word" we might know "the truth" concerning those matters about which we have been instructed (see Luke 1:2-4).[68]

The key phrase from the viewpoint of this investigation is the subordinate clause *quorum historicitatem incunctante affirmat*, referring to the four Gospels, "whose historicity (Holy Mother Church) unhesitatingly affirms". The background of this subordinate clause was the concern of the Pope, Paul VI. He was perturbed at the lack of any statement of the historicity of the Gospels. This he saw as necessary in particular regarding the prevalence of historical scepticism about the Gospels. One of the members of the commission, Cardinal Bea, himself viewed as a "progressive" and indeed the first head of the newly formed Secretariat for Unity, was himself concerned about this form of radical criticism. With these concerns expressed, therefore, the Pope, in a letter of October 17, 1965, wished to add that the Gospels are "worthy of true or historical faith" (*vera seu historica fide digna*).[69]

The Pope's letter explained his position:

> It appears that the first (expression) (i.e. *vera et sincera* with relation to the Gospels) does not give assurance of the real historicity of the Gospels. On this point, as is evident, the Holy Father could not approve a formula which leaves room for doubt as to the historicity of these sacred books.

Cardinal Bea supported the Pope's letter at the next meeting of the Commission. But many objected that the Pope's formula was itself open to difficulties. Bultmann and his followers talk about *the fides historica* ("historic faith"), "identifying it with the act of the believer projecting his existential experience into a fictitious narrative from which the exegete must eliminate every mythical element". The formula, therefore, could be interpreted in a "Bultmannian way": the Gospels lead us to existential, that is, historic faith in our present existential situation, but are not historically reliable documents. They are rather a fiction of the early faith-community.[70]

The Commission therefore proposed what it saw as a much less ambiguous formula:

> And so it seemed to us preferable to assert the reality of facts and events in a concrete way by adding the term historicity which is not ambiguous; Holy Mother Church has held and still holds firmly and with the utmost constancy that the four Gospels, the historicity of which she asserts without hesitation, faithfully hand on.[71]

The Pope accepted this formula as better than his own. The way was clear for the final draft to be accepted by the Council. "*Historicity*" was a felicitous choice by the Council Fathers. In English as well as in Latin and in other European languages, "historicity" is synonymous with "*facticity*", claiming that a given account is fact rather than fiction. *The Concise Oxford Dictionary* defines "historicity" as "historical character, genuineness of alleged event, etc."[72] In other words, if the historicity of the Gospels is affirmed, the claim is made that the four Christian canonical Gospels, Matthew, Mark, Luke and John are fact rather than fiction, and presumably every part of them.

Dei Verbum 19 affirms that the four Gospels "faithfully hand on what Jesus Christ, while living among men, really did and taught for their eternal salvation until the day He was taken up into heaven (see Acts 1:1)". This does not, in my opinion, limit the historicity of the four Gospels only to the public ministry of Jesus, as has been argued.[73] The context of this statement of *Dei Verbum* 19 is a rebuttal of those who claim that the Gospels do not tell us what Jesus said and did while on earth (the "historical Jesus"), but only primarily about what the early Christians believed about Jesus ("the Christ of faith"). On the contrary, says *Dei Verbum* 19, the four Gospels tell us about what Jesus really said and did. They tell us about the historical Jesus.

There is no intention, therefore, by this affirmation, to limit the historicity of the Gospels to the adult ministry of Jesus. Rather, the statement about historicity, *expressed as a subordinate clause*, is clearly intended by the Council Fathers to cover all four Gospels, and every part of them.

Pope Paul VI himself spoke strongly on the historicity of the Infancy Gospels.[74] He complained that some "try to diminish the historical value of the Gospels themselves, especially those that refer to the birth of Jesus and His infancy. We mention this devaluation briefly so that you may know how to defend with study and faith the consoling certainty that these pages are not inventions of people's fancy, but that they speak the truth."

We must admit that, by the same token, the statement "whose historicity she unhesitatingly affirms" is a general one, and does not specify further the *degree* of historical content in the four Gospels as a whole, or indeed in any part of them. Thus is it possible that the scholar may decide how far, in a generally historical body of literature such as the Council Fathers affirm the four Gospels to be, there are also present elements of later interpretation, or even some fictional elements recorded without historical verification by the author, for theological reasons? A small number of fictional narratives within the content of the four Gospels, it might be argued, would not of itself imply that their general character was not that of history.

But it is at this very point that the use of the criterion of "historical presumption" becomes reasonable, even decisive. If at the conclusion of a rigorous examination of the evidence, it is clear that the infancy narratives in general are not proven fiction, and harmonisation of apparent historical inconsistencies in the stories is possible, we may presume that they are fact. Christian tradition has always asserted the "apostolic origin"[75] of the Gospels. Even if the apostles themselves were not witnesses of the events surrounding the birth and infancy of Jesus, nothing would prevent them verifying sources of those events, as we shall see soon regarding the virginal conception itself.

Luke's introduction 1:1-4

Indeed, it is arguable that one of the earliest Christian testimonies, the Gospel of Luke, maintains that the whole of his Gospel, including the Infancy narratives, is historical:

> Seeing that many others have undertaken to draw up accounts of the events that have reached their fulfilment among us, as these were handed down to us by those who from the outset were eyewitnesses and ministers of the word, I in my turn, after carefully going over the whole story from the beginning, have decided to write an ordered account for you, Theophilus, so that your Excellency may learn how well founded the teaching is that you have received. [Luke 1:1-4]

In his fine detailed commentary on the Gospel of Luke, Howard Marshall concludes regarding the Introduction that "Luke's purpose was to give an historical account which would form the basis for a sound Christian faith on the part of those who had already been instructed, perhaps imperfectly and incompletely, in the story of Jesus. Throughout the preface there is a stress on the historical accuracy of the material presented."[76] Luke is going to recount events (*pragmatón*): "The thought is of events brought to completion, namely the events leading to salvation; the passive form suggests that these are divine acts which God himself promised and has now fully brought to pass, and the use of the perfect indicates that they are seen as a finished series in past time. *En hémin* will then refer to the members of the church in whose midst these events took place and among whom they retain their lasting, saving significance and power."[77]

Luke has carefully completed his researches, based as he says upon "eye-witnesses and ministers of the word". This surely means much more than "the clear recognition since antiquity that the evangelist was not an eye-witness of the ministry of Jesus".[78] Rather, as Howard Marshall insists regarding *autoptai,* eye-witnesses, "Since Luke distinguishes himself and his contemporaries from them, it follows that the content of their testimony was primarily the story of Jesus rather than of the early church, and also that Luke distinguishes between the writers of the Gospels and the apostolic eye-witnesses on whose testimony they were dependent."[79] Luke refers to the "eye-witnesses" on whom he is dependent to assure Theophilus, possibly a new convert to the Christian faith of some importance socially,[80] that the events he describes actually happened.

René Laurentin correctly notes that Luke underlines with insistence that he is about to recount those events "from the beginning" (*ap'archés:* Luke 1:2). Laurentin concludes that the originality of Luke's Gospel consists in the fact that it does not begin with the baptism of John, but goes back to the very beginning, to the birth of John the Baptist the precursor of Jesus, and to the birth of Jesus himself.[81]

That Luke intends his account to be of historical events beginning as early as the infancy of Jesus, *ap'archés*, receives confirmation by the fact that the very next verse gives an historical reference to that beginning:

> In the days of King Herod of Judaea there lived a priest
> called Zechariah who belonged to the Abijah section of
> the priesthood, and he had a wife, Elizabeth by name,
> who was a descendant of Aaron. [Luke 1:5]

Secondly, there is soon after in Luke's account an historical
reference to the date of the birth of Christ:

> Now it happened that at this time Caesar Augustus issued
> a decree that a census should be made of the whole
> inhabited world. This census—the first—took place while
> Quirinius was governor of Syria, and everyone went to
> be registered, each to his own town. [Luke 2:1]

The third and final historical reference in the third Gospel is
to the date of the beginning of John the Baptist's ministry,
which at the same time marks the beginning of Jesus' own
adult public ministry:

> In the fifteenth year of Tiberius Caesar's reign, when
> Pontius Pilate was governor of Judaea, Herod tetrarch of
> Galilee, his brother Philip tetrarch of the territories of
> Ituraea and Trachonitis, Lysanias tetrarch of Abilene,
> and while the high-priesthood was held by Annas and
> Caiaphas, the word of God came to John the son of
> Zechariah, in the desert. [Luke 3:1-2]

Some would contest that Luke has an interest in emphasising
the historicity of his account. Brown, for instance, would
rather interpret Luke's claim that he has "decided to write an
ordered account for you" [Luke 1:3b] not "that the evangelist
was a follower of the apostles who wrote literal history" but
that "Probably the author means no more than that he traced
things with care and reordered them logically".[82]

Against Brown, it is difficult to see how one would interpret
autoptés in any sense other than that Luke is claiming to base
his account on "eye-witnesses", because that is the precise
meaning of the word, used only once in the New Testament.[83]
This would seem clearly to indicate Luke's intention to write
reliable history. If then we see Luke beginning his Gospel
with three clear historical references, then the intelligent reader
would surely be forgiven in thinking that Luke intends to

write a factual account of the incredible *pragmata* ("events")[84] which have taken place, in order to make Theophilus surer of his faith.

Naturally, this does not necessarily mean, from the viewpoint of historical criticism, that we can exclude the possibility that Luke has committed the occasional factual error, or "material error" as we have discussed earlier, depending upon the reliability of his sources. Nor even does it mean in principle that Luke could not unwittingly have quoted sources which are themselves fictional, if the "eye-witnesses and ministers of the word" themselves on occasion handed on accounts of events without historically verifying them.

Even Howard Marshall, who as we have seen strongly contends that Luke intended to write history, nevertheless concludes regarding the prophecy of John the Baptist's birth [Luke 1:5-23], "the historicity of the present narrative cannot be positively established, since the origin and transmission of the tradition is obscure. Equally, however, the possibility of a historical basis to the narrative cannot be denied, since we have no historical knowledge that contradicts it."[85]

What our study of the Prologue of Luke's Gospel reveals clearly is that the possibility at least of the accounts being historical cannot be excluded, and so that it cannot be presumed *a priori* that they are *theologoumena*. If Luke, who is writing his Gospel at the latest only a century after the events recorded, tells us that he is intending to write a history, then at least he has the right to demand that we take him seriously. It also means that, where there is agreement as to historical data with the only other account we have, that of Matthew, we must take the possibility of the historical authenticity of such data even more seriously.

We are now therefore at an appropriate point to consider the narratives of the Annunciation of the virginal conception in Matthew and Luke in particular, having arrived at a reasonable presumption, from a study in this chapter of the Infancy narratives in general, that those narratives contain substantial historical fact.

1   BM, 36.
2   Wright, Addison G., 1967,74.
3   Brown, BM, 36.
4   BM, 561.
5   BM, 561.
6   ICC, 193,
7   Derrett, D. 1975, 81-108.
8   France, Richard T., 1979; 119.
9   BM, 562.
10 ICC, 248.
11 Howard Marshall, *Luke*, 107.
12 *Ibid.*, 107.
13 Lagrange, *Matthew*, 29."*Schanz...simplement que Mt.se sert d'un terme vague, tout naturel si l'on ne voulait rien préciser*" (JUSTIN, *Tryph.* 1.1.).
14 *On peut supposer qu'après la naissance de Jésus, Joseph a pu lui trouver un abri plus commode...* Ibid., 29.
15 BM, 176.
16 Brown, *John II*, 556.
17 Howard Marshall, *Luke*, 99.
18 Cf. BM, 412-418, Appendix VII, 547-555.
19 Howard Marshall, *Luke*, 102.
20 *Ibid.*, 102.
21 *Ibid.*, 104.
22 DV 11.
23 *Providentissimus Deus*, 20. http://www.vatican.va/holy_father/leo_xiii/encyclicals/documents/hf_l-xiii_enc_18111893_providentissimus-deus_en.html
24 Second Council of Orange, Canon 7: Denzinger 180 (377); First Vatican Council, loc. cit.: Denzinger 1791 (3010).
25 DV 11.
26 Teaching that the Scriptures are limited to matters of faith and morals was considered by his critics to be the teaching of Cardinal John Henry Newman, as expressed in his article *On the Inspiration of Scripture*, which appeared in the February 1884 number of *The Nineteenth Century*, Vol. 15, No. 84. In his reply, in May 1884, (from *Stray Essays on Controversial Points variously illustrated*, by Cardinal Newman, 1890, privately printed, § 33. *Inspiration in matters of Historical Fact*, Newman insisted that this was not his view, but rather that "In this point of view, Scripture is inspired, not only in faith and morals, but in all its parts which bear on faith, including matters of fact". Newman had perhaps confused the issue by his use of the term *obiter dicta*, "spoken in passing", by which he meant *matters* which were not relevant, "mere unimportant statements of fact" para 26.

This gave the impression, even if a false one, that parts of scripture were not inspired. DV avoids saying this by its explicit affirmation of the complete conformity between the assertion of what God wants to say with what the human author actually says, rather than by declaring that some statements of scripture are *obiter dicta*. For a balanced critique of Newman's concept of inspiration, cf. Benoit, P., *La Doctrine de Newman sur la Sainte Écriture,* 1961, 15-18. Benoit's book review, of Jank Seynaeve, W.F., *Cardinal Newman's Doctrine on Holy Scripture, According to his Published Works and Previously Unedited Manuscripts.* Louvain Univ. and Oxford, Blackwell, 1953, appeared originally in Revue Biblique, 1956, 285-287.

27 Hodgson, Ed., 1973, 88.
28 BMG, 41.
29 *Ibid.,* 67
30 Hodgson, Ed., 1973, , 139.
31 *Ibid.,* 139.
32 *Ibid.,* xxxiii, cf. Hodgson, Ed., 1973, 296, 584, 589-90, 596.
33 *Ibid.,* 150.
34 BM, 531.
35 *Ibid.,* 562.
36 *Ibid.,* 505.
37 *Ibid.,* 516.
38 *Ibid.,* 516.
39 *Ibid.,* 511.
40 So Brown, BM, 513. The Rabbinic evidence for such a belief is later, BM, 513, n.2.
41 BM, 514.
42 The introduction of the shepherds (ποίμήν 2:15, 18, 20*) can well be historical". Howard Marshall, *Luke,* 107.
43 BM, 514.
44 BM, 516.
45 BM, 515.
46 BM, 515.
47 Howard Marshall, *Luke,* 125. Lagrange simply concludes that " *Il est donc plus probable qu'il (Luc) n'a pas connu le début de l'évangile de Matthew. D'autre part on ne saurait pretender que les faits qu'il raconte excluent les autres...* 92.
48 Brown in fact agrees that Luke 2:39 has this function, BM, 468-469.
49 Cf. the history of the town of Nazareth, cf. BM, 207, and of the complex discussion as to the meaning of "he shall be called a Nazorean" [Matthew 2:23], cf. BM 210.
50 Harrington, *Matthew,* 47.
51 MJ1, 216.
52 BM, 34-35.
53 For a discussion of the Synoptic Problem, cf. NJBC **40:1-37**, 587-595, which supports the majority view of Marcan priority. For the

view that Matthew's Gospel was first, cf. Orchard B., and Longstaff, T.R., *J.J. Griesbach, Synoptic and Text-Critical Studies, 1776-1976.* SNTS 34, Cambridge University Press, 1978.

54 Mark 1:1, "The beginning of the gospel about Jesus Christ, the Son of God". "The verse is probably intended by Mark as a title... with reference either to the account of the Baptist's ministry... or to the entire Gospel... The second alternative is to be preferred." Vincent Taylor, *Mark,* 152.

55 John 1:1-18, his famous Prologue concerning the *logos.* For the significance of the Prologue as John's statement of apologetic intent, cf. BMG, 184-193.

56 Excluding the Fourth Gospel, which has no substantial verbal agreements with the other three Gospels throughout. The common opinion (with which I agree) is that John wrote his Gospel independently of the other three, even if he was aware of them. Cf. BMG 170-172, where I agree with C.H. Dodd, *The Historical Jesus in the Fourth Gospel,* CUP 1963, that John used sources independent of the Synoptics, even the fourth evangelist's apostolic eye-witness source (for authorship, cf. BMG 156-9). Even C.K. Barrett, who claims some dependence of John on Mark, concedes that "It is certain that John did not 'use' Mark, as Matthew did", *John,* 45. To me, the evidence is sufficiently explained if John knew Mark's Gospel, and followed its general chronological ordering.

57 I summarise Dodd's arguments, with approval, in BMG 170-172.

58 Dodd, 1963, 7-8.

59 MJ1, 214.

60 BMG, 115, MJ1, 174-5.

61 BMG, 117-118.

62 MJ1, 183.

63 *Ibid.*

64 JVG, 533.

65 I devote a whole chapter in BMG in order to follow Wright's method of building up a case beyond the "critical minimum", cf. *Building up a Profile the Wright Way,* Chapter 7, 125-133.

66 E.g. Machen, I Howard Marshall. The label "conservative" is to be distinguished from "fundamentalist", a dogmatic refusal to adopt the historical-critical method. Calling in particular Howard Marshall's commentary on Luke "conservative" I mean to be a compliment, in that he conserves Christian tradition by a balanced critical assessment of the evidence.

67 BMG, Chapter 16, pp. 296-327. Cf. O'Collins, G. *The Easter Jesus.* London, Darton, Longman and Todd, 1973. O'Collins, G. *The Resurrection – What Actually Happened and What Does it Mean?* London, Darton, Longman and Todd, 1987. Wright, N.T. *Christian Origins and the Question of God. Vol. III, The Resurrection of the Son of God.* London, SPCK, 2003.

68 http://www.vatican.va/archive/hist_councils/ii_vatican_council/
    documents/vat-ii_const_19651118_dei-verbum_en.html.

69 Cf. V2AP, 309.

70 V2AP, 310.

71 *Acta Apostolis Sedis* Vatican II, Vol IV, pars.V, 723.

72 Concise Oxford Dictionary of Current English, Oxford, 1944, 541.

73 Cf. Moloney, F. *The Infancy Narratives: Another View of Raymond
    Brown's 'The Birth of the Messiah',* Clergy Review, May, 1979,
    pp.161-166. I had argued that the Infancy narratives were covered by
    the statement of DV 19 that the four Gospels, and every part of them,
    were to be adjudged historical. Redford, J. *The Quest of the Historical
    Epiphany: Critical Reflections on Raymond Brown's 'The Birth of the
    Messiah',* Clergy Review, January 1979, pp.5-11. Moloney contended
    that the affirmation of DV 19 that the four Gospels are historical
    "refers to the public ministry of Jesus, and does not touch the problems
    posed by the infancy narratives". The then Editor of the *Clergy Review*
    did not allow me an opportunity to continue the debate. My present
    position is, I trust, adequately set out in the main text of this book.
    For a view contrary to mine and in favour of Moloney's view, cf.
    Fitzmyer, J.A. *A Christological Catechism,* p.127.

74 Allocution of December 28, 1966, *Insegnamenti di Paolo VI,* IV,
    pp. 678-679, Vatican Press, 1966.

75 DV 18. Cf. BMG, 158-9. Not necessarily "apostolic authorship".

76 Howard Marshall, *Luke,* 40.

77 *Ibid.,* 41.

78 BM, 236.

79 Howard Marshall, *Luke,* 41.

80 Luke 1:4, Marshall favours the view that Theophilus had received
    formal Christian instruction, but was being given the benefit here of
    more careful training in the faith, "and this Gospel itself contains
    material for such training" 43, i.e. The Gospel of Luke was to be an
    important part of Theophilus' post-baptismal or "mystogogical
    catechesis".

81 Laurentin, 1985, 11. *"Luc souligne avec insistence son souci de rapporter
    les événements" depuis le commencement (ap'archés: 1,2) "depuis l'origine"
    (anóthen: 1,3). Cela caractérise bien l'originalité de son Evangile, qui ne
    part pas du baptême de Jean, mais remont à son origine même".*

82 Brown, INT 227.

83 AS, 69.

84 In LXX translates *dabar,* word, thing, event, also "theme, story".
    BDB, 182, col.2. "that which has been done, *a deed,* act…" AS, 375.

85 Howard Marshall, *Luke,* 51.

CHAPTER SEVEN:

ASSESSING THE EVIDENCE AGAINST

We consider the view the story of the virgin birth was a myth, or perhaps it could be true but we can never prove its authenticity one way or another. We conclude that there is no evidence that the main source of the virgin birth tradition was mythical, and we leave open the possibility that we might find a way to authenticate that tradition.

Those who would reject the historical authenticity of the Christian tradition that a young woman called Mary gave birth to Jesus of Nazareth without intercourse with a man could do so for two possible reasons:

(a) The virgin birth is a myth, a story without historical basis. Jesus was in fact born in the usual way. The first Christians invented the story that he was miraculously born without sexual intercourse to exalt his status from a Jewish prophet to none other than the divine Son of God. This, as we have seen, would be the view of D.F. Strauss, and is what we might call the "liberal" or "modernist" Christian position. It would be held today by a not inconsiderable number of Christians influenced by the Enlightenment.

(b) The virgin birth happened, in that "biologically" or "historically" Mary at least possibly had not had intercourse with a man prior to the birth of Jesus. But it is impossible in any way to demonstrate this.

First option: the virgin birth is a myth

The standard post-Enlightenment position, which holds that miracles are impossible, is that the idea of Jesus being born of a virgin is a legend. If so, then the critical interpreter of Scripture will search for the roots of the story of the virginal conception of Jesus in parallel mythical ideas. The early Christians, it then would be held, took these mythical ideas and adapted them to the story of the virgin birth of Jesus.

(i) Pagan ideas

At one time, a very popular idea was that the Christian idea of the virgin birth arose because pagan religions themselves had notions of gods mating with humans, thus divine/human beings emerging. Suggestions have been made that the Christian belief in the virgin birth has its origin in Buddhism, Krishna, Assyro-Babylonian, Zoroastrian, and Mithraic religious ideas of the miraculous births of their heroes. These supposed parallels of gods mating with humans, are well documented and assessed by Boslooper.[1] Such alleged parallels in the field of comparative religion may well be important; but all attempts to demonstrate a direct dependence on such legends by the early Christian community with its beliefs about Jesus have failed to produce any concrete evidence for it.

This failure to establish such dependence is even more complete now than it was when Machen wrote his book in 1930[2], so much so that Boslooper can conclude his chapter on this subject by affirming:

> What is common between Christian and "pagan" traditions is the idea of miraculous birth. In this sense they are parallel or analogous. There is a striking difference, however, between the Christian and non-Christian traditions. The Christian formula is unique. The idea that it contains divine conception and human birth without anthropomorphism, sensuality, or suggestions of moral irregularity is to be found nowhere in the literature of the world outside the canonical Biblical narratives.[3]

Rather than being an idea borrowed from other traditions, a birth from a virgin woman by the power alone of God's spirit is unique to the Christian sources.

(ii) Jewish ideas

Equally negative is consideration of Jewish sources, in particular just prior to and contemporary with the primitive Christian community's growth in the second half of the first century AD. Schillebeeckx[4] maintains that the early Christians began to speak of the virgin birth as a result of meditation on Isaiah 7:14, "starting from the (Greek) late Jewish interpretation of Isaiah 7:14".

This, however, presupposes that we know for certain that the Jews in Alexandria interpreted Isaiah 7:14 as being a reference to the virgin birth of the Messiah, which as Brown argues[5], we do not know with any degree of certainty, since the evidence is entirely lacking. This we have discussed at the beginning of our investigation. We have argued in Chapter Two that it is at least just as likely that the first Christians already believed in the virgin birth of Jesus and interpreted Isaiah 7:14 in the light of that belief.

Recourse in this connection has sometimes been made to Philo of Alexandria, who was an Alexandrian Jew who lived c.15 BC to 50 AD, and who interpreted the Jewish scriptures in terms of Greek philosophy. Philo, in his exposition of the birth of Isaac (Genesis 21:1-7), does not hesitate to call Isaac a "son of God" by virtue of the fact that God plays a special part in the creative process.

However, the miracle in Isaac's birth consisted not in Isaac's being born of a virgin, but of a barren woman; and, as Boslooper says,[6] agreeing with Worcester and Barton, "in Philo the ideas of human parentage and the impregnation of the mother by God are not mutually exclusive." Neither in Philo, therefore, nor in Jewish interpretation of Isaiah 7:14, can we see a demonstrable source for the idea of the virgin birth, even though in Philo we might well admit that there is a certain preparation for it, in the concept of divine begetting. But again, this gives no rational explanation for the unique elements of the accounts of a virginal conception by Matthew and Luke.

(iii) The accusation of illegitimacy

Is it possible that the story of the virgin birth was initiated as a rebuff to a charge that Jesus was illegitimately born? As Brown points out,[7] one common factor between Matthew and Luke's account of the birth of Christ is that Mary was with child unduly early [Matthew 1:18, Luke 2:5]. After all, suspicion that his future wife had been unfaithful even before marriage was Joseph's immediate reaction when he discovered that his wife was with child [Matthew 1:19].

A Jewish tradition which goes back perhaps as early as the beginning of the second century AD,[8] says that Jesus was born of a woman called Mary, who was unfaithful to her husband. The guilty party in the affair was called Pantera, perhaps the same person as the soldier called Pandera, whom Celsus the anti-Christian polemicist who wrote his work c. 177-180 asserted was the natural father of Jesus.

Was this Jewish charge simply a reaction to the Christian claims of the virgin birth, or was the matter the other way round, in other words that Christians began to claim that Jesus was virgin-born as a dodge to avoid the charge that their founder was illegitimate?

We have already discussed John 8:41, where "the Jews" retort to Jesus "we were not born of fornication". Are they implying the sneer "not like you were!"?[9] It is worth pointing out that other exegetes, for example Meier, do not accept that in this retort there is an implicit charge that Jesus was illegitimate. Meier emphasises that in the dialogue with *hoi Ioudaioi*, it is Jesus on the attack, "raising the question of *their* legitimate birth and that he is discussing their legitimacy in spiritual rather than in physical terms (he admits that physically they are sons of Abraham). To see a hidden reference to Jesus' physical illegitimacy in vv. 39-41 is, in my opinion, highly imaginative."[10]

Even if we accept that the illegitimacy charge goes back to the earthly life of Jesus, it is surely much more likely that the charge itself came from the rumours that Jesus was virgin born, rather than the other way round, that is to say that the belief that Jesus was born of a virgin was counter to an illegitimacy charge. Jesus' opponents would surely have made much more of the accusation of illegitimacy during his lifetime if such an accusation was taken seriously in the popular imagination.

If we have to push the date of the accusation of illegitimacy forward to the second-century attacks on the Christian faith, then it becomes even more likely that the illegitimacy charge itself was a slur on the already existing Christian belief that Jesus was virgin born. This is particularly so granted the fact that, as we have seen, the tradition of the virgin birth pre-dates any other account of Jesus' parentage.

(iv) Developing Christology

Many authors, particularly in the German critical tradition, have proposed that the idea of the virgin birth developed in the early Church as a natural development of the idea that Christ was divine.[11] Most famous of these was Dibelius, who saw the idea of the divine begetting of Jesus, together with meditation on Philo, and reflection on Galatians 4:21-31, where Dibelius saw Paul's treatment of the birth of Isaac as parallel with Philo's, leading eventually to the idea that Jesus, like Isaac, was begotten without any human aid.

But the idea of Jesus being virgin born is not necessarily linked with his divinity, nor his divinity necessarily linked with his virginal conception. Catholic theology has never insisted that the virgin birth was necessary in order that Jesus should be the divine Son of God, only that, as we shall see, the virgin birth was most fitting. And, on the other hand, as McHugh argues regarding Dibelius,[12] the belief of Philo and in his turn of Paul, that the person begotten by God (in Philo's case Isaac, and in Paul's case Jesus) is indeed a recipient of God's special activity does not thereby imply that he was virgin-born. It is well known that Moslems accept the virgin birth of Jesus, while of course rejecting any idea of his divinity.

In Raymond Brown's *Birth of the Messiah*, there is a more sophisticated development of this view that the idea that Jesus was virgin born was itself the result of reflection by the Christian community on Jesus as Son of God. Brown's view is that there was in the earliest history of the formation of the

Christian tradition a gradual evolution in the understanding of Jesus as Son of God:[13]

1. The earliest Christology saw Jesus as the adopted Son of God only after his Resurrection. This would have been the primitive Christology; although it finds its expression in literary form only in Acts (80-100 AD), Romans (67 AD) and Philippians (63 AD).

2. The next stage was to see Jesus as the adopted Son of God only after his baptism, Mark 1:1 (64 AD).

3. The third stage was to see Jesus as the adopted Son of God only after his birth in the womb of the Virgin Mary (80 AD).

4. The final stage was to see Jesus as the Son of God from all time as the eternal logos (100 AD).

Davies/Allison gives this view of Brown short shrift:

> This thesis, in its essentials already propounded by J. Weiss and A. Harnack, is no doubt simplistic. For not only does the Son of God Christology play a relatively minor role in the birth narratives, but the birth of Jesus was an important Christological moment from the earliest times, as is evident from the pre-Pauline materials preserved in Romans 1:3-4 and Galatians 1:15 (cf. Hebrews 1:6). In addition, one need not look any further than the prophetic tradition, where election is from the womb (Jeremiah 1:5, Isaiah 49:1, Galatians 1:15) to understand how the conception of Jesus could early on have come to hold Christological significance. To find moreover, as have many, an adoptionist Christology in Mark 1:9-11 or its parallels, one must read too much between the lines, and the motifs of Spirit and sonship in these narratives do not represent a retrospection of resurrection language (see on 3:16-17). Finally, the interpretation of Mary's pregnancy as due to the Holy Spirit can be assigned to the confluence of other factors...[14]

Brown's view, that the Christology of the early church moved upwards from low to high, would also be judged simplistic by such as John McDade. I crave the indulgence of repeating the quotation from McDade's article which I have already quoted in *Bad, Mad or God?*:[15]

> It (Life of Jesus Research) also often makes the assumption that early Christology is "low" and later Christology is "high", and therefore the Christological categories closest to Jesus and perhaps deriving directly from him, are the "low" end of the Christological spectrum. Yet the earliest Christian writings, those of Paul, give no evidence that the Christology of the 40s and 50s was "low": quite the reverse, in fact. I sometimes wonder if "early low Christology" is not a fantasy of modern exegesis.[16]

In favour of Brown, it does seem fairly obvious that the disciples of Jesus did not immediately perceive that he was the divine Son of God. This awareness dawned only after the Resurrection. In that sense, there was a movement upwards in their Christological understanding, from low to high. What would be naïve would be to consider that this movement upwards was unilinear.

Rather, as John P. Meier amusingly insists, Christological ideas were mixed up together in a "grab bag", or, as we would say over here, packed in the same supermarket trolley:

> Instead of engaging in artificial rectilinear patterns of development, we should recognise that, once the early Christians believed that Jesus had been raised from the dead, a theological explosion was set off that assured both creativity and disorder for the rest of the first century AD. When it comes to understanding New Testament Christology, it is best to recite this mantra: in the beginning was the grab bag. The next couple of centuries would be taken up sorting out the grab bag. Many early Christians were quite content to make both "low" and "high" affirmations about Jesus, with no great concern about consistency, systematisation, or synthesis. Hence we need not be surprised to find in a pre-Marcan and pre-Johannine miracle story a presentation of Jesus that basically depicts

him as Yahweh bestriding the waters of chaos in a theophany and proclaiming his identity with the words of Yahweh in Deutero-Isaiah: "It is I [or I am]; fear not". The same Mark who takes over this portrayal of Jesus has no difficulty in speaking of Jesus' inability to heal people because of their unbelief or of Jesus' ignorance of the date of the parousia. In the beginning was the grab bag.[17]

Our contention in *Bad, Mad or God?* was that "high" Christological ideas could, and indeed were, present from the beginning of the post-resurrection Christian community precisely because the historical Jesus had himself communicated those ideas about his person and his work during his lifetime. A prime example is the disciples' experience of Jesus Walking on the Water. We argue to the historical authenticity of that miracle in Chapter 12 of *Bad, Mad or God?*,[18] Jesus' calling out to the terrified disciples in the New Jerusalem Bible translation 'It's me. Don't be afraid.' [John 6:20] sounds more like "don't worry, chaps, it's me". But modern scholars do not miss the deep theological undertones of that call from Jesus in the dark of the Sea of Galilee. The background is that of YHWH bestriding the sea, and calling out "Fear not, I AM WHO I AM", in the context of Exodus 3:14-15 and Isaiah 43:1-13.[19]

The disciples' Christological faith was based first and foremost upon what Jesus had said and done. It was not the faith-creation of the primitive community. Thus the movement upwards in the primitive Church, if we grant such, towards the understanding of the full divinity of Christ as expressed in St John's Gospel, was not a pure creation from its own subjective idealism.[20] It came from reflection upon the life and teaching of a man entirely unique in the history of the human race.

Indeed we can go further than Meier himself to pursue this analogy. He is saying that, at the beginning of the life of the Christian Church, there were a number of Christologies operating, both "low" and "high". But we must ask, is not this existence of the various Christologies at least to some extent inherent in the very doctrine of the Incarnation itself, which affirms that Jesus is fully God and fully Man, in a single divine identity of person? In the fourth century, the Alexandrians such as Athanasius and Cyril tended to pull the Church too far towards the divinity leading to the heresies of Apollinarianism and Monophysitism, the denial of the full humanity of Jesus; while Antiochenes such as Diodore of Tarsus and Theodore of Mopsuestia pushed the humanity of Jesus so far that Adoptionism and Nestorianism almost inevitably arose to deny effectively full divine identity of Jesus.[21]

It is not only "in the beginning was the grab bag", but the grab bag was there throughout the history of Christology. Any presentation of the Incarnation has to some extent to be a "grab bag". The pre-scientific mind loved unexplained paradoxes, riddles *hyda* by for instance Samson's riddle, devised from his seeing a dead lion which bees had made into a hive, to catch out the Philistines: "Out of the eater came something to eat. Out of the strong came something sweet." [Judges 14:14]. This is close to the Hebrew meaning of "parable" *mashal*. Cf. Proverbs 1:6 "to understand a proverb (*mashal*) and a figure, the words of the wise and their riddles" (*hyda*). When we have relieved the tension in one area, then we find that we have discovered a new set of opposites, even of apparent contradictions, but which, as we have seen, are essential elements of the one mystery.

In the Hebrew mind, a parable is far from just being a story with a meaning. It is an enigma, which conceals as well as reveals. The parables of Jesus are often misunderstood to be no more than catechetical examples. But, in Matthew 13:35 Jesus himself quotes a Psalm, where the two words *mashal* and *hyda* come together in poetic parallelism (a Hebrew literary technique) to describe the whole mystery of Jesus' message: "Give ear, O my people, to my teaching; incline your ears to the words of my mouth. I will open my mouth in a parable (*b'mashal*); I will utter dark sayings (*hydóth*) from of old", [Psalm 78:1-2]. In this sense the Incarnation is a parable, a mystery, even a riddle. But it is not a myth. Each separate statement is true; Jesus is really God, Jesus is really Man. But its truth can only be held in the tension of two apparently opposite truths.[22]

I repeat, this is not to say that there was not some ascent in Christological thinking in the earliest Church, towards a fuller and more explicit Incarnational doctrine. But perhaps it presented the doctrine of the Incarnation better precisely because it left the opposites in tension, and mostly without explanation in the New Testament. It had met Jesus, and that itself was the greatest mystery, if you like the greatest riddle. To do justice to that meeting, they simply described, they did not try too hard to explain.

As Davis/Allison require from Brown, to demonstrate that the idea of the virgin birth arose only in an ascending Christology, he would have to demonstrate much more convincingly the negatives. He would have to show that, in Acts 2:32, etc. to testify that Jesus was proclaimed Son of God at his Resurrection also implies that the early Christians did *not* believe that he was proclaimed Son of God at his baptism, as declares the earliest Gospel of Mark, 1:11; or to believe that, with Mark, Jesus was declared Son of God at his baptism denied implicitly that he was Son of God at his birth. It is this which the scholars find unproven, indeed, imposing an anachronism upon the early Christology, reflecting back the Christological controversies of a later age upon the primitive Church.

Ebionism,[23] the belief that Jesus was the Messiah but not the divine Son of God, was in evidence as a movement in the second century. But we have no idea whether this Christian heresy was a reaction to the Christian faith clearly expressed by the end of the first century that Jesus was true God become true man, the apostolic faith, or that Ebionism was part of the developing Christology of the first decades of the infant Church. Failing such evidence, again we must draw the line as "uncertain" regarding any unilinear theory of Christological development from low to high as the most important catalyst for the development in the primitive church of belief that Jesus was virgin born.

Second option: the virgin birth possibly really happened, but we cannot prove it

This would be the position of distinguished Catholic biblical scholars such as Brown and also Meier, in his massive work *Marginal Jew*. The virgin birth may well have genuinely happened, in that "biologically" or "historically" as a matter of fact Mary had not had intercourse with a man prior to the birth of Jesus. But it is impossible in any way to demonstrate this. The origin of the Church's faith in the virgin birth, therefore, must remain unhistorical, in the sense that it grew up as a *theologoumenon*. Yet it can remain the faith of the Church, only by faith alone.

Brown became convinced that "the *scientifically controllable* biblical evidence leaves the question of the historicity of the virginal conception unresolved."[24] By "scientifically controllable biblical evidence" he means "the type of evidence constituted by tradition from identifiable witnesses of the events involved, when that tradition is traceably preserved and not in conflict with other traditions".[25]

Brown on the one hand rejects the theory that the idea of the virginal conception came from pagan gods mating, or from Isaiah 7:14, or from Philo. [26] But the doubts he expresses about the so-called "family tradition" which supposedly handed on the historical tradition of the virginal conception, plus the theory which we have discussed previously that he sees a Christological upward ascent in the thinking of the early Church as a possible source of the story of the virginal conception, makes him agnostic concerning its historical demonstration. "Thus, the idea of the virginal conception of God's Son may have resulted from an interplay of many factors: a credal affirmation (designated or begotten Son of God through the Holy Spirit), stemming from the early preaching, and a theology of sinlessness coming together to interpret the historical fact of conception by Jesus' mother before she came to live with her husband – a mixture leavened perhaps by an ingredient of family tradition."[27]

John P. Meier reaches a similarly nuanced conclusion:

> The end result of this survey must remain meagre and disappointing to both defenders and opponents of the doctrine of the virginal conception. Taken by itself, historical-critical research simply does not have the sources and tools available to reach a final decision on the historicity of the virginal conception as narrated by Matthew and Luke. One's acceptance or rejection of the doctrine will be largely influenced by one's own philosophical and theological presuppositions, as well as the weight one gives to Church teaching. Once again, we are reminded of the built-in limitations of historical criticism. It is a useful tool, provided we do not expect too much of it.[28]

In this connection, Meier introduces us to four possible grounds for faith in the virgin birth, or for rejection of it; historical evidence, philosophical presuppositions, theological presuppositions, and Church teaching.

Meier, in terms of his own theory of historical investigation, is particularly keen to keep such issues logically separate. He insists that, at the conclusion of any historical investigation into the virgin birth, "What the historian or exegete cannot hope to do by historical research is to resolve what are really philosophical questions (e.g. whether miracles do take place) or theological questions (e.g. whether God has indeed acted in this particular "miracle", thus calling people to faith). Such questions, while important, simply go beyond the realm of history proper."[29]

Without doing a head count, one suspects that such historical agnosticism might be a common opinion among scholars today. It is certainly the conclusion of Davies/Allison, who provide us with the most comprehensive contemporary historical/critical commentary on Matthew's Gospel:

> It is, certainly, the doubtful character and meagre number of the extant sources and the limitations of historical research in general which disallow a final verdict on the issue at hand. The origin of belief in the virginal

conception and birth of Jesus remains unclarified. Yet, this being said, it should be plainly stated that to say that no satisfactory mundane explanation has so far procured a critical consensus is not to say that the historical evidence clearly confirms the miraculous conception of Jesus. The apparent silence of most of the New Testament, particularly Mark and John and Paul, the number of possible even though imperfect parallels in the history of religion, the fact that Mary and her family show no special understanding of Jesus during the ministry, and the non-historicity of so much in the infancy narratives all point rather strongly in one direction: affirmation of the virgin birth entangles one in difficult dilemmas. Hence if the traditional belief be maintained, it will have to be on the basis of strictly theological considerations; historical reasoning offers little support.[30]

It is at least encouraging that modern scholars have retreated from the utter rejection of the historicity of the virginal conception so dogmatically expressed by David Friedrich Strauss. As we have seen, the historical evidence for the virgin birth is complex and difficult to interpret. Strauss' total scepticism and universal reduction of the Gospels to myth appears to us now as just as immature as fundamentalism. Two hundred years of critical study have at least achieved this positive result.

But is it correct to separate completely the theological and philosophical considerations from the historical? Davies/Allison, in their "concluding observations",[31] quote Joseph Pieper:

> Anyone who treats the charged expressions encountered in cultural history exclusively from the "historical standpoint" is in that very measure incapable of genuine interpretation.[32]

But what is the "historical standpoint"? Must it of necessity exclude the miraculous? Cannot philosophical and theological presuppositions be part of the making of a strictly historical investigation? If not, why not?

Conclusion

We must conclude this chapter by saying that, in the nature of the case, it could never be proved absolutely that it is impossible that the narrative of the virgin birth arose from pagan ideas, or a developing Christology, or Philo of Alexandria, or any combination of such fictional factors. Historical investigation does not admit of such absolute certainties.

One of the main reasons why the Christian faith has found it hard to adapt to a critical/historical methodology is precisely because historical arguments are unlike the abstract scholastic arguments for the existence of God as proposed by such as Aquinas or Anselm, which conclude that it is absolutely necessary that God does exist. Even if there have always been those who have disputed such arguments, the terms of the debate are agreed as concerning absolutely certain conclusions.

But, as we shall now discuss more in detail, it is the nature of the investigation into the authenticity of ancient documents not to be able to come to such absolutely certain conclusions. We can never conclude that alternative solutions are utterly impossible. We can only argue that alternatives are most unlikely, or regarding the virgin birth of Christ at least that this or that supposed fictional origin is demonstrably unproven. That, I submit, we have already demonstrated.

In arguing for the historical authenticity of the story of the virginal conception, therefore, we now hope or need only to demonstrate that the accounts in Matthew and Luke that Mary gave birth to Jesus without intercourse with a man are in themselves credible, and furthermore *are more credible than the alternatives which we have just discussed.* That, I submit, is fully in keeping with the limitations of any historical investigation into the nature of ancient documents.

We must also discuss, as we did already at length in *Bad, Mad or God?*,[33] how such less-than-absolutely-certain but reasonable historical conclusions can possibly be the foundation of the act of faith, which Christianity has always insisted is founded upon the absolute certainty of the testimony of God himself, not upon the shifting sands of tentative historical conclusions.

1   Boslooper, 1962, 135-186.
2   Machen, 1930, 317-379.
3   Boslooper, 1962, 185-186.
4   Schillebeeckx, 1970, 556.
5   BM, 149.
6   Boslooper, 1962, 194.
7   BM, 530.
8   BM, 536.
9   But cf. Schnackenburg John II, 212.
10   MJ1, 228.
11   cf. BV, 207-223.
12   For a full discussion of Dibelius' theory, cf. MJNT, 309-321.
13   BM, 29-32, 140-2.
14   Davies/Allison, *Matthew I,* 200.
15   BMG, 183.
16   McDade, 1998, 502.
17   MJ2, 919.
18   Cf. BMG, 222.
19   BMG, 215.
20   The worst culprit in this supposed idealised ascending Christology is
     Schillebeeckx's complex, even bewildering, account of the evolution
     of the idea of the virgin birth in early Christian thinking up towards
     its zenith in the account of the virginal conception in Matthew and
     Luke. "What was first, as a result of the Easter experience, associated
     with Jesus' resurrection – his being Son and being completely filled
     with the Spirit – is on subsequent reflection affirmed as the reality of
     the emergence and actual constitution of his being as man". 1979,
     555. But every step in Schillebeeckx's upwardly ascending Christology
     is pure Hegelian hypothesis.
21   Cf. Kelly, J.N.D., *Early Christian Doctrines,* London, Adam and
     Charles Black, 1968. Kelly, throughout his book, presents a masterly
     outline of the paradoxes yet the logic of the development of
     incarnational doctrine in the early Christian centuries.
22   It seems to me that J.A.T. Robinson, *The Priority of John,* London,
     SCM, 1985, 367, falls into the trap of not admitting the paradoxes of
     incarnational doctrine. He argues that the full humanity of Christ
     would be incompatible with his full divinity, whereas the affirmation
     of the full divinity and the full humanity of Christ is precisely the
     faith of Chalcedon, 451. Cf. BMG, 241.
23   ODCC, 438.
24   BM, 527.
25   *Ibid.,* 527, n.26a.
26   *Ibid.,* 524.
27   *Ibid.,* 527.

28 MJ1, 222.
29 *Ibid.*, 220.
30 ICC, 216.
31 ICC, 219-221.
32 Quoted in ICC, 221, from Ben F. Meyer, *Theological Studies* 47 (1986), 382.
33 BMG, Chapter 17, 328-366.

CHAPTER EIGHT

ASSESSING THE EVIDENCE FOR

> **We conclude that the tradition handed on to Matthew and Luke that Mary gave birth to Jesus without intercourse with a man is most plausibly historically authentic.**

An historical tradition?

We first must clarify terms used. We have already established that the story that Mary was a virgin when she gave birth to Jesus existed prior to the writing of the Gospels of Matthew and Luke.

As we have already established, the accounts of the virgin birth in those Gospels are based upon what C.H. Dodd called "an historical tradition", which existed prior to the written Gospel accounts.

In his epoch making book *Historical Tradition in the Fourth Gospel*,[1] Dodd came to the firm conclusion that "behind the Fourth Gospel lies an ancient tradition independent of the other gospels, and meriting serious consideration as a contribution to our knowledge of the historical facts concerning Jesus Christ".[2]

Dodd gives many examples of what he calls this "historical tradition", independent of the Synoptic tradition and available to and used by the author of the Fourth Gospel.[3] For example, "the pre-Johannine tradition had a full and detailed account of the Passion and the events immediately preceding it".[4] All his examples manifestly show John drawing upon his historical tradition, which tradition goes back for him before 66 AD.[5]

For Dodd, this is not the end of the investigation. The question remains, how based upon *fact* is this material from the Fourth Gospel's own historical tradition? By "historical tradition", Dodd means no more than that the tradition in question is a story or saying relating to Jesus prior to the writing of the Gospel:

"For unquestionably the tradition, in all its forms, *intends* to refer to an historical episode, closely dated *sub Pontio Pilato*, apart from which (this is the uniform application) there would have been no church to shape or hand down such a tradition. It is in this sense an historical tradition, whatever degree of absolute historical or factual value may attach to various parts of it."[6]

In this investigation we wish to go further than Dodd in his investigation into the Fourth Gospel. We have already shown, as Dodd showed regarding the Fourth Gospel, that the Infancy narratives of Matthew and Luke are dependent upon a pre-written Gospel tradition.

We wish now to demonstrate that this pre-Gospel historical tradition attests to an *historical fact* that Mary gave birth to Jesus without intercourse with a male. We would therefore wish to show that the Gospel narratives of the virgin birth are what we might call a "factual historical tradition". We wish not only to show that Matthew and Luke intended to write a substantially factual narrative in their accounts of the virgin birth. This, I submit, we have already done; or at least that there is no evidence whatsoever that they did *not* intend to recount a miraculous historical event, and some good evidence that they did so intend. There is no evidence whatsoever that Matthew and Luke intended to write a myth or *theologoumenon*. We wish now to show that their accounts were based upon a reliable factual source. That is our task in this chapter.

The "Family Tradition"

In recent years, the belief that the idea of the virgin birth came down to Matthew and Luke by means of a "family tradition" going back originally to Mary and Joseph has not had an easy passage in New Testament scholarship. E. Schillebeeckx, for instance, was quite firm in rejecting any such idea:

Recent exegetical studies have made it clear that elsewhere, in other early Christian communities, this was unknown (or actually refuted) and there is no question of "historical information" here, for instance, information acquired via Mary's private family tradition, as is often said.[7]

Brown is, rightly, more cautious in his assessment, concluding that "the family tradition thesis is not impossible, but it faces formidable difficulties".[8] I intend to go still further in the opposite direction to Schillebeeckx, to show that the "difficulties" regarding the family tradition have been greatly exaggerated; and, on the contrary, that the "family tradition thesis" is the most reasonable explanation of the evidence to hand.

In our chapter on *The "silence" of the New Testament apart from Matthew and Luke* we have already dealt sufficiently with Schillebeeckx's view that "in other early Christian communities, this (the virgin birth) was unknown (or actually refuted)". The virgin birth was certainly never refuted. The most we can say is that in the remainder of the New Testament, apart from Matthew and Luke, there is a silence regarding the virgin birth of Christ. We have examined those texts, as in Paul's writings, in which scholars have found a possible reference to the natural birth of Jesus, and found none such.

As we have argued, these New Testament authors did not at all necessarily signify by their silence that they did not accept the virgin birth. They just did not mention it, probably because it was not theologically relevant in the context of their writing; or, possibly at the stage of the development of early Christian thinking which they represent, they just did not know of the doctrine. It is even possible, as we have seen when discussing Mark's Gospel, that expressions were avoided which might have more easily implied that Jesus was born from natural intercourse (e.g. Mark's use of "Son of Mary" rather than "Son of Joseph"[9]). And a scholar such as C.K. Barrett[10] is convinced from his study that the writer of St John's Gospel believed in the virgin birth. We saw that these exegetical efforts to see the virgin birth implicitly even if not explicitly expressed in New Testament writings other than Matthew and Luke have not convinced all scholars. But such efforts at least indicate that the New Testament "silence" apart from the Matthean and Lucan infancy narratives can equally be seen as favouring the early acceptance of the virgin birth rather than being evidence of an initial belief that Jesus' birth was from natural intercourse.

On the contrary, we have seen that whatever explicit testimony we have regarding the birth of Jesus in the first Christian century, whether in Matthew and Luke or in the apostolic father Ignatius of Antioch, is witness to the effect that Jesus was virgin born. Justin the Martyr early in the second century was already defending the virginal conception of Jesus against his opponent Trypho, before Irenaeus of Lyons at the end of the second century, that there were groups of Christians who denied the virgin birth. The Ebionites, we have argued, could have opposed the virgin birth because their Christology was too low, as an early reaction to orthodox Christian faith. But there is no evidence whatsoever that such a low Christology which denied the virgin birth was part of the development of apostolic Christianity in the first century.

Still more, all our studies have indicated a consensus among the scholars that the accounts in Matthew and Luke of the virgin birth presuppose an "historical tradition" in C.H. Dodd's sense of the word prior to the writing of those Gospels, which are by critical consensus dated at the latest towards the close of the first century. The story of the virgin birth is pre-Matthew and pre-Luke; and there is no demonstrable dependence of one evangelist upon the other's account. Hence that tradition must go back realistically to the middle of the first century, to the first generation of the Christian church. That would be at the most half a century after the birth of Christ.

Finally, in our previous chapter, we have seen that at least we cannot rule out the possibility that the infancy narratives in Matthew and Luke in general are history rather than *theologoumena*. Matthew's Jewish but highly individualistic use of the Old Testament as proof texts for stories connected with Jesus' birth, we have demonstrated, could equally

153

presuppose an historical event underlying that interpretation (e.g. the actual Slaughter of the Innocents) rather than the event itself being a midrashic creation of the evangelist. And Luke's expressed concern in his Gospel prologue to write history, even if, as we have seen, his sources as for instance regarding the famous census could be problematic, must make us cautious before dismissing his account of the infancy as fiction.

We have shown that the difficulties of harmonising Matthew's and Luke's infancy accounts are exaggerated, especially if we remember that these accounts have been transmitted as popular stories, and not as scientific biographies. "Popular" does not mean necessarily "mythical". Facts can be communicated in such popular modes of transmission.

It is now therefore time to consider more in detail the possibility that the story that Jesus was born of a young woman called Mary who had not had sexual intercourse with any man was handed down in Christian tradition not as fiction or *theologoumena* but as an authentic historical fact.

What is a "Family Tradition"? Mary herself

It is first necessary to establish more clearly what we mean by a "family tradition" as the source of the doctrine of the virgin birth. I would first suggest that even the term "family tradition" could cause misunderstanding.

We could, for example, consider that the family of Jesus passed on the story to the Christian community that Mary was still a virgin when Jesus was born. But even this would not necessarily make it "an authentic historical tradition", since the family could conceivably be making the story up, particularly, in view of the "illegitimacy" charge, to preserve its good name.

Even if Joseph handed on this tradition, it would not thereby make it a "historical tradition", if by that we mean a tradition based upon eye-witness testimony. All that Joseph could testify was the fact that *he* had not had intercourse with Mary his wife before Jesus was born. He might have every reason to believe in divine revelation to the effect that Mary had not had intercourse with anyone, and even that there were no physical signs that she had had such intercourse; but she was the only person ultimately who could testify as an "eye-witness" that she had not had intercourse with any man to her knowledge (thereby confirming Matthew 1:25), and yet that Jesus was born of her. *What we mean, therefore, by a "family tradition" of the virgin birth is a tradition going back to Mary herself and to no other person on earth.* Otherwise the "family tradition" would itself be valueless historically.

This is the precise difficulty of the verification historically of the virgin birth. In our previous book, *Bad, Mad or God?* we were concerned with verifying public events; the miracles of the adult Jesus, his preaching, his self-identification as the divine Son of God. Even the Resurrection itself, although an event well beyond the normal, was according to Paul verified by five hundred witnesses [1 Corinthians 15:6].

But only one person, Mary herself, could have known that she had not had intercourse with a man before Jesus' conception and birth. Joseph according to Matthew knew this by a divine vision; but only Mary knew it from her knowledge of the *historical fact* that the birth was without male intercourse.

Mary, witness to her own virginal conception of Jesus?

From Mary, the historical tradition of the virginal conception could have been handed down immediately from her after the Resurrection to the first Christian community in Jerusalem. Mary the "mother of Jesus" is explicitly mentioned, together with the "brethren of Jesus" as being present with the disciples of Jesus in "an upper chamber" in Jerusalem after the ascension of Jesus into heaven [Acts 1:13-14]. That Mary herself was the source of the story of the Annunciation is the simplest explanation, even if, as we shall soon see, many have found difficulties with it.

René Laurentin asks:

> "Did he (Luke) know Mary directly? That is not impossible… But it seems more probable that he only knew of the memoirs of Mary by intermediaries. Was that by oral tradition or in written form? One lacks the means of deciding. But, whatever the mode and whoever the intermediaries, Mary is indeed the source on which Luke depends for the accounts of the infancy."[11]

Laurentin's point is crucial here. In claiming that Mary was the ultimate source of the tradition that she gave birth to Jesus without prior intercourse with a man, we are not thereby claiming that Mary stood over Luke while he wrote the account of the Annunciation. That is an easy Aunt Sally which scholars might use to pooh-pooh the idea that Mary was the source of Luke's account.

Such an idea is by no means impossible; in fact, it is just as plausible as some of the gratuitous critical theories proposed to find the origin of Luke's Annunciation narrative. Brown, for instance, suggests that Luke obtained the Magnificat of Mary [Luke 1:46-55] from a group of Jewish *Anawim* (poor) who had been converted to Christianity, a group that unlike the sectarians at Qumran would have continued to reverence the Temple and whose messianism was Davidic. Jesus came blessing the poor, the hungry, the downtrodden, and the persecuted [Luke 6:20-22].[12]

What is remarkable about the Magnificat is its Jewishness, as indeed is the Benedictus, sung by Zechariah the father of John the Baptist [Luke 1:68-79], and the Nunc Dimittis, sung by Simeon the old man in the Temple [Luke 2:29-32]. The Magnificat seems rather to be Jewish pre-Christian, even if Messianic in hope:

> [46]And Mary said: My soul proclaims ((*magnificat anima mea)* the greatness of the Lord
> [47]and my spirit rejoices in God my Saviour;
> [48]because he has looked upon the humiliation of his servant. Yes, from now onwards all generations will call me blessed,

⁴⁹for the Almighty has done great things for me. Holy is his name,
⁵⁰and his faithful love extends age after age to those who fear him.
⁵¹He has used the power of his arm, he has routed the arrogant of heart.
⁵²He has pulled down princes from their thrones and raised high the lowly.
⁵³He has filled the starving with good things, sent the rich away empty.
⁵⁴He has come to the help of Israel his servant, mindful of his faithful love
⁵⁵– according to the promise he made to our ancestors – of his mercy to Abraham and to his descendants forever.

This song is certainly not in Luke's own Greek style. Thus scholars who cannot accept that Mary composed the song herself, and that it was handed on by her family and by the first apostles, have to account for the primitive nature of the Magnificat linguistically and theologically.

But any alternative hypotheses as to the origin of the Magnificat are equally if not more without solid historical evidence. Brown protests that "The existence of these Jewish Christian Anawim is not purely hypothetical."[13] But in fact it is. He quotes as evidence Acts 2:43-47 and 4:32-37, about the first Jewish Christians, converted after Peter's sermon on the Day of Pentecost:

⁴⁴And all they who believed were together; and whatever belonged to them, was of the community.
⁴⁵And they who had a possession, sold it, and divided to each one as he had need.

But this is a substantially historically reliable description of the whole of the first Jewish Christian community in Jerusalem, even if, as Brown says, "with some historical simplification".[14] It was not a description of a group within the primitive Christian Church. It is entirely plausible as Brown says, that those first Christians lived a life like the Anawim of Qumran in the early days.

157

But it is pure hypothesis to suggest that this group remained as a sect of Anawim within the later more mixed and developed Jewish and Gentile Church out of which came the Gospel of Luke.

Anyone could readily accept that there was an element of primitive idealism in the earliest Christian Church which was later modified as the reality of the imperfection of its members, even if converted Christians, was realised. The story of Annas and Sapphira [Acts 5:1], the couple who deceived the apostles by pretending to hand over their property when they had not, must have been a stark reminder to the early Church that with human members there was always the possibility of abuse and corruption within the Church.

According to Acts 6:1, there were problems as to the distribution of social care, when "the Hellenists made a complaint against the Hebrews: in the daily distribution their own widows were being overlooked". By the time the letters of Paul were written, there is no evidence whatsoever that Christians were expected to share their property; although Paul made no financial demands on the churches under his direction. It was two or three centuries later before the renunciation of property, typified by Anthony of Egypt (251?-356),[15] became an institutionalised form of the ideal of *koinónia* first practised in those early days of the Jerusalem Church. There is no evidence whatsoever that this ideal of poverty found institutionalised expression in the Lucan apostolic Church, and certainly not in a sect such as the Anawim.

On the one hand, there is no need to claim that Mary composed the Magnificat herself immediately after the angel came to her giving her the good news that she would be giving birth to a child without intercourse with a man. There are what we might call stylised responses to divine activity, a literary *genre*, in the Old Testament, for instance the Song of the Three Holy Children [Daniel 3:51-87]. It is most likely that the Song was composed well after the Book of Daniel, as a stylised hymnic response.

On the other hand, there is no reason to think that the Magnificat, along with the Benedictus and the Nunc Dimittis, was not a primitive Christian hymn going back to the origins of the apostolic faith even prior to the Resurrection, with its origins even in Mary herself. One does not have to invent a sect contemporary with Luke's writing of the Gospel called the Anawim to account for its primitive Jewishness.

There is a strong tendency within modern Gospel scholarship to propose any theory, however gratuitous, which avoids having to say that in this or that respect the Gospels are actually rooted in the historical event of the life, death and Resurrection of Jesus. We found this in writing *Bad, Mad or God?*

For instance, scholars reject the authenticity of the Son of Man claim of Jesus in Mark to be the "Son of Man coming in the clouds of heaven" [Mark 14:64], which led to the high priest declaring that Jesus had committed blasphemy.[16] They opt rather for an early and entirely hypothetical Jewish Christian community which elevated Jesus to being the divine "Son of Man". And scholars propose an equally hypothetical "Johannine Community" as accounting for the high claims of Jesus in John "Before Abraham was, I AM" [John 8:58]. On the contrary, I demonstrated, the most credible source of these sayings is in the self-consciousness and in the public proclamation of the historical Jesus himself.[17] These alternative hypotheses are, I proposed "unnecessary beings" to be excised by Occam's razor,[18] the principle enunciated by William of Occam to the effect that *entia non sunt multiplicanda praeter necessitatem*, "beings are not to be multiplied without necessity".[19]

Again, I insist, I am not claiming that I can prove that Mary composed the Magnificat immediately after the Annunciation. The Church, in its conviction of the historicity of the Gospels does not necessarily lend implicit support to such a simplistic idea. The insertion of the Magnificat could have been part of the "synthesis",[20] the combination sometimes artificially of different sources, from which Luke ultimately produced the Gospel. What is a most reasonable presumption, however, is that the Magnificat was an early Christian hymn, part of the tradition handed on to Luke from those first Christians, even from Mary herself.

As Howard Marshall says, "The lack of Christian colouring suggests that the present hymn fits no situation better than Mary herself,[21] although this does not necessarily mean that Mary herself composed the hymn at the precise occasion in the text."[22] And this is not mere hypothesis. It is part of the claims of Luke in the introduction to his Gospel that the accounts of the events of the life of Jesus which he included were handed down to him by "eye-witnesses and ministers of the word" [Luke 1:2-4].[23]

It is time to consider this tradition. If the ultimate source of the Christian story that Mary was a virgin before she gave birth to Christ was Mary herself, then could we trace hypothetically the process by which that story made its way from the months before the birth of Christ when the Holy Spirit formed the embryo of Jesus in Mary's womb until the moment when Luke put his Gospel together for publication?

First stage: birth and early life of Jesus

Let us begin with the hypothesis that the accounts in Matthew and Luke concerning the annunciation to Joseph and to Mary respectively are substantially accurate, that Mary gave birth to Jesus without prior intercourse with any man.

The first presumption is that Mary and Joseph, and the whole family circle of Mary and Joseph, would not wish this information to be widely known. Before Jesus was understood to be claiming to be the Messiah, that is, during his adult life, stories about his virgin birth would be ridiculed as masking the fact that he was illegitimately born. We have seen earlier that stories that Jesus was born illegitimately were current at least by the second century, and even possibly during the public ministry of Jesus; that is if we take the view that the Jews' angry response to Jesus "we were not born of fornication" [John 8:41], is an oblique reference to a common view that Mary gave birth to Jesus from all-too-natural intercourse, but with a man other than her husband Joseph.[24]

If this accusation of illegitimacy was current during the earthly life of Jesus, then it might have its source, again presuming on the substantial historicity of the Gospel account, in gossip arising from the family circle that Joseph was not the natural father of Jesus. All this points to the need, from pure common sense, to keep the fact of the virgin birth secret. According to Matthew 1:18-25, Joseph needed a divine revelation to convince him that Mary was not pregnant from an unfaithful relationship. The citizens of Nazareth, bereft of any such revelation, would draw a very different conclusion from stories of the virgin birth of Jesus, which would do the family reputation of Joseph and Mary no good whatsoever.

Also, the knowledge which Mary had that she had not had intercourse before Jesus was born did not necessarily imply that she initially believed in the full divinity of her Son, but simply that he was the Messiah to come. Roman Catholics believe that Mary was without sin, a privilege given to her as the Mother of the Saviour. But this did not necessarily imply that she was aware that Jesus was "God from God, light from light" as we say in the Creed. Her knowledge was subject to development, as was that of her divine son, who "increased in wisdom, in stature, and in favour with God and with people" [Luke 2:52].

We saw above that Davis/Allison have argued, indeed in my opinion have demonstrated, that Matthew's evident belief in the virgin birth was not first of all dependent on belief in the full divinity of Christ. Rather, "the interpretation of Mary's pregnancy as due to the Holy Spirit can be assigned to the confluence of other factors", for example to the fact that Jesus was the Messiah and so was most apt in Old Testament terms to be "associated with the Holy Spirit".[25]

We may well accept, as we have earlier discussed, that Matthew's assertion that Jesus would be called "Emmanuel, God-with-us" was an indication of his own developed knowledge that Jesus was the divine Son of God.[26] But Matthew is careful not to make the angel, or Joseph in reply, make so bold an assertion. Jesus would "save the people from their sins" an instrument of God's forgiveness,[27] but not necessarily as in Mark 2:5: one who claims to be able himself to forgive sins, so incurring the charge of blasphemy.[28] This is most credibly a later development awaiting the public ministry of Jesus, not an understanding given to Mary and Joseph at his birth.

The growth of the Messianic idea in the Old Testament is complex, but had reached some clear lines by the time Jesus was born. As expressed in the Psalms of Solomon 17:23-26, written according to scholarly opinion 70-40 BC,[29] it was both religious and political. In this thinking, the one who "saves his people from their sins" would be such a messianic deliverer, not a *divine* Saviour, but a *human* mediator of the cleansing of God's people:

> Behold, O Lord, and raise up to them their king, the son of David, in the time which thou, O God, knowest; that he may reign over Israel thy servant; and gird him with strength that he may break in pieces the unjust rulers; may purge Jerusalem from the heathen which trample her down to destroy her; in wisdom and righteousness may he thrust out sinners from the inheritance, crush the proud spirit of the sinners as potter's vessels; and with a rod of iron shall he break all their substance. He shall destroy the ungodly nations with the word of his mouth so that at his rebuke the nations shall flee before him, and he shall convict the sinners in the thought of their own hearts. And he shall gather together a holy people whom he shall lead in righteousness, and shall judge the tribes of the people that has been sanctified by the Lord his God. And he shall not suffer iniquity to dwell in the midst of them; and none that knoweth wickedness shall abide with them. For he shall take knowledge of them that they are all sons of their God, and shall apportion them in the land according to their tribes; and the stranger and the sojourner shall dwell with them no more. He shall judge the nations and the peoples with the wisdom of his righteousness; and he shall hold the nations under his yoke to serve him. And he shall glorify the Lord in a place seen of the whole earth; and he shall purge Jerusalem and make it sacred as it was at the beginning; so that the nations shall come from the ends of the earth to see her glory, bringing as gifts her sons which had fainted, and

they shall see the glory with which God has glorified her. And he as righteous king, taught by God, shall be over them, and there shall be no unrighteousness among them in his days, because they are all holy and the Messiah of the Lord is their king.[30]

Entirely in the same vein, Luke in his infancy accounts manifests a similarly low Christology but a strong sense of supernatural deliverance through the Messiah. We noted above the Jewishness of the Magnificat, pre-Christian in its theology. It conforms particularly to Jewish expectation of the Messiah at the beginning of the first Christian century, when Jesus was born.

So, in Luke's account of the Annunciation, the child prophesied to come out of Mary's womb is the Davidic Messiah from God "He will be great and will be called Son of the Most High. The Lord God will give him the throne of his ancestor David" [Luke 1:32]. And Luke has the angel answering Mary, "The Holy Spirit will come upon you, and the power of the Most High will cover you with its shadow. And so the child will be holy and will be called Son of God" [Luke 1:35].

There is nothing here inconsistent with what we might call an "orthodox Jewish Messianism" contemporary with the time of Christ, and in Judaism after it. Brown claims that in Luke's account, "the way in which these ideas are combined in 1:35 takes us out of the realm of Jewish expectation of the Messiah into the realm of early Christianity. The action of the Holy Spirit and the power of the Most High come not upon the Davidic king but upon his mother".[31]

We may freely admit that Luke, in writing his Gospel, has Christological ideas of his own, in line with the developed Christology of his own day, and reads those ideas into the narratives he writes. But on the other hand, Davis/Allison make a comparison from Jewish sources between Mary and Moses' sister Miriam (Miriam being the Hebrew form of Mary). "…it becomes important to observe that in LAB 9.10 we read that 'the spirit of God came upon Miriam at night and she saw a dream…'"[32] For Mary herself, the Holy Spirit, the source of miracles, the direct action of God in the Old Testament, [Judges 13:25, 14:6, 19:15] was the cause of Jesus' birth, without the necessarily understood implication that her Son was God become man.

Nothing in the term "Son of God" in its Old Testament context implies the full divinity of the Son of David.[33] Rather, "Son of God" in its Messianic context simply means that the anointed king in the line of David will have an especially intimate relationship with God giving him a unique divinely bestowed authority to fulfil the will of YHWH for his people. The prophet Nathan puts in the mouth of God regarding David's successor, "I shall be a father to him and he a son to me" [2 Samuel 7:14]. This is only a prophetic guarantee of the eternity of David's dynasty. It in no way implies that this Davidic Messianic "Son of God" has a relationship *in nature* with God his Father.

This was, I am sure, the limitation of the understanding initially of Mary as a woman of Jewish faith regarding the wonderful child she gave birth to without male intercourse. On the other hand, Luke goes on to tell us that an event in the life of her child Jesus possibly made her think more deeply as to what it meant that her son was truly "Son of God". When his parents took Jesus to the Temple, when he was twelve years old, they lost him for three days, then they found their son discussing with the Rabbis "listening to them, and asking them questions". His mother instinctively said to him, "My child, why have you done this to us? See how worried your father and I have been, looking for you.' [Luke 2:48]. He replied, "Why were you looking for me? Did you not know that I must be in my Father's house?" [Luke 2:49].

Luke tells us that "His mother stored up all these things in her heart" [Luke 2:51]. Was it at that point that she began to wonder whether the virgin birth of her son meant more even than that he was a special person initiating a new act of God? Was her son aware that God was his own Father? If, as we have argued in *Bad, Mad or God?*,[34] Jesus was aware that he was truly God, then it would be most consistent that as a boy he would develop a consciousness that God was his special Father, a consciousness which would develop in his adult life so that he would eventually say to the startled Jerusalem crowd, "Before Abraham was, I AM" [John 8:58].[35]

Raymond Brown insists that "whether one is liberal or conservative, one must desist from using the present scene to establish a historical development (or lack of development) in Jesus' self-awareness".[36] But I just fail to see why. Luke's account of Jesus manifesting a child's understanding of his own self-consciousness as divine fulfils the *Criterion of Coherence*, namely "A saying of Jesus in the Gospels is likely to be historically authentic if it coheres with other sayings and deeds of Jesus."[37] Luke 2:49 coheres with other texts in all four Gospels where Jesus claims to be God, either explicitly or implicitly, as we demonstrate throughout *Bad, Mad or God?*.[38] Brown insists that "The appreciation of Jesus' divine sonship was post-resurrectional."[39] But why is it incredible that there were words and deeds of Jesus, even of the child Jesus, which before, even long before, his Resurrection,[40] expressed the truth of his divine claims, and were the historical foundation for the growth of the Church's consciousness of his divine status?

I repeat that I do not think that Matthew's or Luke's account of the infancy of Jesus was word for word accurate in a fundamentalist sense. But, whatever redactional theories are proposed, the text as we read it, presented only one hundred years after the infancy of Jesus itself, is credible *in se*. Both Mary and Joseph believed that Jesus was born from the womb of Mary without intercourse with any man. This virgin birth was to them not at first a proof of the divinity of Christ, but rather a divine sign, a miracle wrought by the Holy Spirit, showing that the Messiah was born, who was come to deliver Israel from sin and into freedom. And they would have no reason to publicise this fact at least during the early life of Jesus, since he himself had not yet manifested his Messiahship. Preaching the virgin birth would lead only to scandal and ridicule.

The public ministry of Jesus

The same situation regarding the non-publicising of the virgin birth of Jesus would have applied throughout his public ministry, right until the Resurrection. The story of the virgin birth would have been an unnecessary distraction from the challenge of the miracles and the teaching of the adult Jesus.

Some might argue that, in the context of Jewish belief in miracles, the public announcement that the new prophet had been virgin born would have been an added sign that he was the Messiah. But this would only have aroused suspicion and ridicule, before there was sufficient belief established in his Messiahship for the virgin birth to be an asset rather than an obstacle to faith.

We have argued earlier[41] that the friends and relatives of Mary and Joseph in Nazareth might well have known of the birth of Jesus in Bethlehem without drawing any significant theological conclusions from that place of birth. If the story of the census is substantially historical (as we have argued that it is[42]), then that would have been sufficient reason for Mary and Joseph to go down to Bethlehem for the birth of Jesus without any whiff of messianic pretensions. Joseph was "of the house and lineage of David" [Luke 2:4], as were hundreds or more of Jewish men at that time. That was reason enough to go to Bethlehem.

Regarding the virgin birth, my own opinion is that Mary and Joseph tried to keep the true story as secret as possible throughout the life of Jesus, perhaps allowing only the closest and most trusted family such as Elizabeth to know what really happened. Only this would focus minds on what the adult Jesus was performing wonderfully, his miracles as signs of the kingdom [Matthew 12:28], and his teaching as the Gospel to the poor [Matthew 11:5].

The need for Mary and Joseph to keep the true story of Jesus' birth secret is at least an initial pointer to the silence of the rest of the New Testament concerning the virgin birth, which we have discussed in Chapter 4. Most of Jesus' hearers, as also some if not most of his disciples, would have thought that Jesus was born from a natural union between Mary and

Joseph. They would have had no reason to believe otherwise, since there was no tradition that we are aware of contemporary with Jesus which considered that the Messiah would be virgin born. We have discussed at length Isaiah 7:14 in Chapter One, and have looked in vain for any pre-Christian Jewish interpretation of that text "a virgin will conceive and bear a son" which saw it as a prophecy that the Messiah to come would be born of a virgin.[43]

This easily explains the use of the term "son of Joseph" in the Gospels to describe Jesus, rather than "son of Mary"; simply because most people considered that Joseph was Jesus' natural father. We have also noted earlier that Jesus was in any case "son of Joseph" in the legal sense that he was Joseph's heir; thus even those who believed that Jesus was virgin born could in this sense call him "son of Joseph", even if he was not his natural son.

In Chapter 4, we entered into the complex discussion as to whether Jesus was called originally "son of Joseph" or "son of Mary". We discussed Miguens' view, that Mark deliberately avoided calling Jesus "son of Joseph" because he believed that Jesus was "son of God" exclusively, so deliberately avoids using the term that Jesus is "son of Joseph". We argued that, particularly granted Mark's high Christology, which we have made a pivotal part of our case in *Bad, Mad or God?*, Miguens' view is feasible, but not proven.[44] Brown's view is also a possibility, that Mark's use of "son of Mary" was not necessarily redactional, but could have been for other historical reasons, for instance that, like the dead son of the widow of Nain being called "the only son of his mother", Jesus could have been called "son of Mary" because Joseph was dead and Mary was a widow.[45] Brown explains Mark's refusal to call Jesus "son of Joseph" on the more mundane grounds that "Joseph was dead and Mary, the one living parent, was well known to all the villagers."[46]

We rather conclude that John's Gospel once more reflects the historical reality of Jesus' own time, being generally and understandably called "son of Joseph" [John 6:42]. But, as we have demonstrated, this in no way negates the early tradition of the virgin birth.

A real problem for Mary, with her orthodox first century Jewish expectations of the Messiah, must have been the behaviour of her son right from the beginning of his public ministry. Instead of promising to lead the armies of Israel to crush their enemies (albeit with the spiritual purification of the people and the welcoming of the Gentiles in the future), as in the prophecy we have quoted above from the Songs of Solomon, her son Jesus focused entirely upon his miracles and his preaching. The sermon of her son at the synagogue in his home town of Nazareth would have sounded strange in the ears of all the congregation including his own mother's:

> [16]He came to Nazara, where he had been brought up, and went into the synagogue on the Sabbath day as he usually did. He stood up to read, [17]and they handed him the scroll of the prophet Isaiah. Unrolling the scroll he found the place where it is written:
> [18]The spirit of the Lord is on me, for he has anointed me to bring the good news to the afflicted. He has sent me to proclaim liberty to captives, sight to the blind, to let the oppressed go free, [19]to proclaim a year of favour from the Lord. [20]He then rolled up the scroll, gave it back to the assistant and sat down. And all eyes in the synagogue were fixed on him. [21]Then he began to speak to them, "This text is being fulfilled today even while you are listening." [Luke 4:16-21]

This is almost as far as it could have been from the iconic Messiah in the Psalms of Solomon. Again, even if Roman Catholic teaching regarding the sinlessness of Mary is accepted, that does not mean that she could not have difficulties being rebuffed by her son when he was busy, as in Mark's account:

> [31]Now his mother and his brothers arrived and, standing outside, sent in a message asking for him. [32]A crowd was sitting round him at the time the message was passed to him, "Look, your mother and brothers and sisters are outside asking for you." [33]He replied, "Who are my mother and my brothers?" [34]And looking at those sitting in a circle round him, he said, "Here are my mother and my

brothers. [35]Anyone who does the will of God, that person is my brother and sister and mother." [Mark 3:31-35]

Her son is forming a new community, not based upon blood line, but upon submission to God's will. That must have been a painful idea for her to accept. Most of all, as a mother she must have found it difficult when instead of her son crushing God's enemies prior to the spiritual renewal of the elect, he would himself suffer an ignominious death.

Here we follow the well argued view of N.T. Wright in *Jesus and the Victory of God*, who is rightly convinced that the historical Jesus foresaw the Destruction of Jerusalem, which actually took place in 70 AD, when the rapacious Roman army crushed a futile Jewish revolt, destroying the Temple and ravaging the city. With Vincent Taylor, Wright sees the prophecy of Jesus "Not one stone will be left here upon another, all will be thrown down" [Mark 13:2] as historically authentic, not as a "prophecy after the event" *(vaticinium ex eventu)*.[47] For Wright, Jesus foresaw not only the Destruction of Jerusalem, but the hope following it of a new community, Christ's own body, the true renewal of Israel.[48]

How much of her son's revolutionary concept of Messiahship did his mother understand during his life? Of course, we shall never know. But we have no reason to doubt John's account that his mother stood at the foot of her son's cross while he writhed in his final agony.[49] Her faith that her son had some special destiny, which had been initially generated by the strange event of his birth, might well have been tested almost to breaking-point at various points in his ministry [Mark 3:31-35, John 2:3-4]. Now, as he died a crucified criminal, rather than, as in the Psalms of Solomon, leading the victorious Israelites to freedom, that faith must have been most of all put to the test. But we all know that the faith of mothers in their children often still stands firm because of their deep love for them, when everyone else's fails. Perhaps she was able to understand and accept with a mother's heart what kind of a Messiah her son was, when the male disciples of Jesus had fled.

Faith in the virgin birth after the Resurrection

We will proceed on the hypothesis, in agreement with Laurentin,[50] that after Pentecost, when the Spirit came upon the apostles, Mary first told the Jerusalem community of Christians that she had given birth to Jesus without male intercourse. Mary the "mother of Jesus" is explicitly mentioned, together with the "brethren of Jesus" as being present with the disciples of Jesus in "an upper chamber" in Jerusalem after the ascension of Jesus into heaven [Acts 1:13-14].

This community did not use the virginal conception of Jesus as part of its preaching, which was focused upon the Resurrection itself, as the climax of the *public ministry* of Jesus. But the miracles of Jesus, together with his Resurrection, were an essential element in the apostolic preaching as manifested in the first speech of Peter in Acts 2.[51] It is therefore most appropriate that the faith of those early Christians should have been confirmed by the further proof of his Messiahship rendered by his miraculous birth. If Mary had truly conceived Jesus in her womb without natural intercourse, as we contend actually happened, then it is difficult to see how she could have kept this fact quiet among the first Christians after Pentecost and the Resurrection. Nor presumably would she have wished to do so.

Nor need it have been too long a time before a written record of the virginal conception was compiled. There is an endless discussion among the scholars concerning the sources of the four Gospels. Even if the final edition of Luke and Matthew did not appear until towards the close of the first Christian century,[52] all the scholars admit that the Gospels contain traditions going back to the beginning of the Christian Church in Jerusalem, not to say back to the time of the historical Jesus himself. New Testament scholarship presumes that the earliest traditions were oral; but it may have not been very long before there were pre-Gospel written accounts.[53]

Thus Brown concludes concerning the speculative literary history of Matthew 1:18-25 that Matthew wrote his account using "a pre-Gospel narrative of the annunciation of the

Davidic Messiah's birth from a virgin through the creative power of the Holy Spirit".[54]

He does not hold a similar view concerning Luke's account, 1:26-38. Rather, Brown thinks "that the whole annunciation scene was composed by Luke and that the specific angelic prophecy of Mary's virginal conception of Jesus (i.e. verses 34-35) were always part of it".[55]

But, if, as we have demonstrated throughout this study, the narrative of the virgin birth pre-dated Matthew's and Luke's account of it, how can we verify its truth?

How much can Jones swallow?

We can only go so far with literary and form-critical analysis. We have already demonstrated that the tradition that Luke's Gospel was written by Luke the companion of Paul is well founded.[56] We have already shown, with Laurentin,[57] that the source of Luke's account could well have been Mary herself, even if Luke did not have Mary as the direct literary source but only as the source of the historical tradition of the virginal conception handed on by her from the early days of the Jerusalem Christian Church.

We have used all the tools of modern biblical research to demonstrate that the tradition of the virginal conception is the earliest account of the mode of Jesus' birth, after the New Testament going back at least to the beginning of the second century with Ignatius of Antioch and Justin Martyr.[58] It pre-dates any account that Jesus was born of natural intercourse between Mary and Joseph, or between Mary and any other man, apart from the natural presumption during Jesus' lifetime that he was born of a sexual union between Mary and Joseph (or even, possibly, that he was illegitimate).

As we demonstrated, the mere calling of Jesus "son of Joseph" might not be any kind of threat to the historicity of the tradition of the virgin birth. It may have meant that those who believed that Jesus was virgin born were referring to Jesus' rights as firstborn, not inferring that he was the natural son of Joseph. It may have meant that, lacking any other information, it was the general presumption that Jesus along with the rest of the human race was the issue of sexual union between a husband and his wife. And we saw that there may even have been a tradition, proceeding from rumours of a virgin birth, that Jesus was in fact illegitimate.[59]

The "silence" of the rest of the New Testament, we have reasonably concluded in Chapter 4, cannot be used as an argument that there was an early contrary tradition that Jesus was not born of a virgin. We have on the contrary concluded that there are possible hints quite apart from the infancy narratives of Matthew and Luke that God was the only Father of Jesus, and that his birth was "not of the will of the flesh but of God himself". We have argued that these hints of virginal conception, even if not fully demonstrable, certainly provide us with negative proof that we cannot demonstrate from the earliest Christian tradition that Jesus' birth was from natural intercourse.

We have shown in Chapter 5 that these accounts are not demonstrably fiction or *theologoumena*. They cannot be proven to arise from pagan myth or from the subjective evolution of Christian consciousness upwards towards the affirmation of Jesus' divinity. Rather, as far as literary and form criticism can determine, they *could well* be factual accounts, even if written from Old Testament and Rabbinic sources and with theological motivation.

We can make one further point from Christian tradition, as represented in *Dei Verbum*, the Dogmatic Constitution on Divine Revelation. The literary *genre* is not clearly myth or *theologoumenon*, as we have demonstrated. The Council Fathers affirmed the historicity of the four Gospels. Could we not therefore argue that it is at this point that the Criterion of Presumption becomes relevant? This Criterion states that a saying of Jesus in the Gospel is presumed to be from the historical Jesus (in this case can be presumed to be factual) unless proved otherwise.[60] Since they are not proven to be myth, then cannot we presume the historicity of Matthew's and Luke's accounts regarding the virgin birth?

We saw earlier[61] how cautious we have to be in the use of this Criterion. But we saw also there that the Criterion of

172

Historical Presumption comes very much into play as we build up a cumulative case for the historical authenticity of the Gospels. We could argue that at this point we have now already carefully built up such a cumulative case in this book for the historical character of the tradition that a baby called Jesus was born by the power of the Holy Spirit to a virgin called Mary.

But we can be sure also that many of our readers will be making extra demands for an account in the Gospels which states that a miraculous birth occurred, only once it seems in the history of the human race. The demands will be even greater in the context of a post-Enlightenment society which, if it no longer believes that miracles are impossible absolutely, will take a great deal of persuading that an event outside of the ordinary course of nature has actually occurred. We need now therefore to consider the virginal conception as a miracle, and attempt to find criteria to verify or falsify it.

NOTES – CHAPTER EIGHT

1   Dodd, 1963.
2   Dodd, 1963, 423. Cf. BMG 170-172 for a discussion of Dodd's "historical tradition".
3   Dodd identifies this distinctively Johannine oral tradition such as John's use of an Aramaic tradition. He tends to use *Messias* [John 1:41] and *Képhas* instead of *Christos* and *Petros*. There are allusions to well attested Jewish beliefs (Dodd, 1963, 425) such as the fact that the Messiah would remain unknown until Elijah identified him (Dodd, 1963, 266. John 1:26), and the High Priest's gift of prophecy by virtue of his office (Dodd, 1963, 425, John 11:47-53).
4   Dodd, 1965, 430.
5   "The basic tradition, therefore, on which the evangelist is working was shaped (it appears) in a Jewish-Christian environment still in touch with the synagogue, in Palestine, at a relatively early date, at any rate before the rebellion of AD 66" Dodd, 1965, 426.

6   Dodd, 1965, 7-8.
7   Schillebeeckx, 1979, 554.
8   BM, 526.
9   Miguens, 1975, 6-27.
10 Barrett, *John*, 184.
11 Laurentin, R., 1985, 51.
12 BM, 352.
13 BM, 354.
14 BM, 354, cf. n.46. "It is not reasonable to consider these Lucan
    summaries as totally fictional idealization. Luke's description of the
    structure and ideals of the Jerusalem community comes remarkably
    close to what we know of Qumran structure an ideals, and so Luke
    was describing a way of life that was entirely plausible in early first-
    century Judaism".
15 ODCC, 67.
16 BMG, 147.
17 I argued the authenticity of Mark 14:64, BMG 146. I argued the
    authenticity of John 8:58 and the other *egó eimi* sayings in BMG
    Chapter 14, 253-266.
18 Regarding the authenticity of Mark 14:64, BMG 146. Regarding the
    "Johannine Community", BMG 175-177.
19 BMG, 117.
20 DV 19.
21 Machen, 1958, 75-101.
22 Howard Marshall, *Luke,* 79.
23 Cf. above, 127.
24 Brown, *John I*, 357.
25 ICC, 201. E.g. Isaiah 11:2.
26 Cf. above, 41, n.41.
27 ICC, 210. "The subject could admittedly be God (cf.Psalm 130:8),
    especially as 'Jesus' might be rendered, 'Yahweh is salvation'. But
    Matthew will have thought of Jesus..."
28 Regarding Mark's high Christology, cf. BMG 141.
29 http://www.1911encyclopedia.org/Psalms_Of_Solomon
    The date of the Psalms of Solomon is discussed by
    http://www.earlyjewishwritings.com/psalmssolomon.html.
30 Landman, L., ed., 1979, 78-9. I follow here that translation of the
    Songs of Solomon which appeared originally in the article by
    H.P. Smith, *The Origin of the Messianic Hope in Israel,* American
    Journal of Theology, vol.14, 1910, 340-341.
31 BM, 312.
32 ICC, 201.
33 Benoit, P., 1961, 126-128 gives a full account of the OT use of
    "Son of God".

34 BMG, 254-258.

35 Cf. the long discussion in Laurentin, 1957, 38-72. I find as so often Howard Marshall's view balanced: "...the whole context (of Luke 2:49) suggests that a deeper significance is present. It is not simply the 'official' position of the Messiah, but a personal consciousness of God which finds expression both in worship and learning in the temple, and also in private communication with God". *Luke*, 129. This we could call the "childhood consciousness" which Christ had of his own divinity, which was of course to develop into expressions such as the absolute I AM as in John 8:58 which Jesus used of his own self-consciousness during his adult life.

36 BM, 483.

37 BMG, 116.

38 BMG, 147, 240.

39 BM, 492.

40 Meier admits the complex nature of the development of primitive Christology, cf. "his mantra", "In the beginning was the grab bag", BMG 259, MJ2, 919. It seems to me most credible that part of that "grab bag", perhaps its most important content, was the divine self-consciousness of Jesus himself.

41 Above, p.112.

42 Above, p.103.

43 Above, p.18. BM, 149. So also Harrington, *Matthew,* 35.

44 Miguens, 1975. 6-27. Above, 83-86.

45 BM, 540-1, above, 85.

46 BM, 541.

47 JVG, 416-417, BMG, 128.

48 BMG, 130, JVG, 222-3.

49 Against Barrett, *John,* 551, that the soldiers would not allow relatives near to the crucified criminal for security reasons. Carson, *John,* 615-6, rightly responds, "But apart from the fact that four Roman auxiliaries were unlikely to be terrified by a few women in deep mourning, the Roman authorities, if we are to judge by Pilate, were well aware that neither Jesus nor his disciples posed much of a threat."

50 Laurentin, R., 1985, 51.

51 F.F. Bruce is convinced of the substantial historicity of Peter's speech, as indeed of the other speeches in Acts Bruce, *Acts,* 96. against Haenchen, *Acts,* 185. With Bruce, it seems as clear to me as regards the Magnificat that Luke is quoting an early source going back to the first Jerusalem Christians.

52 Cf. above, 103.

53 Cf. BMG, 68-72.

54 BM, 161.

55 BM, 303.

56 *Ibid.*, 303.
57 Above, 156.
58 Above, 65, 153.
59 Above, 72, 75, 78-85.
60 Above, 81.
61 Above, 120-1.

CHAPTER NINE

THE VIRGIN BIRTH: A MIRACLE

> **We conclude that, in conformity with Christian belief, Mary did give birth to Jesus without prior intercourse with a man.**

In *Bad, Mad or God?*, we outlined a number of criteria for assessing whether or not a given event recounted as history actually occurred. We started from the assumption that to accept an event in the past as historical is nothing other than to make an act of faith in the veracity of the witness or witnesses concerned.

We should not be at all surprised that the act of faith is necessarily associated with the authentication of events as historical. We demonstrated in Chapter 4 of *Bad, Mad or God?* that the acceptance of any event in the past as factual can only be because we accept on faith that the event has occurred from human witnesses to that event. We proposed the formula "X told me that Y happened, and I believe X".[1] This has always been called in traditional Catholic apologetics the act of *historical faith*. We believe the thousands of witnesses of the battle who told us that the Battle of Hastings was won by the Normans. We believe the registration authorities when they provide us with documents telling us that our great-grandmother died in 1876. Someone had to write the death certificate. We believe the clerk who wrote it when he affirmed what he knew as an historical fact, namely the death of great-grandmother.

We complained in *Bad, Mad or God?*[2] that the problem afflicting Western thinking since the eighteenth century Enlightenment is that all forms of legitimate investigation are linked to the laboratory, and cannot be designated "scientific" unless they are. Our precise point was that historical investigation is a probe into the testimony of *human witnesses*. As a human science, therefore, historical science is more to be compared with the processes of a courtroom rather than of a laboratory. The conclusion of such an investigation can only be compared with the judgement of a court, which assesses the testimony of the witnesses and draws a human conclusion as to whose testimony is to be accepted or not.

We will conclude this investigation with the judgement that the Gospels of Matthew and Luke, in asserting that Mary gave birth to Jesus of Nazareth without prior intercourse, were stating authentic historical fact.

In the early stages of our investigation in *Bad, Mad or God?*, we accepted provisionally the commonsense definition of *The Concise Oxford Dictionary* which defines 'historical' as "1. Of or concerning history (*historical evidence*). 2. Belonging to history, not to prehistory or legend."[3] In this Oxford Dictionary definition, it appears very clear that what is "historical" is simply "what has actually occurred". At the close of the investigation, I saw no need to change this understanding of what constitutes an "historical event". Thus history for us is not a closed continuum of events purely in the natural order. To concede this from the beginning is already to preclude any serious discussion as to whether miracles actually occur, or as to whether or not they can be identified as miracles. On the contrary, we wish to investigate whether the miracle of the virgin birth actually happened, that is to say precisely that it was an historical event.[4]

This brings us immediately to discuss the various criteria by which we may judge the authentication of an historical event, as we did in *Bad, Mad or God?*, and to apply those criteria to our investigation of the accounts of the virgin birth in Matthew and Luke. The first and perhaps the most important criterion is whether a miracle may ever be *per se* credible.

A. Is the event of the virgin birth per se impossible to believe?[5]

The first criterion is that of the credibility of the event *per se*, we might say its "natural credibility". If a member of the staff here told me that she had a cup of coffee at 10.30, that would be *per se* credible because coffee time is 10.30 here at Maryvale. If her husband sends a message to us that the baby she was expecting has duly arrived in good health, that is *per se* credible. It is naturally to be expected, and therefore it is naturally credible, *per se* credible.

But if a teenage girl told me that she was to give birth to a child, and that she had had no intercourse with any man, that would be hardly *per se* credible. It is naturally in general not to be expected. Our first instinct is to disbelieve her story, and look to her relationship with a boyfriend as the cause of the pregnancy. This was indeed the reaction of Joseph when he was told that his future spouse was pregnant, but not by him. It had happened miraculously.

Our natural instinct therefore is quite correct in disbelieving a story which is not *per se* credible. But nevertheless, we realise also that events which we disbelieve at first may turn out ultimately to be true. My own football team Charlton Athletic is, at the time of writing this book, in desperate straits attempting to avoid relegation from the Premier League. But if someone with a crystal ball told me that not only did they avoid relegation, but finished half way up the league table, and they were not joking, I would be ecstatic. It would be *per se* difficult to believe, but not impossible to believe.

On the other hand, if someone looking into the same crystal ball told me that Charlton won the League Championship, then I would disbelieve them because even now it is mathematically impossible for them to acquire enough points. This would be not only *per se* **difficult** to believe, but would be *per se* **impossible** to believe.

Clearly, any miracle is difficult to believe. Anyone involved with the Vatican investigations of miracles knows how sceptical the Church is when first a miracle is reported. It is quite correct that we should be sceptical when extraordinary events are reported to us.

The Enlightenment philosophy, which has strongly influenced investigation into the life of Jesus,[6] took the view that miracles are absolutely impossible, and consequently absolutely incredible.[7] We quoted Strauss earlier, who dogmatically insisted that "…the absolute cause never disturbs the chain of secondary causes by single arbitrary acts of interposition".

But why "never"? Who says that the "absolute cause" is incapable of directly acting upon events without an intervening secondary cause? We saw that the reason why Strauss posited the absolute incredibility of the miracle was that he was a Hegelian pantheist, seeing God as the absolute Idea, revealing itself in the historical process and as its dynamism, but not transcending it. And we saw also in *Bad, Mad or God?* that Reimarus and those who began the Quest of the Historical Jesus at the close of the eighteenth century were Deists,[8] believing that God only acted through secondary causes, and never through direct divine causality.

But if the monotheistic religions Judaism, Islam, and Christianity are right, God is omnipotent. God cannot be limited to working through the causes he has already created as their First Cause. Thus, for an orthodox monotheist, miracles, even if they are *per se* difficult to believe, cannot be absolutely incredible.

In *Bad, Mad or God?*, we outlined a philosophy of miracle. With René Latourelle,[9] we affirmed that a genuine miracle is not a myth, and is therefore not apt for "demythologising" (Bultmann's famous *Entmythologisierung*[10]), but is rather something which happens in human experience, again through our senses, in the real world, which causes wonder, and which cannot be explained in the usual way by natural cause and effect.

The birth of Jesus from the womb of Mary who did not have intercourse with a man is a "one-off". As far as we know, apart of course from the modern technology of IVF, it has not happened before, and is unlikely to happen again; at least in us humans.

Natural science can give us instances in the animal and insect world of parthenogenesis, i.e. virgin birth:

> Parthenogenesis (from the Greek παρθενος *parthenos*, "virgin", + γενεσις *genesis*, "birth") describes the growth and development of an embryo or seed without fertilization by a <u>male</u>. Parthenogenesis occurs naturally in some species, including lower <u>plants</u> (called agamospermy), <u>invertebrates</u> (e.g. water fleas, aphids, some bees and parasitic wasps), and vertebrates (e.g. some reptiles, fish, and, very rarely, birds).[11]

This would at least make belief in the single instance of a virgin birth in the history of the human race at least less difficult. If parthenogenesis already happens routinely in the natural world, then the birth of Jesus from a virgin must be adjudged much lower on the Richter scale of miracles than for instance, the multiplication of the loaves or even more the Resurrection of the body of Jesus from the dead with no remains of his physical corps testified by the discovery of the empty tomb.[12]

Yet, we must repeat, in humans it was and is a unique occurrence. For this reason alone, eighteenth century Enlightenment thinking would dismiss any account of the miraculous simply on account of its one-off character. But this is precisely unscientific, as the distinguished molecular scientist Denis Alexander, in his excellent study on science and faith *Rebuilding the Matrix: Science and Faith in the 21st Century*, argues. He accuses the Scottish empiricist, David Hume, of having a closed mind. "Scientists are supposed to be open to the evidence, wherever it leads, rather than pretending they already know the answer. Hume's stance suggests that, even if the evidence for something is overwhelming, you still shouldn't believe it. That jars."[13]

Alexander goes on to note in the same newspaper article that "science is good at investigating and explaining reproducible phenomena, but ill-equipped to answer questions about unique events (such as what really happened at the Battle of Hastings). That is the province of historians and lawyers".

And philosophers and theologians, I would add. We surely cannot reject the historical authenticity of the conception of Jesus in the womb of the Virgin Mary simply because it is a one-off event. As Alexander rightly insists, such a position would be unscientific. More serious would be the hypothetical explanation that the virginal conception of Jesus was just a freak event, a chance deviation from the normal, not the result of direct divine causality. On this supposition, by a whim of nature, a human birth resulted from parthenogenesis, in this single instance aping a similar asexual process of birth in lower species of life.

In historical investigation very little can be judged absolutely impossible. But a chance freak of nature leaves the scientist dissatisfied. It is a "black hole" in our human knowledge, which longs to be filled. Another presupposition, which again we would say is metaphysical, which the scientist brings into his investigation, is that the world is rational, and therefore that events should be explained as part of the total process of being and becoming in the world.

Miracles such as the virgin birth, therefore, may be difficult to believe, but they cannot be adjudged impossible. For a monotheist, they are instances of God's direct activity in the world where we mainly experience God working through secondary causes.

In post-Newtonian science, the world has been seen rather like a machine. But a better analogy for the world might be that of the human body. There are many mechanisms in the body which work whether we are conscious of them or not; digestion, waste disposal, life-blood beating through our veins. That would be an analogy for secondary causality.

A person observing these functions, if that was all that person did observe, might come to the conclusion that the human body works mechanistically and automatically. But, when the body stands up and begins to act as if apparently freely, "telling" its feet and hands to move, then we realise that there is a "higher intelligence" not breaking the order but directing the body to a higher end than just eating and digesting.

Likewise the miracle does not rupture the order of phenomena, but indicates that directing the universe there is a God, its transcendent supreme intelligence, who has a higher plan, and who sometimes acts directly according to that higher plan.

B. Are the circumstances credible?

We obviously need more evidence to persuade us of the truth of a miraculous event than of a normal event. We can only verify the virgin birth if the circumstances surrounding that event are as extraordinary as the event itself. The circumstances of an event, when it happened, to whom it happened, and why it happened, make a great difference regarding its credibility.

1. Who

Thus, if we ask the question "is the story in Luke and in Matthew that Mary gave birth to Jesus without sexual intercourse with a man credible?" then we can answer that it is credible because of the person to whom it happened, namely the infant Jesus. If it was any human being who was born, then a case of parthenogenesis would at first sight be assumed to be a freak of nature. But here we are referring to the Son of God, born for our salvation. If it is appropriate that he should have a special means of birth without human male intervention, then this in itself would be a verification of the historicity of the story of the virgin birth of Jesus. That is of course provided we have already run through the thorough tests which we have in fact made in this book regarding the historical origins of the story.

The primary reason theologically for the virgin birth has always been seen as a sign both of the divinity and the humanity of Christ: the most "fitting" sign of it, even if not absolutely necessary. Catholic theology has always asserted that Christ could have been both God and human even if born of a natural intercourse between man and woman. We cannot restrict the possibilities with an omnipotent God.

But as a miracle, the virgin birth is a *sign* that God is the true Father of Jesus; and, as a real conception and a real birth, this means that Christ has something entirely in common with all of us, human birth into our world "completely like his brothers so that he could be a compassionate and trustworthy high priest of God's religion, able to atone for human sins" [Hebrews 2:17]. Far from the humanity of Jesus being lessened by the virgin birth, therefore, in the early centuries it was used to support the real humanity of Jesus.[14] As the *Catechism of the Catholic Church* states:

> CCC 496. From the first formulations of her faith, the Church has confessed that Jesus was conceived solely by

the power of the Holy Spirit in the womb of the Virgin Mary, affirming also the corporeal aspect of this event: Jesus was conceived "by the Holy Spirit without human seed".[15] The Fathers see in the virginal conception the sign that it truly was the Son of God who came in a humanity like our own. Thus St Ignatius of Antioch at the beginning of the second century says: You are firmly convinced about our Lord, who is truly of the race of David according to the flesh, Son of God according to the will and power of God, truly born of a virgin... he was truly nailed to a tree for us in his flesh under Pontius Pilate... he truly suffered, as he is also truly risen.[16]

We have already seen that in Luke's account Elizabeth, announced by an angel as the mother of John the Baptist, is barren, and so miraculously gives birth: so, argues Brown, a greater miracle (hence the virginal conception) heralds the birth of a greater one than John the Baptist, i.e. Jesus the Messiah. The greatness of the person to be born, the Son of God, requires an even greater miracle than the barrenness of Elizabeth as a sign of the greatness of John the Baptist to come.[17]

2. When

The announcement of the angel to Joseph and to Mary that Jesus was to be born came after a long preparation for the people of God; eighteen hundred years after Abraham set out from Ur of the Chaldees to find a land and a blessing [Genesis 12]; twelve hundred years since Joshua and the Judges invaded the Promised land and settled there; a thousand years since the great King David conquered Jerusalem and made it a place of worship for YHWH, and his son Solomon built the Temple there. Seven hundred years since Isaiah prophesied that a baby called Emmanuel would be born of an ʿalmah; six hundred years since the disastrous exile to Babylon; five hundred years since the return from Exile and the rebuilding of the Temple with the beginning of messianic expectation; two hundred years since large numbers of Jews emigrated to the Hellenistic city of Alexandria and imbibed Greek culture; one hundred years since the Roman yoke both united an empire and created a yearning for freedom under the promised Messiah.

As the phenomenal success of Paul the Pharisee converted to become the first Christian missionary demonstrates, the time was ripe for Christ to come, ripe for a very special birth as the sign of a new beginning. The time was ripe for this very special act of God, as N.T. Wright says with his usual perception:

> What matters is the powerful, mysterious presence of the God of Israel, the creator God, bringing Israel's story to its climax by doing a new thing, bringing the story of creation to its height by a new creation from the womb of the old. Whether or not it happened, this is what it would mean if it did.[18]

At this stage in his argumentation for the virgin birth in his article *God's Way of Acting*, Wright is only working on hypothesis. But hypothesis is an important part of any demonstration. We may come to the conclusion that it did happen from the principle made famous by John Henry Newman of *antecedent probability*. An event is credible if the mode of its happening is what we would probably expect in the circumstances. Matthew and Luke tell us that Jesus was born of a virgin. We can believe them, because it is the kind of act which we would expect God most probably to perform to draw our attention to the birth of his own Son for our salvation, to signal a wonderful new beginning in the history of salvation.

3. Where

Jesus' home town was Nazareth, even though the evangelists insist he was born in Bethlehem south of Jerusalem. Geographically, Jesus was a Galilean, living in "Galilee of the Gentiles" [Matthew 4:15]. Some have even conjectured that Jesus might have known Greek, so cosmopolitan was that region, much of it today part of Syria. Culturally, therefore, Jesus was a member of the chosen people of God, but with an awareness of a wider world beyond his own country.

But the most important fact about the "where" of Jesus' birth was the link that being born in Bethlehem made with his Davidic lineage, and his being a member of the tribe of Judah. If Jesus had been of any race other than that of the Jews, he could not have saved the human race, since God had chosen the Jews for that purpose, to bring forth the Messiah.

That is why it was so important for Jesus to end his public ministry in Jerusalem, where he preached his final message inviting his people to follow him "the light of the world" [John 8:12]. Jesus had to go to Jerusalem to fulfil the prophecy that "the law would go forth from Zion, and the word of the Lord from Jerusalem"[Isaiah 2:3]. It was there he had to die, in order that his own people who refused to accept his message, not to mention the Gentiles, "will realise that I AM HE",[19] and that I do nothing on my own, but I speak these things as the Father instructed".[20] When he was risen from the dead, then people would realise his true identity as the Son of God.

4. How

How was the virgin birth of Jesus effected? The apocryphal proto-Gospel of James, second century, introduces a midwife's testimony that Mary showed all the physical signs of being a virgin, a method of procedure, which Schillebeeckx claims[21] is "shunned" by the canonical Gospels. Or, more obviously, did the Gospels not include such evidence since it was not available? Ultimately the kind of scientific testing which would be required, which would of course include examination of Mary herself, would not be possible.

The nature of the Gospels themselves, that of human testimony to events, means that we have to trust the veracity of the witnesses of those events, in this case Mary herself. The ultimate "how" of the virgin birth God alone knew. Mary knew that she had not had intercourse with a man, and testified to that for us. For traditional Christian theology, that is an essential part of Christian faith. Our trusting of those witnesses, the witnesses to the events of Christ's birth, life, death, and Resurrection, links us in faith, hope and love to the apostolic community which first proclaimed the good news that spread throughout the Roman empire.

The good news was given to ordinary people, and handed on in an ordinary human way. We are quite able today, two thousand years later, to use the ordinary means of historical testing, which we have attempted to use systematically throughout this book. We have demonstrated at the very least that the historical evidence can be interpreted in a way favourable to faith, and even that it should be. Then, ultimately, we are confronted with the testimony of ordinary people such as Mary, who simply present us with the challenge of mystery, and of faith, to which we ourselves must personally respond.

This is precisely what we mean when we say that the Christian faith is an apostolic faith. It depends upon the testimony of those sent out by Jesus after his Resurrection to proclaim the good news of salvation. As we have seen, though Mary was not described in the New Testament as an apostle, she qualified eminently as an "eye-witness and minister of the word" [Luke 1:1], namely as a testimony to the apostolic faith. We have argued earlier that it was in Jerusalem,[22] at the very beginnings of the church after Pentecost, that she was most likely to have handed on the truth to which she bore witness that Christ was born of her without male intercourse.

C. Is the witness credible?

We have demonstrated earlier that, in the final reckoning, the only possible witness to the virginal conception was Mary herself.[23] Only she knew that she had had no sexual relations with any man prior to the birth of her son Jesus.

Far from the credibility of the witness being questioned, an enormous devotion has sprung up in traditional Christianity to the one who gave birth to the Saviour. This has been a great source of controversy among Christians. The Second Vatican Council, while promoting this liturgical devotion, "exhorts theologians and preachers of the divine word to abstain zealously both from all gross exaggerations as well as from petty narrow-mindedness in considering the singular dignity of the Mother of God."[24]

But it is surely a valid point that the supreme dignity of the Son must reflect honour also on the mother. Mary's cousin Elizabeth, receiving a visit from Mary and being told of the coming birth of her son Jesus …gave a loud cry and said, 'Of all women you are the most blessed, and blessed is the fruit of your womb. Why should I be honoured with a visit from the mother of my Lord?" [Luke 1:42-43]. Elizabeth was the first to manifest a genuine and authentic devotion to the Mother of the Saviour.

Similarly, the virginity of Mary has no doubt fostered many millions of Christians over the centuries to live a life of consecrated virginity. There is no evidence that the propagation of virginity was linked to the virginity of Mary in the earliest days of the Church. St Paul, while unmarried himself, did not pressurise his newly converted Christians at Corinth, to whom he wrote his First Letter c.67 AD, to take vows of celibacy. He left them entirely free, even though he presented the advantages of being unmarried in difficult times, so that the Corinthians would be "free from all worry". [1 Corinthians 7:32]. St Anthony of Egypt (251?-356),[25] to whom we made reference earlier,[26] also promoted the virtue of a chaste religious life, in compensation for the fact that literal martyrdom was less likely for the Christian, thus presenting the ideals of poverty, chastity and obedience as spiritual martyrdom. By this time, the virginity of Mary was an additional motivation for a life of chastity, as was also the commendation of "eunuchs for the kingdom of heaven's sake" [Matthew 19:12] by Jesus himself.

No doubt the Church in its history has sometimes tended to denigrate marriage in favour of celibacy. But no doubt also that consecrated virginity and celibacy have borne enormous fruit in the Church, not only in the contemplative life, but in those devoted to education and healing. Does this not itself make Mary's witness to the virgin birth credible in terms of its inspiration to a life of self-sacrifice and holiness?

Boslooper castigates both what he calls the Protestant

fundamentalist perversion of seeing it as a historical event, and the Catholic perversion of seeing it as the basis of a "docetic theology of Mary". He says that, on the contrary, it is a "positive affirmation of the sanctity of marriage", since, in the midst of a polygamous society, "Christ proposed the necessity of one marriage for life."[27]

In response to Boslooper's provocative comments, one can agree that if virginity is promoted, marriage itself becomes sanctified, because no longer can man see himself as the sole creator, dominating his wife in the sex act [Cf. Genesis 3:18], but rather as the creative sign of new relationships not from flesh and blood "but from God himself" [John 1:13]. One can now see that God can work other than through the relationships established by nature; "who is my brother, and sister, and mother?" [Matthew 12:50, Mark 3:35]. Thus, paradoxically, as Boslooper says, by the virgin birth sexual love itself becomes sanctified; but, I would maintain, precisely because of the fact that the virginity of Mary is real, and not mythical. It is difficult for one who understands traditional devotion to Mary to see it as "docetic". Mary's *body* was sanctified by the Holy Spirit overshadowing her [Luke 1:35], as is the body of every person who consecrates his or her life, body and soul, to the Creator God.

In the present age, almost all forms of sexual activity are encouraged; homosexual and heterosexual, even to the point that laws are increasingly in place which threaten those who dare to say that, for example homosexual acts are wrong. The virginity of Mary is a prophetic statement to the modern world that sex is not a compulsive necessity, and certainly not a compulsive necessity for happiness.

This evolution of a life of consecration which has affected millions of people is surely itself also an authentication of the reality of Mary's virginity, which she testified to by handing on the tradition of the angel's visit to her and the subsequent birth of her divine Son without prior intercourse with a man.

But at this point, many will possibly be saying "Yes, that is a nice story. Mary's virginity admittedly has had some good effect in the history of the Church and of the world. But would not there have been the same effect if it was just a story, a myth, a *theologoumenon*? So now we will run through the negative tests outlined in *Bad, Mad or God?*,[28] to see whether the story of Mary giving birth to Jesus while still a virgin continues to hold water.

1. Is the witness deceiving?

As we saw earlier, even that marauding sceptic Strauss drew back from asserting that Mary herself had pretended to have given a virgin birth when in fact she had been unfaithful to her espoused husband.[29] But many, as we have seen in our investigation, have accused the early Christian community of exalting their leader Christ by positing him as having a miraculous birth. The Christian community is what we might call an "intermediate witness" between Mary and ourselves. It is that intermediate witness, some say, which has deceived for two thousand years.

We have gone painstakingly through all those hypotheses, beginning with the contention of Geza Vermes that the first Christians had created the myth of the virgin birth from a reading of Isaiah 7:14, "A virgin will conceive and bear a son", in order to promote the idea that Christ was the fulfilment of scripture. In a sense, the whole of this book has been a reply to such a contention. On the contrary, I have argued, all the evidence admits of the positive interpretation that the early Christian belief that Jesus was actually virgin born underlies the tradition. The myth did not create the story of the virgin birth. To summarise our position, again we turn to N.T. Wright:

> To put it another way. What would have to have happened, granted the sceptic's position, for the story to have taken the shape it did? To answer this, I must indulge in some speculative tradition-history. Bear with me in a little foolishness. Are they tradition critics? So am I. Are they scholars of ancient history? So am I. Are they reconstructors of early communities? So am I. Are they determined to think the argument through to the end? I speak as a fool – I am more so.

This is how it would look: Christians came to believe that Jesus was in some sense divine. Someone who shared this faith broke thoroughly with Jewish precedents and invented the story of a pagan-style virginal conception. Some Christians failed to realise that this was historicised metaphor, and retold it as though it were historical. Matthew and Luke, assuming historicity; drew independently upon this astonishing fabrication, set it (though in quite different ways) within a thoroughly Jewish context, and wove it in quite different ways into their respective narratives.

And all this happened within, more or less, 50 years. Possible? Yes, of course. Most things are possible in history. Likely? No.[30]

In historical investigation, as we have insisted more than once, we deal with likelihoods and rarely with impossibilities. But to me, after this investigation, it is close to impossible that the story of the virgin birth was so invented, rather that it was historically authentic.

2. Has the witness been deceived?

Only those who espouse the theory that Mary gave birth to Jesus from intercourse with a man other than Joseph would maintain the opinion that Mary was deceived; namely, that a man crept into her bed and had sex with her when she was still asleep, and she was not aware of it. Joseph would have told her, of course, if he had had intercourse with her. It is surely impossible that no impression, physical or emotional, was left upon Mary after such an act of surreptitious sex. Thus, as Mary became aware of what had happened to her, she would have had to become a deceiver herself, and we are faced with the previous objection, that Mary herself pretended that Jesus was virgin born. She does not come over in the New Testament as a deceiving type. That is why this objection is most generally not even hinted at.

Catholic, and of course also Orthodox, devotion to Mary is controversial. Protestants do not accept either the perpetual virginity of Mary, nor her Immaculate Conception, that she was free from all sin from the first moment of her conception. While again these doctrines cannot be directly proven from scripture, and Catholic and Orthodox believers have to accept the living tradition of the Church rather than explicit biblical evidence, yet the scriptural data for her life, meagre though it is, does not in any way contradict these traditions. She does not appear as deceiver, nor as deceived. She only "stored up all these things in her heart" [Luke 2:51], to give to all generations after her.

To add to all the complex exegetical arguments we have engaged upon in this book, can we not add the instinct of Christians for two thousand years that this woman, "full of grace", was the first human being to get it all right, to say to the angel in wonderment yet faith, "Be it done unto me according to thy word". [Luke 2:38]? The mediaevals said *Tota pulchra es, Maria* ("Mary, you are completely beautiful"). Cannot the perception of the beauty of Mary's love of her divine Son, her lifelong fidelity to him, her motherhood of all believers, be the final argument for the veracity of her historical testimony? It can, if what is beautiful is also true.[31]

3. Has the witness been misunderstood?

As we have discussed earlier, many scholars would see the literary genre of the infancy narratives of Matthew and Luke not as fact, but as theological fiction, *theologoumena*. They would therefore conclude that we have misunderstood Matthew and Luke when we take their accounts as historical. This has obvious implications for the accounts of the virgin birth within the context of those infancy narratives.

We have carefully considered all these arguments in Chapter Six. Certainly, we have shown that the infancy narratives are not demonstrably fiction from their *form*. Parallels with rabbinic *midrash* are not decisive concerning the historicity or non historicity of Matthew's infancy narrative in particular. It could equally be that Matthew reflected in midrashic mode on past historical events connected with the infancy (e.g. the flight into Egypt), as that he invented the whole story as a fictional *midrash*.

The Infancy narratives of Matthew and Luke are written in popular story mode, but that does not mean that they are fiction. The difficulties in reconciling the chronology of the infancy of Jesus comparing Matthew and Luke are not impossible. This is especially the case if we assume, as in for instance the case of the census, that the evangelists writing almost a century from the events concerned have made minor factual errors, transmitting a popular account without intending that those facts should be critically evaluated. We have shown how such an idea is not contrary to the doctrine of the divine inspiration of scripture.

The points where Matthew and Luke agree, for example that Jesus was son of David, and was born in Bethlehem, should make us even more confident that they are communicating fact rather than fiction particularly regarding the fact that those two evangelists do not depend on each other from a literary viewpoint. Luke's Introduction [1:1-4] we have shown to be a serious indication to us of his literary genre, a history based upon eye-witnesses and ministers of the word. The presumption can be legitimately made, therefore, that they are fact, as is the assertion of Christian tradition.

What is true in general regarding the Infancy narratives is true in particular regarding the narratives of the annunciation of the virgin birth to Joseph in Matthew and Mary in Luke. Neither account gives the impression of being fictional. In Chapter Seven, we challenged, I submit successfully, all the sceptical theories which have been proposed since the Enlightenment, that the idea of the virgin birth came from pagan ideas, from a developing Christology, or as a counter to the charge that Jesus was born illegitimately.

We therefore examined more closely in Chapter Eight the so-called "family tradition", finding that phrase somewhat misleading. We concluded that ultimately Mary was the sole witness of the virgin birth in that she alone knew for certain that she did not have sex before Jesus was born. We then followed through the hypothesis that Mary herself handed on the knowledge of this wonderful fact of the virgin birth through the birth, childhood, adulthood and death of her Son. We found that the evidence was coherent with the historical fact of the virgin birth, and found it most credible that Mary communicated to the first Christians in Jerusalem the joyful news after the Resurrection that she had given birth to Jesus without intercourse with a man.

We must conclude, therefore, that in no way are we misunderstanding those apostolic authors Matthew and Luke when we affirm that their account of the virgin birth is substantially historical, while not necessarily arguing that Mary was the immediate source of Luke's account, and Joseph of Matthew's.

4. Are the documents false?

If the documents which record the miracle of the virgin birth are inauthentic, then the miracle itself is not verified. If the Gospels of Matthew and Luke were demonstrated to be as late as the third century, more than two hundred years after the historical Jesus, then the story of the virgin birth would be historically valueless.

On the contrary, we have demonstrated that both Matthew and Luke are to be dated at the latest at the end of the first century AD, a century after the event described, the birth of Jesus. That is well within the life span of at least those who were eyewitnesses of the fact. We showed in Chapter Three, against Ehrman, that the manuscripts are substantially reliable, namely that we have the text which was written by the evangelists. We saw that there is no reason to reject the traditional authorship of Luke's Gospel as being by the companion of St Paul of that name. And whereas the authorship of Matthew's Gospel is more disputed, no one doubts that the author, and/or the later redactor(s), was within the apostolic tradition of those first Christians, with links to the teaching of the historical Jesus.

Conclusion: the Miracle

As the nineteenth century ran its course, even the growing number of sceptics in Europe found it difficult to maintain the position that miracles are absolutely impossible, therefore absolutely incredible. By the early twentieth century, even science itself became less dogmatic as to what events could or could not occur , with Heiselberg's Uncertainty Principle, "the impossibility of determining exactly the position of particles at the same time as their momentum", [32] and then with Einsteins's theory of relativity.

Thus by the turn of the nineteenth and twentieth centuries, the view that miracles were impossible of occurrence was replaced by the view that only non-miraculous events could be scientifically investigated. This is the source of the modern view that Scripture studies in general do not decide for or against miracles, which has been dominant since Bultmann in the early twentieth century right up to the present new millennium. The great Albert Schweitzer was disgusted with this position:

> That does not mean that the problem of miracle is solved. From the historical point of view it is really impossible to solve it, since we are not able to reconstruct the process by which a series of miracle stories arose, or a series of historical occurrences were transformed into miracle stories, and these narratives must simply be left with a question mark standing against them. What has been gained is only that the exclusion of miracle from our view of history has been universally recognised as a principle of criticism, so that miracle no longer concerns the historian either positively or negatively. Scientific theologians of the present day who desire to show their "sensibility," ask no more than that two or three little miracles may be left to them – in the stories of the childhood, perhaps, or in the narratives of the Resurrection. And these miracles are, moreover, so far scientific that they have at least no relation to those in the text, but are merely spiritless, miserable little toy-dogs of criticism, flea-bitten by rationalism, too insignificant to do historical science any harm, especially as their owners honestly pay the tax upon them by the way in which they speak, write, and are silent about Strauss.[33]

This is a quotation from Schweitzer's masterly outline, published in 1906, of the whole of Gospel criticism up to his own day, *Von Reimarus zu Wrede*, translated into English in 1910 with the title *The Quest of the Historical Jesus*. No doubt at least partly as a result of his disillusion with the development of critical theology in his own day, Schweitzer abandoned the study of theology and went out to Africa as an equally brilliant surgeon founding a missionary hospital. He could no longer find the historical Jesus as a man relevant for our time in Scripture and in the teaching of traditional Christianity. He could only find Jesus in his own experience, as one "without a name",[34] with him as the surgeon wielding his healing scalpel, rather than what he had come to see as the theologian scratching his critical but futile pen.

I submit that we have achieved in this investigation into the miracle of the virgin birth of Christ what Schweitzer abandoned as an impossible task in the early twentieth century. We have been able to "reconstruct the process by which a series of miracle stories arose". We have shown that, regarding the accounts of the angelic annunciation of the virgin birth, it is not true that "series of historical occurrences were transformed into miracle stories". We have on the contrary shown that they were in fact miracle stories in the first place. And at the end of our investigation, I submit that it is not true that "these narratives must simply be left with a question mark standing against them", but rather we have shown that they are authentic accounts of the greatest event in the history of the human race, the birth of the Son of God from the womb of the Virgin Mary.

The decision of Faith

As we have also seen earlier, many today would see the acceptance of a miraculous event in the past as purely a matter of faith.[35] We cannot prove that a miracle has occurred, Meier would say, we can only accept it or not accept it as believers or as non-believers "e.g. whether God has indeed acted in this particular 'miracle', thus calling people to faith". Meier would seem to be saying, with Bultmann, that whether a miracle has or has not occurred is strictly speaking not a question for the historian. History deals with a closed continuum of secondary causes, not with direct divine causality.

Our own position, as worked out in *Bad, Mad or God?*, is rather that miracles can be verified or non-verified by critical historical investigation. We concurred in this matter with the methodology of the theologians Latourelle[36] and Malevez,[37] and with the Cambridge scientist Denis Alexander.[38] Our investigation into the miracle of the virgin birth has both used this method and verified it.

Our position is not that miracles may be assessed purely by reason, or purely by faith. Rather, as with the Bishops of the First Vatican Council, which met in 1870 to counter what they saw as the errors of growing materialism and secularism, reason works together with faith to come to a reasonable conclusion that God in this instance has revealed his saving purpose through miracles and prophecies, which are genuine signs of revelation. Having asserted that we cannot accept God's revelation without the Holy Spirit's gift of faith, the Fathers of the Council go on to say:

> Nevertheless, in order that the submission of our faith should be in accordance with reason, it was God's will that there should be linked to the internal assistance of the Holy Spirit outward indications of his revelation, that is to say divine facts (*facta divina*), and first and foremost miracles and prophecies, which clearly demonstrating as they do the omnipotence and infinite knowledge of God, are the most certain signs of revelation and are suited to the understanding of all.[39]

Our conclusion therefore would be that the ultimate verification of the miracle of the virgin birth is our understanding of the place which this event had in God's plan of salvation. Because Jesus Christ was truly God become man, it was more than appropriate that God should signify this event by making the birth of Jesus a unique birth, with God as his only Father and Mary as his true Mother.

Is this invalidly introducing theological considerations into the investigation? For such an understanding, we freely admit, faith is necessary. I would agree with Meier that "Decisions on this tradition, limited within the NT to the Infancy Narratives, will largely be made on the basis of one's philosophical views about the miraculous and the weight one gives to later Church teaching."[40]

But is it "unscientific" to use those theological arguments to tip the scales in favour of the miraculous event having actually occurred? Surely not if, as we have seen, the judgement about the authenticity of any historical event involves in any case an act of historical faith. The fact that the virgin birth has a *theological coherence*, namely that it harmonises with God's plan, is a valid reason why we should accept it as fact, even though it is a unique, one-off, event. "X told me Y happened. I believe X". I can believe X, namely Matthew's and Luke's account of the Annunciation of the virginal conception, because the happening of the miracle is made credible by its being in conformity with God's plan, the creator of the universe, who has both the power and the reason to perform that direct action of the birth of his Son Jesus by the power of his Holy Spirit.

We saw earlier that what David Friedrich Strauss, whom Hodgson calls the "alienated theologian", thought was that there can never be any direct activity on the part of God. Thus the Incarnation itself was impossible. But on the contrary, in the orthodox theology of the Incarnation, God acts directly to create what is called the "grace of union", whereby the divine and human nature of Jesus are united substantially:

> And that a higher gift than grace,
> Should flesh and blood refine
> God's presence and his very self
> And essence all divine.[41]

That is the supreme miracle of all miracles. That is a scandal to our post-Enlightenment world. God is not acting according to natural laws. He is transcending them in the very act of the Word becoming flesh.

How fitting it is then that the whole process of our salvation should begin with a miracle which is visible to the whole human race, a sign of the greater miracle still of the Incarnation. The Holy Spirit overshadows Mary, and she gives birth to Jesus without human intervention. Once more, it is a sign that her Son is truly God become Man, divine because God is his only Father, and human, because he is born of a woman. And it is the sign, as the early Fathers taught, that there was a new beginning. Jesus was not from the seed of Joseph, but from the seed of the Word who directly created him in the womb of the Virgin Mary. Thus the bonds of original sin were broken, and a new life of grace was initiated, with a unique act of the virginal conception of Mary drawing attention to the greatest wonder of all, her Son the Incarnate Word of God.

This act of faith goes beyond the mere historical evidence yet completely in harmony with it, as we have demonstrated in *Bad, Mad or God?*,[42] to belief in the God who has so revealed in the virgin birth the greatness of the Son of Mary who is in fact the Son of God come to save us.

We give the last word to Gerald O'Collins, who gives an explanation of the virginal conception which is both an inspiring theological understanding of it, and a reason for its reality as an historical event:

> Finally, in his *Quod unus sit Christus* Cyril of Alexandria would encourage us to read the story of the virginal conception in its significance not only for divine self-revelation but also for human salvation. Christ's conception, in initiating the saving drama of new creation, shows that redemption comes as divine gift. Human beings cannot inaugurate and carry through their own salvation. Like the original creation of the world, the new creation is divine work and pure grace – to be received on the human side, just as Mary received the new life in her womb.[43]

1   BMG, 84.
2   BMG, 100.
3   *The Concise Oxford Dictionary,* Oxford, Clarendon Press, 1990, 558, has other meanings for "historical", e.g. '4, belonging to the past, not the present'. But here, regarding Christian tradition's concept of the four Gospels, we take the prime meaning as relating to history, and so to fact.
4   There is a much fuller discussion of what constitutes "history" in BMG, 92-97, where I express my dissatisfaction with John P. Meier's definition of "history" and "historical".
5   Cf, BMG, 86.
6   Cf. BMG, Chapter 2.
7   Above, 108. Hodgson, Ed., 1973, 88.
8   BMG, 40-42.
9   *Ibid.,* 345, Latourelle, 1988.
10 *Ibid.,* 341.
11 http://en.wikipedia.org/wiki/Parthenogenesis
12 I discuss fully the Resurrection of Jesus in BMG, Chapter 16, pp.196-327.
13 *The Daily Telegraph,* 21.11.01, 18. Quoted in BMG, 347.
14 BM, 529.
15 Council of the Lateran (649): DS 503; cf. DS 10-64.
16 St Ignatius of Antioch, *Ad Smyrn* 1-2: Apostolic Fathers, ed. J.B. Lightfoot (London: Macmillan, 1889), II/2, 289-293; SCh 10, 154-156; cf. Romans 1:3; John 1:13.
17 Above, 62.
18 N.T. Wright, 1998, 1217.
19 This is Jesus asserting his divine identity, *ego eimi,* I AM. The Hebrew form was *'ani hu,* "I (am)he". Jesus is claiming to be God. Cf. BMG, Chapter 13, 233-249.
20 BMG, 389-390. In that Chapter 15 of BMG, I discuss the meaning of what it was for Jesus to be a "Jew", and the meaning of that term.
21 Schillebeeckx, 1979, 554.
22 Cf. above, 155.
23 Cf. above, 154-5.
24 Tanner I, *Lumen Gentium,* 67, 897.
25 ODCC, 67.
26 Cf. above, 158.
27 Boslooper, 1962, 235.
28 BMG, 85-7.
29 Hodgson, Ed., 1973, 139.
30 Wright, 1998, 1217.
31 Hans Urs Von Balthasar, in his massive seven volume work *The Glory*

of the Lord, develops *A Theological Aesthetics,* published by T. and T. Clarke, Edinburgh. This is an important re-focussing of theology.

32 Malavez, 1958, 134.
33 Schweitzer A., 1954, 111.
34 *Ibid.,* 401.
35 MJ1, 145, 220.
36 MJTM.
37 *The Christian Message and Myth,* London, 1958.
38 *Rebuilding the Matrix: Science and Faith in the 21st Century.* Oxford, Lion, 2001.
39 Tanner, II, *807, Vatican I, Dogmatic Constitution on the Catholic Faith, Chapter III, *de Fide.* Cf. BMG, 18.
40 MJ1, 230.
41 Newman, J.H. From the hymn, *Praise to the Holiest in the Height.*
42 BMG, 353-360.
43 O'Collins, 1995.

BIBLIOGRAPHY

Alexander, D., *Rebuilding the Matrix: Science and Faith in the 21st Century.* Oxford, Lion, 2001.

Aquinas, Thomas, *The Summa Theologica,* Benziger Bros. edition, 1947. Translated by Fathers of the English Dominican Province, http://www.ccel.org/a/aquinas/summa/home.html

Barrett, C.K., *The Gospel According to St. John: An Introduction with Commentary and Notes on the Greek Text.* Second Edition. London, SPCK, 1978.

Beare, F.W., *The Gospel According to Matthew.* Oxford, Basil Blackwell, 1981.

Benoit, P., *Exégèse et Théologie.* Paris, du Cerf, 1961.

Boslooper, T., *The Virgin Birth.* London, SCM, 1962.

Brooke, George J., *The Birth of Jesus: Biblical and Theological Reflections.* Edinburgh, T. and T. Clark, 2000.

Brooks, W., *The Immanuel Prophecy,* http://www.iclnet.org/pub/resources/text/m.sion/brooalma.htm#_Toc387811425

Brown, P.B., *Problems with Allegorical Interpretations of Prophecy,* http://www.newwine.org/Articles/Allegorical.htm.

Brown, R.E., *An Introduction to the New Testament.* New York, Doubleday, 1997.

Brown, R.E., *The Birth of the Messiah: A Commentary on the Infancy Narratives in Matthew and Luke.* New York, Doubleday, 1979.

Brown, R.E., *The Gospel According to John, i-xii.* Anchor Bible, London, Chapman, 1966.

Brown, R.E., *The Gospel According to John, xiii-xxi.* Anchor Bible, London, Chapman, 1966.

Bruce, F.F., *The Acts of the Apostles: The Greek Text with Introduction and Commentary.* Michigan, Eerdmans, 1952.

Clarke, A.C., *Born of the Virgin Mary,* The Way Supplement, 25 (1975), 34-45).

Daube, D., *The New Testament and Rabbinic Judaism.*
London, 1956.

Davis, W.D., and Allison, D.C., *The Gospel According to
Saint Matthew: A Critical and Exegetical Commentary.
Volume 1.* Edinburgh, T. and T. Clark.

De La Potterie, I., *Interpretation of Holy Scripture in the
Spirit in which it was Written (Dei Verbum 12c).*
R.Latourelle, Ed. *Vatican II Assessment and Perspectives,
Twenty-Five Years After (1962-1987),* Volume One,
New York, Paulist Press, Mahwah, 1988, pp.220-266.

De La Potterie, I. *Mary in the Mystery of the Covenant.*
Transl. B. Buby. New York, Alba House, 1992.

Derrett, D. *Further Light on the Narratives of the Nativity,*
Novum Testamentum, 1975, vol 17/2, pp.81-108.

De Turrecremata, J., *Tractatus de Veritate Conceptionis
Beatissime Virginis.* Impression Anastaltique Culture et
Civilisation, Brussels, 1966.

Dodd, C.H., *The Interpretation of the Fourth Gospel.*
Cambridge University Press, 1953.

Dodd, C.H., *Historical Tradition in the Fourth Gospel.*
Cambridge University Press, 1965.

Doney, W. Ed., *Descartes: A Collection of Critical Essays.*
University of Notre Dame Press, 1968.

Edwards, D., *The Virgin Birth in History and Faith.*
London, Faber and Faber, 1943.

Ehrman, Bart D., *Whose Word Is It? The Story Behind Who
Changed the New Testament and Why.* London,
Continuum, 2006.

Fitzmyer, J.A., "The Virginal Conception of Jesus in the
New Testament." *Journal of Theological Studies,* 34
(1973).

Fitzmyer, J.A., *The Gospel According to Luke: Introduction,
Translation and Notes.* New York, Doubleday, 1981.

France, Richard T., *Herod and the Children of Bethlehem,*
Novum Testamentum, Vol 21/2, April 1979, p.119.

Gray, G.B. *A Critical and Exegetical Commentary on the
Book of Isaiah I-XXXIX.* Edinburgh, T. and T. Clark,
1912.

Gray, J., *I and II Kings, A Commentary*. 3rd Revised
Edition, London, SCM, 1977.

Harrington, D.J., *The Gospel of Matthew. Sacra Pagina
Series Vol. 1*. Minnesota, Liturgical Press, 1991.

Haenchen, E., *The Acts of the Apostles*. Oxford, Basil
Blackwell, 1971.

Hodgson, Peter C. ed., *David Friedrich Strauss. The Life of
Jesus Critically Examined*. London, SCM, 1973.

Jackson, Wayne, *Did Isaiah Prophesy the Virgin Birth of
Christ?* Christian Courier Questions,2002,http://
www.christiancourier.com/questions/
virginProphecyQuestion.htm.

John Paul II, Pope, *Fides et Ratio: Encyclical Letter* Fides Et
Ratio *of The Supreme Pontiff John Paul II To The Bishops
Of The Catholic Church On The Relationship Between
Faith And Reason*, 15 September 1988.
http://www.vatican.va/holy_father/john_paul_ii/
encyclicals/documents/hf_jp-ii_enc_15101998_fides-et-
ratio_en.html

Kelly, J.N.D., *Early Christian Doctrines*. London, Adam and
Charles Black, 1968.

Kraus, H.-J., *Geschichte der Historisch-Kritischen Erforschung
des Alten Testaments*. 2nd Edition, Neukirchener Verlag,
1969.

Lacocque, A., *The Book of Daniel*. Transl. D. Pellauer.
London, SPCK, 1979.

Lagrange, M.-J., *Évangile selon Saint Matthew*. Paris,
Gabalda, 4th Ed., 1927.

Latourelle, R., *The Miracles of Jesus and the Theology of
Miracles*. Transl. M.J. O'Connell. New York, Paulist
Press, 1988.

Laurentin, R., *Court Traité sur la Vierge Marie*. 5th Edition,
Paris, Lethellieux, 1968.

Laurentin, R., *Structure et Théologie de Luc I-II*. Paris, 1957.

Laurentin, R., *Les Évangiles de Noël*. Paris, Desclée, 1985.

Levie, J., *The Bible, Word of God in Words of Men*. Transl.
S.H. Treman. London, Geoffrey Chapman, 1961.

Levine, Ê., *The Targums: Their Interpretative Character and Their Place in Jewish Text Tradition.* Saebo, M. Ed., *Hebrew Bible/ Old Testament: The History of its Interpretation. Vol. I: From the Beginnings until the Middle Ages (Until 1300). Part 1, Antiquity.* Göttingen, Vandenhoek and Ruprecht, 1996, 323-331.

Livius, T., *The Blessed Virgin in the Fathers of the First Six Centuries.* London, Burns and Oates, 1893.

Machen, J. Gresham: *The Virgin Birth of Christ.* London, James Clarke, 1930.

Maier, J., *Early Jewish Biblical Interpretation in the Qumran Literature.* Sbø, 108-129. Saebo, M. Ed., *Hebrew Bible/ Old Testament: The History of its Interpretation. Vol. I: From the Beginnings until the Middle Ages (Until 1300). Part 1, Antiquity.* Göttingen, Vandenhoek and Ruprecht, 1996.

Malavez, L., *The Christian Message and Myth.* Transl. Olive Wyon, London, SCM, 1958.

Marshall, I.H., *Luke: A Commentary on the Greek Text.* Exeter, Paternoster Press, 1978.

McDade, J., *Jesus in Recent Research, The Month,* Second New Series, 31/12, December 1998, 495-505.

McHugh, J., *The Mother of Jesus in the New Testament.* London, Darton, Longman, and Todd, 1975.

McNamara, M., *Targum and Testament: Aramaic Paraphrases of the Hebrew Bible: A Light on the New Testament.* Michigan, Eerdmans, 1972.

Meier, John P., *A Marginal Jew: Rethinking the Historical Jesus. Volume I. The Roots of the Person and the Problem.* Anchor Bible Reference Library. New York, Doubleday, 1987.

Meier, John P., *A Marginal Jew: Rethinking the Historical Jesus. Volume II Mentor, Message, and Miracles.* Anchor Bible Reference Library. New York, Doubleday, 1994.

Meier, John P., *A Marginal Jew: Rethinking the Historical Jesus. Volume III. Companions and Competitors.* Anchor Bible Reference Library. New York, Doubleday, 2001.

Miguens, M., *The Virgin Birth: An Evaluation of Scriptural Evidence.* Westminster MD, Christian Classics, 1975.

205

Neirynck, F., *L'Évangile de Noël selon S. Luc* (Paris: Pensée Catholique, 1960).

Newman, J.H., *Newman on the Inspiration of Scripture*, from *The Nineteenth Century*, Vol. 15, No. 84, [Feb. 1884.], also his reply, in May 1884, from *Stray Essays on Controversial Points variously illustrated*, by Cardinal Newman, 1890, privately printed, § 33. *Inspiration in matters of Historical Fact*, http://www.newmanreader.org/works/miscellaneous/scripture.html

Nahigan, K.E., *A Virgin birth Prophecy?* The Skeptical Review, 1993, No. 2. http://www.infidels.org/library/magazines/tsr/1993/2/2virgi93.html.

Orchard, B. and Longstaff, T.R.W., *J.J. Griesbach: Synoptic and Text-Critical Studies 1776-1976.* SNTS, 34, C.U.P., 1978.

Palmer, P., *Mary in the Documents of the Church.* London, Burns Oates, 1953.

Paredes, J., *Mary and the Kingdom of God. A Synthesis of Mariology.* Transl. Daries, J. and Martinez, M., Slough, St Pauls Publications, 1990.

Rahner, K., *Mary Mother of the Lord. Theological Meditations.* Transl. W.J. O'Hara. London, Nelson, 1962.

Redford, J., *The Quest of the Historical Epiphany: Critical Reflections on Raymond Brown's 'The Birth of the Messiah'.* Clergy Review, January 1979, pp.5-11.

Robinson, J.A.T., *Redating the New Testament.* London, SCM, 1976.

Robinson, J.A.T., *The Priority of John.* London, SCM, 1985

Sbo, M. Ed., *Hebrew Bible/ Old Testament: The History of its Interpretation. Vol. I: From the Beginnings until the Middle Ages (Until 1300). Part 1, Antiquity.* Göttingen, Vandenhoek and Ruprecht, 1996.

Scheeben, M.J., *Mariology.* Volume 1. Transl. Geukers, T.L.M. London, Herder, 1946.

Schillebeeckx, E., *Jesus: An Experiment in Christology.* Transl. H. Hoskins. London, Collins, 1979.

Schürmann, H., *Das Lukasevangelium,* I Herders
Theologischer Kommentar zum Neun Testament. 3;
Freiburg: Herder, 1969.

Schweitzer, A., *The Quest of The Historical Jesus. A Critical
Study of its Progress from Reimarus to Wrede.* Transl. W.
Montgomery, London, A & C Black, 3rd Edition, 1954.

Taylor, V., *The Gospel According to Mark: The Greek Text,
with Introduction, Notes and Indexes.* 2nd Edition,
London, McMillan, 1966.

Trocmé, E., *The Formation of The Gospel of Mark.* Transl.
Pamela Gaughan, London, SPCK, 1963.

Vögtle, A., "Offene Fragen zur Lukanischen Geburts-
und Kindheitsgeschichet," *Bibel und Leben* 11 (1970),
51-57.

Von Campehausen, H., *The Virgin Birth in the Theology of
the Ancient Church.* Studies in Historical Theology
No.2. London, SCM, 1964.

Weinandy, T.G., Keating, D.A., and Yocum, J.P., *Aquinas
on Scripture: An Introduction to his Biblical
Commentaries.* London, T. and T. Clark, 2005.

White, A.D., *A History of The Warfare of Science with
Theology in Christendom.* New York D. Appleton and
Company, 1898 (text in the public domain),
http://abob.libs.uga.edu/bobk/whitewtc.html

Wright, Addison G. *The Literary Genre Midrash.* Alba
House, New York 1967.

Wright, N.T., *Christian Origins and the Question of God.
Volume I, The New Testamenet People of God.* London,
SPCK, 1992.

Wright, N.T., *Christian Origins and the Question of God.
Volume II, Jesus and the Victory of God.* London, SPCK,
1996.

Wright, N.T., *The Resurrection of the Son of God.* Volume 3
of *Christian Origins and the Question of God.* London,
SPCK, 2003.

Wright, N.T., *God's Way of Acting.* The Christian Century,
December 16, 1998, pp.1215-17.

Wright, N.T., and Borg, M., *The Meaning of Jesus.* London,
SPCK, 1999.

ABBREVIATIONS

AS   Abbott-Smith, *A Manual Greek Lexicon of the New Testament.* Edinburgh, T & T Clark, 3rd Edition.

BDB   Brown, F. Driver, S. and Briggs, C. *The Brown-Driver-Briggs Hebrew and English Lexicon, Coded with Strong's Concordance Numbers.* Massachusetts, Hendrickson, 2003.

BI   Megivern, J.J. *Bible Interpretation. Official Catholic Teachings.* Consortium Books. North Carolina, McGrath.

BM   Brown, R.E. *The Birth of the Messiah: A Commentary on the Infancy Narratives in Matthew and Luke.* New York, Doubleday, 1979.

BMG   Redford, J. *Bad, Mad or God? Proving the Divinity of Christ from St. John's Gospel.* St Pauls, London, 2004.

BV   Boslooper, T. *The Virgin Birth.* London, SCM, 1962.

CCC   *Catechism of the Catholic Church.* English translation London, Burns and Oates, 1994. http://www.scborromeo.org/ccc/ccc_toc.htm

DV   *Dogmatic Constitution of the Second Vatican Council on Divine Revelation Dei Verbum ("The Word of God").* Quotations are from the Vatican website, http://www.vatican.va/archive/hist_councils/ ii_vatican_council/documents/vat-ii_const_19651118_ dei-verbum_en.html.

ET   Benoit, P. *Exégèse et Théologie.* Les Éditions du Cerf, Paris, 1961.

ICC   Davis, W.D. and Allison, D.C., *The Gospel According to Saint Matthew: A Critical and Exegetical Commentary. Volume I.* Edinburgh, T & T Clark.

INT   *Introduction to the New Testament.* Preceded by name of author, and followed by page reference, e.g. Klijn, INT, 23.

JVG   Wright, N.T. *Christian Origins and the Question of God. Volume II, Jesus and the Victory of God.* London, SPCK, 1996.

LAB   *Liber Antiquitatum Biblicarum* (Pseudo-Philo).

LJ   Hodgson, Peter C. ed. *David Friedrich Strauss. The Life of Jesus Critically Examined.* London, SCM, 1973.

LXX   *The Septuagint Greek Version of the Old Testament.*

MJ1 Meier, John P. *A Marginal Jew: Rethinking the Historical Jesus. Volume I. The Roots of the Person and the Problem.* Anchor Bible Reference Library. New York, Doubleday, 1987. MJ2 and MJ3 refer to Volumes 2 and 3 of this book. For fuller references, cf. the Bibliography.

MJNT McHugh, J. *The Mother of Jesus in the New Testament.* London, Darton, Longman and Todd, 1975.

MJTM Latourelle, R. *The Miracles of Jesus and the Theology of Miracles.* Transl. M.J. O'Connell. New York, Paulist Press, 1988.

NBD Douglas, J.D. et al. *The New Bible Dictionary.* London, Inter-Varsity Press, 1962.

NJB H. Wansbrough, Ed. *The New Jerusalem Bible*, Standard Edition.

NJBC Brown, R.E. Fitzmyer, J.A., and Murphy, R.E., *The New Jerome Biblical Commentary.* London, Geoffrey Chapman, 1968.

NTHIP Kümmell, W.G. *The New Testament: The History of the Investigation of its Problems.* Transl. S. Mclean Gilmour and Howard C. Kee. London, SCM, 1973.

ODCC Cross, F.L. & Livingstone, E.A., Ed. *The Oxford Dictionary of the Christian Church*, Oxford University Press, 1974.

ST Aquinas, T. *The Summa Theologica* translated by the Fathers of the English Dominican Province, Benziger Bros. edition, 1947. http://www.ccel.org/a/aquinas/summa/home.html.

Tanner Tanner, N.P., Ed. *Decrees of the Ecumenical Councils.* II Vols. London & Washington, DC, Sheed & Ward and Georgetown University Press, 1990.

V2AP R. Latourelle, Ed. *Vatican II Assessment and Perspectives, Twenty-Five Years After (1962-1987),* Volume One, New York, Paulist Press, Mahwah, 1988.

RSG Wright, N.T. *The Resurrection of the Son of God.* Volume 3 of *Christian Origins and the Question of God.* London, SPCK, 2003.

\\ Where a text is paralleled in all three Synoptic Gospels, the convention is to give only the reference in Matthew, followed by e.g. Matthew 21:1\\, rather than giving all three references in full.

INDEX OF AUTHORS AND SUBJECTS

A

Abraham 44, 73, 75, 81, 88, 96, 137, 157, 159, 165, 184.
Adoptionism 142.
Ahaz King of Judah 26-29.
Alexander, Denis 181, 197, 202.
Almah 16-7, 27-8, 184.
Anakephalaiósasthai 37.
Anawim 156-159.
Annunciation 21, 60-2, 72-3, 89, 93-4, 99, 111, 113, 129, 155-6, 159-60, 163, 170-1, 175, 193, 196, 198.
Antecedent Probability 185.
Anthony of Egypt 158, 188.
Apollinarianism 142
Aquinas, Thomas 37, 147, 202, 207, 210.
Ascension 123, 155, 170.
autoptai 127

B

Barrett, C.K. 80, 82, 91, 132, 174.
Benedictus 156, 158.
Bethlehem, Jesus' birth at 15, 94-6, 98-104, 107, 109-116, 166, 185-6, 193, 203.
Betulah 16-7, 64.
Boslooper, T. 68-9, 135-6, 148, 188-200, 202, 209.
Brown, Philip 32, 35, 41-2, 202.
Brown, Raymond E. 18, 22, 27-8, 42, 59-64, 67, 74-5, 79, 81, 84-5, 91, 94, 96-7, 99-102, 108-113, 115, 128, 130-1, 133, 135-7, 139-40, 143-4, 152, 156-7, 163, 167, 170-1, 174-5, 184, 202, 209-10.

C

Calvin, John 20, 31.
Cardinal Augustine Bea 123-4.
Catechism of the Catholic Church 20, 37-8, 183, 209.
Celsus 81, 137.
Census 103-4, 111, 114, 122, 128, 154, 166, 175, 193.
Cerinthus 64-5.
Christology, Christological 41, 64-6, 70, 85-6, 88-9, 96-7, 133, 138-41, 142-4, 147-8, 153, 163, 167, 174-5, 193, 206.
Church in Jerusalem 170.
Clement of Alexandria 30.
Coherence, Criterion of 165, 198.
Complete Fictionality 107.
conception through the Holy Spirit 40, 115.
Constantine, Emperor 44, 100.
Cyril of Alexandria 142, 199.

D

date of Luke 58.
date of Matthew 57-8, 93, 122.
Davidic descent 109, 115.
Davis, W.D., and Allison, D.C. 74, 96, 99, 143, 161, 163, 203, 209.
devotion to Mary 189, 191.
Dibelius, M. 138, 148.
Divino Afflante Spiritu 33, 48, 105.
Dodd, C.H. 119, 150-3, 173, 203.
Dogmatic Constitution on Divine Revelation, Dei Verbum, (DV) 32, 34-5, 93, 104, 122, 133, 172, 203, 209.
Douay Rheims Version of the Bible 49, 51.

E

Ebionites 66, 153.
Edwards, Douglas 75, 90, 203.
eggenésan 73-4.
Ehrman, Bart D. 45-54, 84, 194, 203.
ek spermatos Daueid 77.
Eliot, George 86.
Elizabeth, Mother of John the Baptist 14, 62, 96, 108, 128, 166, 184, 188, 200.
ending of Mark's Gospel 50-51, 53.
Epiphanius 20.

F

faith, decision of 79, 196.
family tradition 122, 144, 151-2, 154-5, 193.
Farmer, W.R. 56.
Feeding of the Multitude 86, 94.
Finding of Jesus in the Temple 72, 113.
Fitzmyer, J.A. 61-2, 68, 79, 90-1, 133, 203, 210.
Flight into Egypt 94, 98, 113-4, 192.
Formal Error 105-6.
France, Richard T. 97, 130, 203.
Fundamentalism 24-5, 33, 146.

G

Galilee, return to 112-3.
genomenou 77.
ginomai 78.
Gray, G.B. 27-8, 41, 203.

H

Harnack, A. 139.
Harrington, Daniel 17, 22, 28, 42, 114, 131, 175, 204.
Healey, Nicholas M. 37.
Hegelian 88, 148, 180.
Helvidius 20.
Herod the Great 15, 39, 60, 95, 97, 100, 103, 113, 116-7, 122, 128.
historical agnosticism 145.
historical faith 124, 177, 198.

historical presumption, criterion of 120-2, 126, 173.
historical tradition 58, 72, 97, 119, 144, 150-1, 153-5, 171, 173, 203.
historicity of the Gospels 122-5, 159.
historicity, absolute 98-90, 102.
historicity, substantial 88, 98, 102-3, 113, 166, 175.
Holtzmann, M. 86-7, 93.
House of David 13, 26, 40, 61, 67.

I

Ignatius of Antioch 55, 65, 153, 171, 184, 200.
illegitimacy charge 82, 85, 91, 137-8, 154, 160.
Immaculate Conception 191.
Immanuel 13, 16-7, 25-9, 40, 42, 202.
inerrancy of Scripture 104-6.
Infancy Narratives 75, 89, 93-9, 101-4, 107-9, 115, 119-21, 126, 129, 133, 146, 151, 153, 172, 192-3, 198, 202.
inspiration and revelation 35-7.
Irenaeus of Lyons 22, 42, 64, 68, 77, 153.
Isenbiehl, Johann 33.

J

Jackson, Wayne 24-8, 41, 204.
Jerome 20, 47, 53-4, 210.
Jerusalem, Fall of 57.
Jewish Messianism 163.
Johannine Comma 51.
Johannine Community 159, 174.
John the Baptist 61-2, 94, 96, 116-8, 127, 156, 184, 200.
Joseph, Husband of Mary 13, 15, 20-1, 27, 40, 61-4, 67, 70-5, 78-85, 88-90, 94-6, 99-101, 103, 112-3, 115, 130, 146, 151-2, 154-5, 160-2, 165-7, 171, 179, 184, 191, 193-4, 199.
Justin the Martyr 16-7, 23, 29, 65, 69, 130, 153, 171.

K

Karris 59-60.
King James Authorised Version of
   the Bible 49.
Kümmel, W.G. 59, 67, 91, 210.

L

Lagrange, M.-J. 42, 50, 113, 130-1,
   204.
Last Supper 101-2.
Lateran, Council of 649 20, 22, 200.
Latourelle, René 180, 200, 203-4,
   210.
Laurentin, René 127, 133, 156,
   171, 174-5, 204.
Logos Doctrine 30, 82, 88, 132,
   139.
Luke's Gospel Introduction 59, 123,
   126-8, 133, 160, 187.
Luther, Martin 20, 31.

M

Machen, J. Gresham 17, 22, 27-28,
   41, 132, 135, 148, 174, 205.
Magi 94-5, 97-8, 100, 102, 114.
Magnificat 156-9, 163, 175.
Maier, J. 31, 42, 205.
marriage and celibacy 76, 188-9.
Marshall, I. Howard 63, 68, 72, 90,
   100, 102-3, 113, 126-7, 129-33,
   160, 174, 205.
Mary as Witness of the Virgin Birth
   155-6, 160, 186, 188, 190, 192-3.
mashal and *hyda* 142.
Massoretic Scribes 46.
material error 106, 129.
McDade, J. 140, 148, 205.
McHugh, John 68, 76-8, 90, 138,
   205, 210.
Meier, John P. 114, 120-1, 137,
   140-1, 144-5, 175-6, 196-8, 205,
   210.
Midrash 5, 95-7, 121, 192, 207.
Miguens, M. 68, 79, 82-6, 91, 167,
   173, 175, 205.
miracles 86-8, 108, 119, 134, 145,
   155, 164, 166, 168, 170, 173,
   178-82, 195, 197-8, 204-5, 210.

miracles and science 179-82.
Monophysitism 142.
multiple attestation, criterion of
   120.
Muratorian Canon 58, 60.

N

Nadab King of Israel 36.
Nativity, Church of, Bethlehem
   100.
Nazareth 11, 13, 72, 78-9, 94-5,
   100-01, 111-16, 131, 134, 161,
   166, 168, 178, 185.
Newman, J.H. 130-1, 185, 201,
   206.
Non liquet 121.
Nunc Dimittis 156, 158.

O

Occam's Razor 159.
oikos 100, 102.
Old Latin Manuscripts 47, 63.
Old Syriac Version of the Bible 73,
   75.
onus probandi 120-1.
Orchard, Bernard 56, 66, 132, 206.
'oth 26.

P

pagan ideas the source of the story
   135, 144, 147, 193.
Pandera 137.
Papias, Bishop of Hieropolis 55-6,
   58.
Parthenogenesis 180-1, 183, 200.
parthenos 16-7, 22, 24, 27-9, 40,
   180.
Passover 101-2.
Paul of Tarsus 4, 52, 54-5, 58-60,
   67-8, 70, 75-8, 90, 120, 138, 140,
   146, 155, 158, 171, 185, 188, 194.
Paulus, Heinrich 108.
Pekah King of Israel 26.
Pentecost 157, 170, 187.
Perpetual Virginity of Mary 19-21,
   191.
pesher 31.
phatné 10

Philo of Alexandria 136, 138, 144, 147.
Pieper, Joseph 146.
Pope Damasus 47.
Pope John Paul II 20, 204.
Pope Leo XIII 104-6.
Pope Paul VI 123, 125.
Pope Pius XII 33, 48.
post-Newtonian science 182.
Potterie, Ignace de la 35, 42, 203.
pragmatón 127
Proto-Gospel of James 186.
Providentissimus Deus 104-6, 130.
Psalms of Solomon 162, 168-9, 174.
public ministry of Jesus 70, 94, 101, 116, 125, 128, 133, 160, 162, 166, 168, 170, 186.

Q

Quirinius Governor of Syria 103, 128, 175.
Qumran 31, 156-7, 174, 205.

R

Rabbinic Judaism, Rabbinic Sources 38, 57, 63, 95-6, 121, 131, 172, 192, 203.
Razon King of Syria 26.
Reimarus, Herbert Samuel 108, 180, 196.
Robinson, J.A.T. 56-7, 66, 148, 206.

S

Schillebeeckx, E. 136, 148, 151-2, 173, 186, 200, 206.
Schweitzer, A. 195-6.
Science 177, 180-2, 195, 201-2, 207.
Scripture, inerrancy of 104-5.
Scripture, inspiration of 24, 34, 46, 105, 130, 193, 206.
Second Vatican Council 21-2, 32, 36, 66, 83, 105, 122, 187, 209.
sensus literalis 31.
Septuagint (LXX) 16, 24, 78, 209.
Shepherds 15, 94, 97-8, 111, 114, 131.

Sign 26-7, 29, 41, 165-6, 183-5, 189, 199.
Simon, Richard 32-3.
slaughter of the Innocents 15, 39, 96-7, 113, 121, 154.
Son of God 41, 44, 52, 64, 72, 81-9 91, 97, 117, 132, 134, 136, 138-40, 143-4, 155, 161, 163-4, 167, 183-4, 186, 196, 199, 207, 210.
Son of Joseph 64, 70, 72, 75, 78-85, 88-9, 152, 167, 171.
Son of Man 87, 91, 108, 159.
Son of Mary 83-5, 152, 167, 199.
Song of the Three Holy Children 158.
spiritual sense of Scripture 30-1.
Star of Bethlehem 15.
Strauss, D.F. 86-8, 108-10, 134, 146, 179-80, 190, 198, 204, 209.
Synoptic Gospels 94, 101, 113, 119, 131, 150, 210.
Syria 26-7, 75, 103, 128, 186.

T

Targums 30-1, 205.
Taylor, J.B. 29 30.
Taylor, V. 53, 66, 132, 169, 207.
Textus Receptus 49.
The *Da Vinci Code* 44, 53.
theological coherence 198.
Theologoumenon 99, 110, 115, 144, 151, 172, 190.
Theophilus 59, 126-7, 129, 133.
Tischendorf 45.
tota pulchra es Maria 192.
total inspiration 106.
Transfiguration 87.
Trent, Council of 33, 48.
Trypho 16, 23, 29, 153.

V

Vermes, G. 16, 18, 24, 29, 63, 190.
virgin birth 5, 11, 15-9, 22-4, 26-8, 58, 60, 64-6, 69-73, 75-6, 78-80, 82, 85-6, 89, 93, 97-9, 108, 134-8, 143-55, 160-1, 164-7, 170-2, 176-8, 180-99, 202-8.

virginal conception 11, 17-9, 22-4, 29, 39-41, 52, 61-2, 64-66, 68, 70, 72, 77-80, 82, 85, 89-91, 93, 108-9, 112, 119, 126, 129, 136, 138, 144-8, 153, 170-3, 181, 184, 187, 191, 189-9, 203.

virginity in the history of the Church 188-9.

visitation of Mary to Elizabeth 108.

Viviano, Benedict 55, 58.

Von Campenhausen 65, 68, 71, 79, 89-90, 207.

Vulgate Version of the Bible 48-9, 51, 53.

W

walking on the water 91, 141.

Weiss, J. 139.

Westcott and Hort 45-6, 48.

Western Text 80.

Wrede, William 87-8, 196.

Wright, N.T. 54, 57, 66, 92, 121, 130, 132, 169, 185, 190, 200, 207-9.

Y

yóléd 75.

Young, E.J. 26.

215

OLD TESTAMENT

Genesis
3:18 *189*
12 *184*
13:8 *22*
14:16 *22*
16:11 *67*
21:1-7 *136*

Exodus
3:14-15 *141*
40:34-5 *68*

Leviticus
12:1-8 *114*

Judges
13:3 *67*
13:25 *164*
14:14 *142*
14:6 *164*
16:1 *42*
19:15 *164*

Ruth
2:12 *68*

2 Samuel
5:2 *42*
7:14 *164*

1 Kings
8:10-11 *68*
11:41 *36*
14:19 *36*
15:7 *36*

1 Chronicles
1:34 *75*

Job
14:1 *77*
15:14 *78*
25:4 *78*

Psalms
2:7 *75*
78:1-2 *142*
130:8 *174*

Proverbs
1:6 *142*

Isaiah
2:3 *186*
4:3 *42*
7:4 *26*
7:10-16 *26*
7:13 *61*
7:14 *16-9, 22-25, 28-30,*
33-4, 39-42, 60-1,
67-8, 96, 136, 144,
167, 190.
7:17 *67*
11:2 *174*
40:3-5 *116*
43:1 *71*
43:1-13 *141*
49:1 *139*

Jeremiah
1:5 *139*
26:6,18 *66*
31:15 *42*
44:29ff *27*

Ezekiel
8:1 *34*
33:22 *34*

Daniel
3:51-87 *158*

Hosea
2:21 *68*
11:1 *32*

Micah
3:12 *66*
5:1 *42, 110*

NEW TESTAMENT

Matthew
1-2 *93*
1:1 *70*
1:1-2:23 *118*
1:16 *70, 73-5, 115*
1:1-17 *71*
1:18 *94, 115*
1:18-23 *113, 115, 137*
1:18-25 *13, 40, 74, 161,*
170
1:19 *137*

1:20 *115*
1:20-23 *115-6*
1:21 *116*
1:22-23 *25, 40, 42*
1:23 *41, 115*
1:24-5 *116*
1:25 *63, 115, 155*
2:1 *113, 116*
2:1-12 *94*
2:1-16 *109*
2:1-18 *114*

2:5b-6 *42*
2:11 *99-100*
2:13ff *113*
2:14-15b *32*
2:16 *95, 100*
2:16-8 *94, 97*
2:17-8 *39, 42*
2:19-21 *94*
2:19-23 *114*
2:23 *114, 116, 131*
2:23b *42*

3:1 *116*
3:1-6 *117*
3:3 *116*
3:5-6 *118*
4:15 *185*
9:9 *55*
11:5 *166*
12:28 *166*
12:50 *189*
13:35 *142*
13:55 *22, 83-4*
14:13-21 *94*
19:12 *188*
21:1 *101, 209*
21:12-13 *101*
22:1-10 *57*
22:6-8 *57*
22:7 *57*
26:18 *101*
27:56 *22*
28:1 *22*
28:20 *41*

Mark

1:1 *91, 116, 118, 132, 139*
1:1-3 *116*
1:1-4 *118*
1:1-5 *117-8*
1:9-11 *139*

1:11 *143*
2:5 *161*
2:14 *55*
3:16-17 *139*
3:31-35 *22, 169*
3:35 *91, 189*
6:3 *84-5, 91*
6:32-44 *94*
10:29 *91*
10:29-31 *42*
12:36ff *91*
13:1-4 *56*
13:2 *169*
13:22 *91*
13:32 *86*
14:36 *91*
14:63-4 *86, 159, 174*
16:8 *50*
16:9-20 *50, 86*

Luke

3-3 *93*
1:1-2:53 *118*
1:1 *187*
1:1-4 *59, 61, 126, 133, 193*
1:2 *127*
1:2-4 *123, 160*
1:5 *128*
1:5-23 *129*
1:5-25 *61, 94*
1:23 *160*
1:26 *94*
1:26-37 *61*
1:26-38 *13-4, 94, 111, 113, 171*
1:27 *61, 63, 115*
1:30-35 *115*
1:31 *116*
1:32 *62, 62, 115, 163*
1:34 *61, 115*
1:35 *62, 115, 163, 189*
1:36 *128*
1:37 *62*
1:38 *62*
1:42-3 *188*
1:46-55 *156*
1:68-79 *156*
2: *50*
2:1 *113, 128*
2:1-3 *103,*
2:1-8 *111*
2:2-7 *113*
2:4 *112, 115, 166*
2:4-6 *116*
2:4-15 *109*
2:5-6 *116*
2:7 *99*
2:8-20 *114*
2:11 *116*
2:21-38 *114*
2:22 *113,*
2:22-38 *113*
2:29-32 *156*
2:34-35 *171*
2:38 *192*
2:39 *113, 131*
2:39-40 *114, 116*
2:40-52 *113*
2:41-50 *114*
2:48 *72, 164*
2:49 *164, 165, 174*

2:51 *164, 192*
2:51-2 *114*
2:52 *161*
3:1 *116*
3:1-2 *128*
3:1-4 *117*
3:3 *118*
3:4 *116*
3:23-38 *71*
4:16-21 *168*
4:22 *83-4*
6:20-22 *156*
7:12 *85*
9:10b-17 *94*
14:16-24 *57*
15:7 *50*
15:10 *50*
15:13 *50*
24:45 *42*

John

1:1-18 *118, 132*
1:12-13 *80*
1:13 *189, 200*
1:19 *116*
1:19-23 *117*
1:23 *116*
1:26 *173*
1:41 *173*
1:45 *78, 82, 111*
2:1-10 *94*
2:11 *90*
2:3-4 *169*
2:11 *88, 95*
2:13-22 *101*
2:22 *100*
2:22-23 *95*
2:22-28 *94*
2:23 *101*
2:39 *94, 95, 100*
2:41-50 *94*
3:16 *80*
4:46-54 *90*
5:1 *101*
5:1-14 *119*
5:1-15 *90*
5:7-8 *51*
5:39-40 *37*
6:1-13 *119*
6:1-16 *91*
6:16-21 *91*
6:20 *141*

217

6:42 *79, 82, 84, 167*
7:1 *101*
7:36-50 *50*
7:40-42 *110*
7:42 *110*
8:1-11 *50*
8:12 *80, 186*
8:28 *91*
8:38-41 *81, 137*
8:41 *91, 160*
8:58 *44, 88, 159, 165,
      174-5*
9:1-7 *91*
10:1-13 *37*
11:41-44 *91*
11:47-53 *173*
13:30 *80*
19:31 *101*

Acts

1:1 *59*
1:1-2 *123, 125*
1:13-14 *155, 170*
2:32 *143*
2:43-47 *157*
2:51 *170*
4:32-37 *157*
5:1 *158*
6:1 *158*
13:33 *75*
16:10 *67*

Romans
1:3 *77, 200*
1:3-4 *139*
5 *77*

1 Corinthians
1:5 *76*
5:6-8 *42*
6 *76*
7:32 *188*
9:5 *22*
10:1-11 *42*
14:33-36 *52, 54*
15:6 *155*

Galatians
1:15 *139*
1:18 *76*
1:19 *22*
2:1 *76*
4:4 *77*
4:21-31 *138*

Ephesians
1:10 *37*
5:31-2 *68*

Philippians
2:7 *78*

Colossians
4:14 *60*

1 Timothy
2:11-14 *54*

2 Timothy
4:11 *60*

Philemon
1:24 *58, 60*

Hebrews
1:5 *75*
1:6 *139*
2:17 *183*
5:5 *75*

1 John
5:7-8 *51*

218

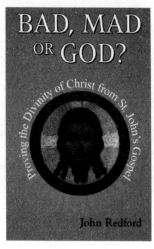

BAD, MAD
OR GOD?

Proving the Divinity of Christ from St John's Gospel

John Redford

By the same author:
BAD, MAD or GOD?
Proving the Divinity of Christ from St John's Gospel

In his new book *Jesus of Nazareth*, Pope Benedict XVI says regarding the historical Jesus: "Unless there had been something extraordinary in what happened, unless the person and the words of Jesus radically surpassed the hopes and expectations of the time, there is no reason to explain why he was crucified or why he made such an impact."

In *Bad, Mad or God?*, published by St Pauls 2004, John Redford fully developed this argument. He demonstrated that, as John's Gospel tells us, the historical Jesus claimed to be God, vindicated his claims by his miracles and his teaching, was put to death for blasphemy and rose bodily from the dead for the salvation of the whole human race.

"...Redford...has produced what must endure as the most impressive, rounded and satisfying achievement of apologetics since Newman's *Grammar of Assent*... Without any condescension, I suggest that this book would make an outstanding text for courses in religion for students..."
Patrick Madigan, *Heythrop Journal*.

"this book... should be read by anyone with an interest in the real Jesus..." Nicholas King, *Scripture Bulletin*.

"All the way through the book the author takes pains to prove that the Gospels are reliable history, and in the process he totally rejects the 'myth theory' of Rudolf Bultmann and his followers... There are not many good books on Christology – books that are truly Catholic and faithful to defined doctrine and tradition. Here is one you can rely on..."
Kenneth Baker, *Homiletic and Pastoral Review*.

ISBN 0-85439-694-2   383 pages   £17.99

Trying my Wings

poems by

Cheri L. Miller

Finishing Line Press
Georgetown, Kentucky

Trying my Wings

ACKNOWLEDGMENTS

My thanks to the following journals and their editors:

Rock & Sling: A Journal of Witness—First Religion
Assisi: An Online Journal of Arts & Letters—Leaving the Lilacs
Penn-Union—Destiny, Dying in a Rented Room
Welter—Fight
Smartish Pace—Flight

Publisher: Leah Huete de Maines
Editor: Christen Kincaid
Cover Art: Sean Tully
Author Photo: Teresa Miller
Cover Design: Elizabeth Maines McCleavy

Order online: www.finishinglinepress.com
also available on amazon.com

Author inquiries and mail orders:
Finishing Line Press
PO Box 1626
Georgetown, Kentucky 40324
USA

Table of Contents

Trying my Wings 1

First Religion 2

Leaving the Lilacs 3

All Summer 4

Remembrance through Mango 5

Passing 6

Shore Country 7

Destiny 8

Pining 9

Mary 10

The Woods Still Accept me as a Little Girl 11

Light Sestina 12

One River 14

Dying in a Rented Room 15

At the Fallen Oak 16

Show Bones Villanelle 17

Leave Me with Laughing Wolf 18

Upon Staying in Your House 19

Lunar Eclipse 20

Waiting for Tea Water 21

In City Traffic Halted by a Funeral Procession 22

Rain Woman Sun Woman 23

Realizing Your Compassion 24

September 25

Hope 26

April 27

Winter 28

Winter II 29

After Winter 30

Fight 31

Flight 32

For Ma

Trying my Wings

A blackbird streaks quickly, soundlessly,
Through a heaven of white confetti,
Dives, almost weightlessly,
Then soars up, up
Into the wide sweet open.

No sound from the trees. No fighting
Of branch and limb. It is windless.
The pond water is newly frozen
Like a quiet bowl in the earth, glazed over
With a thin, translucent lid.

Last night I swept myself up—
So much debris on the path. Afterward,
God settled into me
Like snow settles in grass.

Today I rise with the blackbird,
With the squirrel who treads so lightly
Over the ice crust.
When I reach the hill,
I stop for a moment
To believe my breathing,
And then I try my wings.

First Religion

When the line was blurred between yard and woods,
and crickets sang beneath star-lit leaves,

when the main path was illumined by the moon,
white sand visible as daylight in darkness,

I learned in a game of hide and seek
I needed nothing but shadow to clothe me.

In that dream deep quiet of my life
with the cool grass watering my feet,

I wound my fingers through vines of wild grapes,
tasted bittersweet August on my tongue.

Blackberries drooping with their midnight juice
dropped like answers into my hands.

Leaving the Lilacs

For Ma (1939-2002)

Cool and wet in early spring, the cut grass haunts me.
It reminds me of her hair,
of how the funeral director
cut three small locks for my brother, sister, and me.

Sorrow woven into lilacs, into the green hair of graves,
worries me like a song.
How will I, while the sky is weighted
with the Lenten purple of spring,
leave the magnolia-like clouds, the irresistible fragrance of rain?

I have seen her in her casket.
I have gone into the ground to watch her become the earth.
I have felt the cold drop, ascertained the false stasis.
Today I will move beyond the graveyard.
I'll leave the lilacs, take nothing for my table.

Whatever it takes for a body to become a flower,
that is what I want.

All Summer

All summer I looked forward
to that rose-gold horizon
drawn ahead in the haze,
some place on the other side of this sea.

I waited on the sand in the white sun,
Glided through the jade waves
Attempting to bathe in each moment.

It's always slipping by me,
slipping through me,
love, heat, a rush of days
of warm wind and water,
an ethereal hand
of light on my shoulder.

Remembrance through Mango

*No sooner had the warm liquid, and the crumbs with it, touched
my palate than...An exquisite pleasure had invaded my senses...
and the whole of Combray and of its surroundings, taking their
proper shapes and growing solid, sprang into being, town and
gardens alike, from my cup of tea.*
      —Marcel Proust, Remembrance of Things Past

Now as I sit eating
near the opening of another summer,
age creeping around my eyes
like a snail's path in the sand,

you become a window, mango,
on all of the summers that I ran
lean, brown, and free,
and lived often in the buoyancy of water,

a warm window,
Through which I gaze upon a girl,
As she turns her face to the sun
And rises from her place in the sand.

Passing

Upon my neighbor's loss of his wife

There is nothing mysterious
About a garden gone to grass
Within a circle of stones,
Watched over by a statue of Mary.

That there were flowers here last spring,
All the neighbors know.
Her sun slipped through hyacinth blooms,
Lit the golden wings of butterflies,
And was gone.

Shore Country

Running beside fields of tall corn,
I feel the whir of mosquitoes quicken
As the hot air dampens.

Summer thickets swell with cricket song,
And the road glows
With the gold fire of the setting sun.

I'm sweating, kicking up gravel and feeling
Like I can go on forever—and I do go on forever
Along the trail at the field's edge.

Destiny

A rondel for Sean

I saw your blue eyes fill with sun
when you played like an otter at sea.
In waves your charm spilled over me,
I would no longer live as a nun.

I foresaw our wedding, I'd begun
to skip to Vinny's bakery,
for I saw your blue eyes fill with sun
when you played like an otter at sea.

The goodness of your skin, the utter fun,
how August was a balm that blessed me.
I welcomed you like warm, sugared tea
in the morning light of our balcony,
I saw your blue eyes fill with sun.

Pining

She kicks a can
In the alley where dim light glows.
It clanks across old stones.
In the park he waits to meet her.

He aches, shivers
On a bench by a frozen pond.
Pine branches scrape together.
A cat crosses the alley.

He fingers his change.
Though he has her, he wants her.
The coins are warm in his coat.
She stubs her boot on a rock.

The sky is cream.
She rubs her mittened hands
Together beneath snow's shadow,
A wish of white on pines.

She laughs, blushes,
Forgets winter with him.
She wants him worse than water.
His body is a blanket.

Snow comes and falls
In all the little creases
Between dry blades of grass.

Mary

Sun slants across the floor
Strewing flowers of light.

On my window's ledge,
a cluster of birds
peck briefly, scattering seed,
then hurry off, a flurry of thumping feathers
to the trees.

My room is an empty loft.
All that matters is the love in her face
Pouring over the wooden cross on the wall
Warming to life the small beads
I hold in my hands.

I think I know her in the corner of my heart.
I feel the soft plume of veils dropping away.

The Woods Still accept me as a Little Girl

Lying under garlands of stars,
I feel as if I have feathers.

I look about, and I am warm inside.   .
I laugh, laugh like summer.

I breathe,
And the pine needles
Bring Christmas to my nose.

I roll and let the leaves
Crunch softly in my hair—
I am like a kitten here.

I stretch and rest my back against bark.
I want to rub my skin
Against the velvety moss
Until I am as soft and smooth.

Light Sestina

The bay shimmers in the early sun
As we cross the well-worn bridge
To the calm of the Eastern Shore.
Gulls fly over the quiet waves
In the ever-silent morning light.
We breathe deeply and savor the water.

The untamed, living scent of water
Blends with the gold-suffusing sun.
The bay is a bowl filling with light
As we cross the shining bridge
And watch the new rolling waves
Lap out their lives on the shore.

At one with rhythms of the shore,
Lulled by the sun and music of water,
We watch the willowy sea grass wave,
We feel the sway of wind and sun.
From morning's soft gold we cross the bridge
Into the diamonds of afternoon light.

Across green fields bathed in light,
Rows of corn grow tall on the shore.
In the secluded marshes beyond the bridge,
A heron wades in low water.
Cattails reach through wind to the sun,
Their long stems lean and wave.

You and I have tumbled in the blue waves
And laughed in the summer light.
I've seen your eyes fill with sun
When the ocean lays you like driftwood on the shore.
Your eyes are anchors, cups of cool water,
Sound seas, tiny beacons and bridges.

Together we have risen like bridges
To cross the swells of so many waves.
Now we swim in the folds of silken waters,
And gather shells, keepers of sea and light.
Like sandpipers on the just-wet shore,
We run, almost on air, in a spray of sun.

Crossing this bridge today to the shore,
In the sun above glimmering water,
Our lives seem the whitest waves of light.

One River

Some nights, flushed with French wine,
when even the scents of my own breath
and lipstick are intoxicating,

I lift my skirt a little in the doorway.
I wink at the river, which smells like me.
I swell in my summer clothes.

The river ripples like the muscles of a lean-bodied man,
and I am inclined to merge with the brown water,
to lose my rice-white stain in the brown water.

Dying In a Rented Room

Remains of candlelight flicker
on an iron stand in the corner.
Tears and pools of sweat
swell and roll down my face
like tiny saltwater waves.

How will I be reconciled in this ramshackle room?
I can no longer lift my hands.
I envision pulling my wet sheet around me
and wiping spittle from my mouth
as the day-nurse does,
removing the chin-crust of my meals.

Now is the swan's movement through dusk,
the music of a white moon rising.
Here is my sum total: myself
in a swarm of body odor, on a cot
beneath a smoke-smeared window,
in a room I do not own.

Still, through the screen
oak leaves rustle in the summer wind.
Outside, the walkway is yet warm
with the lemon light of midday.

So many summers come back to me:
graduations and laughter around lamp-lit tables
on porches by the shore,
the golds and silvers of water
in bays, rivers, seas.
I know the fireflies at the edge of the woods
where I sat in the damp grass. I know I wasn't alone.

If only now I would hear
the landlady's sandals on the stair.

At the Fallen Oak

For Tres

In the woods behind our house,
My sister and I prepared a roast.
We tore a chunk of a decaying oak
And arranged it in an old tin pan.

Acorns pressed into the skin on our knees,
Our mouths watered as we knelt in the leaves.
We snapped twigs and laid them in like carrots.
Stones were potatoes, pebbles pearl onions.

We sprinkled spices through our hands
And rubbed them on the roast
As we had seen our mother do.
Wood bits were chopped garlic,
An oak leaf a bay leaf.
Sand was salt and black dirt was pepper.

Happy with ourselves,
We put our roast in an oven
in the hollow of a tree.
We could hardly wait
to taste a piece of the tender beef,
Though we couldn't have known
Nothing would ever taste so good again.

Show Bones Villanelle

All day I think about my size.
I'm a cute pig in lipstick,
A sow if I swallow the lies.

I read a diet book while eating pies,
Marvel over the cover-girl pick.
All day I think about my size.

I've got no bones to show the guys;
I'm much too full for heroine-chic.
I'm a sow if I swallow the lies.

The thinnest woman takes her prize
With the skeletal smile of the sick.
All day I think about my size.

I can't seem to starve my alibis,
Model myself on a stick.
I'm a sow if I swallow the lies.

I shrink until my body cries.
But even my bones are too thick.
All day I think about my size.
I'm a sow if I swallow the lies.

Leave Me with Laughing Wolf

Laughing Wolf is the name of a Native American dancer

Real self, you no longer elude me.
I have followed you into the sleeves
of sun falling like flames
where the wind calls my name,
I resurrect myself again.

Now let me go to Laughing Wolf
to dance the way I saw him dance,
to sweat with him through summer.

Leave me with Laughing Wolf
under a sky so clear the stars seem to sing
and a moon white as bone.

Leave me in the desert just after a rain,
where the greasewoods will cleanse me
of uncertainty,
unravel me with their beauty.

Leave me by the fire where the world's wisdom meets
with that wisdom which is beyond the world.

Because my laughter is long as a June day
and as resilient,
because I will never know how to love tamely,
leave me with Laughing Wolf.

Upon Staying in Your House

Listen to the quiet things:
The way water drips
in a sink downstairs.
The dryer softly shuffles
and turns,
sheets shift and fall
against aluminum.
The refrigerator
hums and drones.

Listen:
Distant cars roll by,
muffled engines purring
along the avenue.
Branches tap glass windows.
Heat stirs and clicks
in the old pipes,
the radiator, a slender accordion,
exudes white rows of warmth.

The house settles
and I settle in it
as if I were born here.
Mirrors hang like gifts
of silver water in the sun.
I have come to life with you,
and peace holds me
like a palm on each side of my face.

Lunar Eclipse

First, there is an entire wafer
Luminescent in the dark.

Then a fraction of the circle
Disappears.

Steadily, a succession of black ribbons
are wound by invisible hands

Until a paper white sliver of moon
Shines, for a moment, like hope,

Then all at once
is swallowed by the throat of night.

Waiting for Tea Water

I raise my head from my arms on the table
as steam begins to rise from the kettle,
a pure stream of white clouds
along walls the color of butter.

Outside, winter slides away
like an ice cube across the counter,
and spring stretches its wide arc
of rain and mist-laden green.

Now sunshine in a seamless path
sails like a god through my window,
strews the floor with flowers of light,
straightens the small bones in my fingers.

In City Traffic Halted by a Funeral Procession

Our cars back up to one another
as far as we can go.
No one is going anywhere.
No one is going anywhere
Until the hearse, deflecting sun,
Commands its following to the grave.

We wave death by,
Quickly, go by,
we feel the sweat
Drip from our necks,
Our lungs pulling hard for breath,
Go quickly so it will be over,
And we can lift our feet from the brakes.

Rain Woman Sun Woman

Mood shaping rain clouds
you swallow me whole
sweet water nursing earth
rain wings spreading wide
holy ocean water
pour over me

Mood shaping sun star
you take up my soul
Sweet light feeding earth
Sun waves stretching out
Sun dances slip
gold into my heart

Realizing Your Compassion

I am like a drunk slumped against the bar door
At dawn, watching the ghost of morning coming
When no one is around.

Here is the bartender
Walking through the fog
With a newspaper under his arm.

I am glad for the steady clip of his shoes
And the clean smell of aftershave.

He doesn't push me aside.
His outstretched hand makes me cry.

September

Nights are cool,
Lusciously full
As melons in the field.

The sun is subdued,
Soft and slanted,
And sinks early into the trees.

At the shore
The rush of summer recedes
Like a long wave going out.

The swimmers have all gone off to school,
Their towels pulled
From balconies and chairs.

Few cars cruise along the coastal road,
As the sea continues to move with the moon,
Shape her sand and call.

Hope

for Sean

When I bloomed with you,
I flung my soul about freely,
And it landed everywhere,
A sprinkling here and a sprinkling there—

There was fire, drops of pure fire,
faces of fire in flowers and trees-
and my adoration for the world in its goodness.

There were journeys in the woods without time,
paths leading everywhere,
The river widening, always widening,
And gardens of every fruit and flower,
A world honeysuckle sweet.

There were roses, dreams,
And honey locusts dropping
their white gifts everywhere,
the smell of spring in everything green,
and the lilacs loving me
through your open window.

April

Nightfall is hushed, dew-laden.
New blades sprout and thicken the grass,
And the stark gaps
Between limbs of maple trees
Have begun to fill in with sticky buds
And small, clean smelling leaves.

Satiny petals of cherry blossoms
Fall like snowflakes in the breeze,
Into my hair and all around me
On my swing in the backyard.

Beyond me,
Just before the woods take over,
Grape vines climb,
Twisting and weaving their slim tendrils
Through the links of the metal fence,
Reaching past the yard,
Clutching the wild wonder
Of barks and branches
In the un-pruned stillness.

The green hose drips from its hanging coil,
After the work of watering the earth,
And there is an outline
Of the lilac in the moonlight,
A purple sketch of its full -grown shape,
With succulent leaves,
And fresh bunches
Of tiny, four-pronged flowers.

My swing sails in the lilac smell,
And I think of how it has always been this way—
When nature begins to hum,
And the silent bells of bleeding hearts open,
I open,
And rush into the arms of spring.

Winter

When the days are shortest yet too long,
The clock a torture and a promise,
When the days are drizzled with gray
And succumb to early darkness,
I claw my way up.
I command my spirit
Through the suffocating quilt of sky,
And tear a hole
Through which I free my soul,
Though exhaustedly, and only for a moment.

Winter II

I know you through your fits and storms,
Winter, and your long, sordid silence.
Your wind howls at my window,
Your icy pond waits in the woods.

But I store summer in my cheeks
Like a squirrel.
I house the hot wind
And the loaded green leaves.
There is always the memory
Of watermelon on my tongue,
And I keep seashells in a saucer year long.

After Winter

I opened myself to the light,
And it didn't take long to notice
The daffodils and the hyacinth.

Though it was still cold,
the sun had breached
the impermanent gray.

I heard a dove,
And my heart moved
After an eternity of stillness.

Here was the hope that green brings,
the path winding through the garden,
the walking stones to another world,
the door at last open.

Fight

Beyond the roses and manicured lawns,
beneath the oak shade
on a day already gray,

beside the fence knitted with new vine,
on the sidewalk littered with grass and trash,

a small bird jumped over and over,
her wings flapping furiously,
all her heart fighting for flight.

And I thought of myself
still thrashing around in last year's leaves,
my spirit not yet able
to get off the ground.

Flight

Beside the magnolia blossoms
Still half-closed in the tentative sun,

Amidst the green growing,
The new bursting through old,

A small bird struggled to fly
Like I struggled to rise
From winter's dank leaves.

She rose, shaken, to the tree on the corner,
so close her wing touched my hand,

And there was a moment
when we were reflections in each other's eyes

both so skittish, so nervous and afraid,
but brave.

Born in Baltimore, Maryland, **Cheri L. Miller** has been writing poetry since childhood. She holds a Bachelor of Arts degree in English from the University of Maryland at Baltimore County and a Master of Arts in Writing from Johns Hopkins University. She has been published in numerous journals, including *Rock & Sling: A Journal of Witness, Assisi: An online Journal of Arts & Letters, The Baltimore City Paper, Poetry Pacific, Welter,* and *Smartish Pace.* In addition to writing a second book of poems, Cheri is working on a collection of short stories, *A String of Pearls,* about coming of age in the 1970's.

CPSIA information can be obtained
at www.ICGtesting.com
Printed in the USA
BVHW041531310522
638449BV00001BA/65